THE THRESHOLD OF DISSENT

THE GOLDSTEIN-GOREN SERIES IN AMERICAN JEWISH HISTORY

General editor: Hasia R. Diner

Is Diss a System? A Milt Gross Comic Reader
Edited by Ari Y. Kelman

We Remember with Reverence and Love: American Jews and the Myth of Silence after the Holocaust, 1945–1962
Hasia R. Diner

Jewish Radicals: A Documentary Reader
Edited by Tony Michels

An Unusual Relationship: Evangelical Christians and Jews
Yaakov Ariel

All Together Different: Yiddish Socialists, Garment Workers, and the Labor Roots of Multiculturalism
Daniel Katz

1929: Mapping the Jewish World
Edited by Hasia R. Diner and Gennady Estraikh

Hanukkah in America: A History
Dianne Ashton

Unclean Lips: Obscenity, Jews, and American Culture
Josh Lambert

Jews and Booze: Becoming American in the Age of Prohibition
Marni Davis

The Rag Race: How Jews Sewed Their Way to Success in America and the British Empire
Adam D. Mendelsohn

Hollywood's Spies: The Undercover Surveillance of Nazis in Los Angeles
Laura B. Rosenzweig

Cotton Capitalists: American Jewish Entrepreneurship in the Reconstruction Era
Michael R. Cohen

Making Judaism Safe for America: World War I and the Origins of Religious Pluralism
Jessica Cooperman

A Rosenberg by Any Other Name: A History of Jewish Name Changing in America
Kirsten Fermaglich

The Threshold of Dissent

A History of American Jewish Critics of Zionism

Marjorie N. Feld

NEW YORK UNIVERSITY PRESS
New York

NEW YORK UNIVERSITY PRESS
New York
www.nyupress.org

References to internet websites (URLs) were accurate at the time of writing. Neither the author nor New York University Press is responsible for URLs that may have expired or changed since the manuscript was prepared.

Please contact the Library of Congress for Cataloging-in-Publication data.

ISBN: 978-1-4798-2931-6 (hardback)
ISBN: 978-1-4798-2936-1 (library ebook)
ISBN: 978-1-4798-2934-7 (consumer ebook)

New York University Press books are printed on acid-free paper, and their binding materials are chosen for strength and durability. We strive to use environmentally responsible suppliers and materials to the greatest extent possible in publishing our books.

Manufactured in the United States of America

10 9 8 7 6 5 4 3 2 1

Also available as an ebook

CONTENTS

Introduction

No Consensus

In the early twentieth-century United States, American Jews, leaders and laypeople alike, explored a diverse array of perspectives regarding what Zionism would mean and how it would fit into American Jewish communal life. Zionism is the movement focused on the establishment, development, and protection of a Jewish state in Israel, and they wondered if this movement should be central or ancillary to American Jewish organizations, including synagogues and philanthropies, activist- and service-oriented work, for all ages of American Jews. After the destruction and horrors of the Holocaust, and especially as Israel became an essential Cold War ally to the United States as well as a beneficiary of American foreign aid, tolerance for these diverse perspectives among mainstream, Zionist Jewish leaders waned. These leaders created and imposed a consensus on Israel and American Zionism that they believed was essential for Jewish survival.

Consensus refers to a decision held together by broad acceptance, an image that served Jewish leaders well but belied a more complex reality. What appeared as a consensus based on shared ideas was, in fact, a manufactured consensus, as Jewish leaders increasingly discounted and marginalized dissent on this issue. They often punished those who criticized Israel, Israeli policies, or American support of Israel or who openly rejected Zionism altogether, castigating them and often denying funding and support for their communal work. A careful analysis of this period reveals the efforts on the part of Jewish leaders to lower the threshold of tolerance for dissenting views on Zionism held by American Jews.

A threshold is a point past which the intensity of something produces a response. At the start of the twentieth century, American Jewish leaders were largely open to dissent from Zionism and engaged in substantive debate over the role Israel should play in American Jewish life. Over the course of the century, these leaders came to see any dissent from Zionism as dangerous. They built a symbolic threshold for this dissent that gradually diminished the space available for intracommunal debate. Any questioning of American Jews' fealty to Israel came to be seen as crossing the threshold, and it produced powerful, negative responses. Critics of Zionism were often accused of disloyalty and even antisemitism. The creation and reinforcement of this low threshold of dissent, then, played a central role in cultivating the image and, over time, the reality of a forced consensus. By the 1980s, as some American Jewish and Zionist organizations rose to positions of power and influence, these leaders had largely sidelined anti-Zionism among American Jews. To avoid these negative, powerful responses, critics had first to affirm their commitment to Israel; only then could they offer any criticism of American Zionism, Israeli policies, or the role of Israel in American Jewish life.

In these same decades, activists and scholars drew attention to the role of Zionism in the *Nakba* ("the catastrophe" in Arabic), the mass displacement and dispossession of Palestinians beginning in 1948, with Israel's founding and with the continued oppression of Palestinians in Israel and its Palestinian territories. As liberal and left-wing social movements and justice coalitions came to include criticism of Israel in their platforms, the forced consensus prevented American Jewish organizations from joining these coalitions. And American Jews who wished to engage in progressive activism *as Jews* were increasingly left with nowhere to go.

For decades, American Jewish historians largely reinforced this imposed consensus, presenting the emergence of Jewish nationalism and unconditional American Zionism as a natural and uncomplicated response to modernity and to the realities of antisemitism and the Holocaust. These scholars equated the triumph of American Zionism with the formation in 1948 of the State of Israel. With few exceptions and well into the twenty-first century, most American Jewish historians portrayed Israel's champions as heroes and largely ignored Israel's critics. As they historicized Jewish communal life in the United States, they largely disregarded the plurality of perspectives on Zionism and Israel. If Israel's critics appear in this scholarship, they do so as afterthoughts; they are dismissed as misguided, as suffering from Jewish self-hatred, or as advocates of the kind of assimilation that leads, inevitably, to Jewish invisibility.

According to this narrative arc, American Jewish critics of Zionism and Israel historically have cared little for the American and global Jewish communities and the future viability of these communities. Those who truly cared for Jewish life and felt authentic solidarity with Jews, it was argued, turned exclusively to Zionism and Israel. Even toward the end of the twentieth century, historians who studied or embraced anti-Zionism often had their work roundly dismissed by American Jewish historians as serving a contemporary agenda. This agenda, they suggested, detracted from the Zionist consensus and, therefore, importantly, from the health of Jewish communal life. The lack of rigorous and respected scholarship on Jewish critics of Zionism in the United States has had far-reaching implications. Perhaps most obviously, the lack of scholarship on these critics has permitted students of American Jewish history to view the development of a certain brand of American Zionism as uncontested.

In the last ten years, shifting sentiments toward Zionism and Israel offer a chilling corrective to the imposed Zionist consensus that is largely still supported by mainstream American Jewish communal leaders. There is a growing understanding of the costs of imposing this consensus, of maintaining a low threshold of tolerance for intracommunal debate over Israel. Among younger Americans of all religions and backgrounds, there is a marked increase in sympathy for Palestinian rights and a corresponding decrease in sympathy for Israel.[1] Among younger American Jews, Israel plays a diminishing role in their Jewish identity.[2] American Jews are more fractured than ever before about Israel: they are more divided about how, or if, the United States should support Israel; about how Zionism should factor into American Jewish identity; about how American Jews can or should interact with Israeli leaders. This evidence suggests that the forced American Jewish consensus on Zionism actually works against communal interests, as many young Jews no longer see their worldviews—their priorities or interests—reflected in mainstream Jewish communal organizations and, as a result, may choose to leave Jewish belonging behind.

These currents also draw strength from and emerge out of world events of the past decade. Israeli leaders have moved increasingly to the right politically, and Israel has encroached still more on Palestinian rights and territory since beginning its occupation of Gaza and the West

Bank in 1967; powerful movements of resistance to Israeli policies, including the Boycott, Divestment, and Sanctions (BDS) movement, modeled on the anti–South African apartheid movement, have gained global support, including among American Jews.

On the seventieth anniversary of Israel's statehood, a gauge of diminishing support for Israel lay in the words of historian and journalist Eric Alterman, long identified as a liberal Zionist and criticized by those on the left and right. In a 2018 column titled "The Fraying Ties between Liberal American Jews and Israel," Alterman wrote that there are only "narrow threads that hold together the alliance between liberal American Jews and the nation they once considered a source of pride and admiration—and today brings only shame and sadness."[3] In 2019 in the *New York Times*, Alterman asked, "Does Anyone Take the B.D.S. Movement Seriously Anymore?" He continued to identify as "a liberal Jew who agonizes over what this endless occupation is doing"—to Palestinians and to Jews, in Israel and around the world. As he lamented Israel's "self-destructive path," he also observed the "rapid growth" of anti-Zionist organizations like Jewish Voice for Peace.[4] As he wrote and as is explored here, "One of the great strengths of the Zionist movement of the 1940s that led to the creation of the state of Israel was its ability to withstand—even encourage—intense internal debate."[5] The title of his most recent contribution to the topic suggests his conclusion: his 2022 book, *We Are Not One: A History of America's Fight over Israel*, traces public debates over Israel, particularly among American Jews.[6]

These debates and developments are largely absent from the annals of American Jewish history. In his 1975 *American Zionism from Herzl to the Holocaust*, historian Melvin I. Urofsky dismissed anti-Zionism as the province of elite Jews and an idea vanquished by the Holocaust.[7] Historian Jonathan Sarna's 2004 book, *American Judaism: A History*, a prominent and much-praised survey work, includes no dedicated analysis of anti-Zionism in its 512 pages, a fact that not one scholar noted in the many positive reviews the book received.[8]

These master narratives do little to help make sense of the historical precedents to the growing contemporary dissent among American Jews (as well as many other groups). *The Threshold of Dissent* analyzes some of the historical actors, all affiliated with Jewish communities, whose actions served as precedents to the dissent so visible today. They criticized or rejected Zionism in diverse contexts, for diverse reasons, across the twentieth century. How did an American Jewish political world that once tolerated debate around Zionism move to one that suppressed it? That suppression often rendered historical criticism of Zionism invisible for future generations, and so these actors imagined that they were writing the first chapter of American Jewish dissent about Israel.

Jewish studies scholar Shaul Magid asserts that without Zionism, diaspora Jews have a lack of "adequate diasporic-identity alternatives." He goes further: "If Zionism . . . is identical to Jewishness, what Arthur Hertzberg called a 'substitute religion,' then challenging Zionism is an attempt to undermine the Jews." In the book *On Antisemitism* by Jewish Voice for Peace, Magid takes on those who have accused Israel's critics of antisemitism: "The accusation of antisemitism (or abetting antisemitism) may be a form of cultural shorthand, a way to avoid confronting a much more complex problem of constructing Judaism or Jewish fidelity outside the conventional Zionist orbit. And by using the term as cultural shorthand it actually makes it easier for real anti-Semites to continue to function because they become part of a more diffuse and shallow use of a malady worth addressing in a more serious and careful manner."[9]

Magid's analysis illuminates one dynamic at work in blocking out voices of Israel's critics and of Zionism, as doing so clears the way for presenting Zionism as the only antidote to very real antisemitism and American Zionism as the truest, most logical evolution of what it means to be an American Jew. Grief for the immense destruction of the Holocaust has, in some ways, inhibited our ability to hear the voices of American Jews who envisioned other antidotes to antisemitism and had alternative visions of what Israel might look like and what role Zionism and Israel might play in American Jewish life.

To listen to the diverse voices of these critics, however, is to learn a more complex and contested history of American Jewish identity. This history raises questions about how the American Jewish community contended with the "malady" of integration and social mobility and how resources were allocated. It also raises questions about the costs of those choices—and of marginalizing dissent. Scholars Noam Pianko and Adam Rovner remind us that some Jews, within and outside of the United States, conceived of Zionism and the possibility of a Jewish homeland in ways that diverged from the ultimately successful movement for a Jewish state in the Middle East.[10]

The Threshold of Dissent builds on both our current historical moment of growing dissent in the American Jewish community and the studies that capture the history of debates over Israel and Zionism in American Jewish history.[11] This analysis examines individuals and organizations who criticized or rejected Zionism and thus dissented from what many American Jewish leaders came to consider a consensus on Zionism and Israel. I identify common themes in the voices of these subjects and analyze how they drew from one another, often unknowingly, as they crafted answers to complex questions about liberation, group belonging, and individual identity across the twentieth century and into our own. They crossed the threshold of acceptable dissent, and many paid a high price.

What grounded these critiques of Zionism and Israel? How did American Jewish leaders contend with critics of Zionism inside of Jewish communal life? How did they build, and then reinforce, the threshold of dissent? What was the appeal of anti-Zionism, and how did it align with other domestic and foreign political commitments, such as American civil rights and global campaigns of anticolonialism? How did Zionists and anti-Zionists face the intense realities of global antisemitism and the destruction of the Holocaust, and how did all groups see their ideas as promoting Jewish safety?

In answering these questions, this work contributes to a fuller portrait of Jewish life in the United States, for, as scholar and activist Tallie Ben-Daniel argues in her history of anti-Zionism in San Francisco, "*both* Zionism and anti-Zionism in the United States took up the question of assimilation and Jewish normalcy."[12] The self-identified anti- and non-Zionist American Jews who appear in these pages shared concern for American Jewish life. They all responded to the Holocaust and to modern antisemitism, balancing particularist commitments to the Jewish community and universalist commitments to the broader world in unique and diverse ways so as to work toward what they saw as the best vision of American Jewish life. Many asserted that American Jewish Zionist leaders did not speak for them. Studying critics of American Zionism illuminates the groundwork for the upsurge in critiques of Zionism and Israel—indeed for the rejection of Zionism—that we see so prominently today. It also illuminates long-standing, and largely unstudied, historical dynamics in American Jewish communal life.

* * *

Jews who criticized or rejected Zionism were not of one worldview or one political persuasion. Jews from across the political spectrum, on the right and left and in between, criticized or rejected unqualified acceptance of Zionism because they feared it would make Jews in their nations of origin *more* vulnerable to accusations of dual loyalties, that it would underscore the idea that Jews were a "race" or nation when their own safe integration rested, they believed, on the rejection of that very idea. Some people feared that massive immigration to Israel would leave the remaining Jewish populations more vulnerable to antisemitism and that investing broadly in Zionism and Israel would drain essential resources from other Jewish communities, which they hoped would continue to flourish. Other critics of Zionism prioritized Judaism's prophetic and universalist teachings about justice and rejected Jewish nationalism as a distraction from that mission. Still others, especially on the political left, rejected the politics of both nationalism and militarism.

The Threshold of Dissent traces how encounters beyond the limits of acceptable criticism of Zionism led some American Jews to ideas outside of the American Jewish mainstream, to Palestinian rights activism, to dissent within a community whose leaders, they argued, did not speak for them. For some, these encounters led to a wholesale reenvisioning of American Jewish identity and communal life, including new ideas about Judaism, gender, and sexuality. This book also documents and analyzes how American Jewish Zionist leaders attempted to marginalize many voices of Jewish dissent. In our current political environment, many seek to equate on-the-rise sentiments of anti-Zionism with antisemitism. *The Threshold of Dissent* shows that these tactics and debates are not new, that American Jews have contested their community's Zionist commitments since before the founding of the State of Israel in 1948.

Two organizations played a vital role in the early history of this struggle. The American Jewish Committee (AJC) was founded by elite Reform Jews in 1906, after the Kishinev pogroms, to support Jews suffering in Eastern Europe. The AJC grew into an advocacy organization to support Jews in the United States and around the world. Its highly elite founders believed that Zionism wasn't compatible with American belonging and so positioned the AJC as "non-Zionist." After the founding of Israel in 1948, they supported the state, and they did not drop the "non-Zionist" label until after the 1967 war in Israel.

The American Council for Judaism (the Council) began in 1942 with a group of Reform Jewish rabbis; they rejected the Zionism that Reform movement leaders were beginning to embrace. The Council was founded as an anti-Zionist organization, as its founders saw Zionism as an obstacle to Jewish integration; they wanted Jewish belonging to be about religion, not the politics of state-building. Many Council members came to accept Zionism's important role in American Jewish life by the 1960s. As this work makes clear, their initial and abiding concerns about Zionism laid the groundwork for later critics.

A Note on History and Terminology: Zionism, Anti-Zionism, Non-Zionism, and the British Example

In 1986, in a series of essays that traced the "chronic ideological controversy about the Zionist idea" in Great Britain, historian Gideon Shimoni authored a brief history of Zionism that offered background on the terminology used throughout this book. Political Zionism, he wrote, asserted that Jews were individuals bound as a religious and a national group and mobilized communal resources to realize what had been a yearning expressed in Jewish prayer liturgies.[13]

The Viennese Jew Theodor Herzl (1860–1904) identified the Jewish problem as rising antisemitism in Europe and worsening conditions for Jews and suggested that the only solution lay in the establishment of an independent Jewish homeland in Zion. Herzl, the founder of modern political Zionism and a major figure in the history of twentieth-century Jews, sought to achieve this through diplomacy and fundraising on the part of Western Jewish leaders.[14] In 1896, he published his famous pamphlet, *The Jewish State*. Soon after he convened the first meeting of the World Zionist Congress in Basel. One year later, it became the manifesto of the modern Zionist movement.

One variant of Zionism, known as classical Zionism, was grounded in the idea that diaspora Jews lived in exile, awaiting their return to the true Jewish homeland of Israel. Diasporic Jewish life would eventually diminish and disappear, it was argued, leaving the authentic Jewish experience to be had in Israel alone. Indeed, categorizing all Jews *not* living in Israel as "diasporic," instead of categorizing them as Jews of the nations of which they are citizens, had political implications. Labeling all non-Israeli Jews as diasporic reinforced the politics of a Zionism in which all Jews are ultimately to act upon their Jewishness by rising (making *aliyah* in Hebrew) to live in Israel.

Shimoni makes clear that classical Zionism posed a dilemma for liberal Jews in emancipated nations. They asserted forcefully that their leaders emancipated Jews with the full expectation that they would shed all attributes that might conspicuously identify them *as Jews* and that they would integrate into their new nations as full citizens. This was the Jews' "moral contract" to embrace Judaism as a religion and to stand with others of diverse religious faiths as good citizens.[15] Rejecting Zionism, from this standpoint, was fundamental to good citizenship and also protected Jews from accusations of dual loyalties and racial difference. Integration in the many nations in which Jews claimed citizenship was the best solution to the problem of antisemitism. Reform movement rabbis in the United States crafted similar arguments as part of their initial rejection of late nineteenth-century Jewish nationalism.

In contrast, Zionists argued that there had long been a nationalist component to Jewish identity. Zionism, therefore, was compatible with all national citizenships. After World War I, British Zionists celebrated the 1917 Balfour Declaration, the published pledge of the British government to support "a national home for the Jewish people" along with the promise of no diminishment of Jewish rights at home. The Declaration was included in the terms of the British Mandate for Palestine after the war and the dissolution of the Ottoman Empire. The war's victors, including Britain, gained what was essentially colonial control of the former empire's territories. While other nations were to be under the mandate until they achieved independence, Palestine was set apart as a "Jewish National home." Though Jews represented a small percentage of the population in 1917, under the British Mandate, this percentage rose.

Shimoni traces the history of the League of British Jews, an elite group founded in 1917 whose members first articulated the idea that political Zionism represented the rejection of emancipated Jews' "moral contract." The League moved from a stance of "anti-Zionism" in the early years after the Balfour Declaration to non-Zionism, terms Shimoni defines carefully. "Anti-Zionism," he contends, is "active opposition to the Zionist organization," while non-Zionism is "willingness to desist from active opposition and to enter into some degree of cooperation with the Zionist organization."[16] Another scholar defines non-Zionists as those who supported the resettlement of refugees in Palestine but opposed the creation of a "Jewish sovereign political entity on that land."[17] Non-Zionists saw Palestine as a safe haven for Jews during the Holocaust but opposed Jewish state-building for a multitude of reasons, among them a fear of destroying Arab/Palestinian communities and displacing the communities that lived in Palestine for generations; some also cited a belief in the separation of religion and state-building.

Through the 1920s, League members came to feel more assured that Palestine was to be a center for Jewish culture and life, not a Jewish state. They tempered their rejection of Jewish nationalism and embraced what became known as cultural Zionism, in the tradition of Ahad Ha'am. Cultural Zionism meant that Palestine would become a cultural homeland, a source of inspiration for Jews rather than a physical home.[18] Although their eyes remained fixed on securing and protecting Jewish rights in Britain and elsewhere, they contributed to cultural and commercial ventures in Palestine. They even cooperated in the leadership of the Jewish Agency, which was instrumental in the establishment of Israel and then became the primary group that connected the world's Jewish population, the population of Palestine, and the British Mandatory Powers that ruled the region until Israel's independence in 1948.

These definitions are instructive when we trace a history of American encounters with Zionism, perhaps especially for an examination of American critics of Zionism. Also instructive are the sticking points that remained between Zionists and non-Zionists throughout their tumultuous coexistence in the League, including representation of the Arab majority in Palestine for any legislative body.[19] Non-Zionists strenuously rejected partition, the plan to create one Jewish and one Arab state, proposed by the British Royal (or Peel) Commission of Inquiry in 1937, because they saw it as undermining their fundamental belief that individuals of all backgrounds and nationalities and religions could live together peacefully. They also saw partition as one step on the road to a Jewish state, which they continued to reject. After 1937, however,

Shimoni finds, the non- and anti-Zionist opposition was "overridden by the Zionists who allowed the enlarged Jewish Agency to atrophy."[20]

Shimoni's history of non-Zionists in Britain is useful for not only his clear definitions of terminology but also his dismissal of perspectives critical of Zionism. He writes, for example, that non-Zionists wanted only to protect their own status as emancipated and integrated into the broader British population and labels their fears "unfounded," a result of their "residual sense of insecurity in English society." Further, he writes that they showed "selfish disregard for the needs of the displaced and the distressed Diaspora Jews." Though the "assimilationist case was neater and more logically consistent . . . in reality the untidier Zionist case has been vindicated."[21] More recent work suggests that understanding British anti- and non-Zionism proves central to understanding British political commitments in the Middle East.[22] *The Threshold of Dissent* analyzes the worldviews, agendas, and values that led American Jews to their criticism of Zionism and Israel and argues that their dissent is essential to understanding American Jewish history and American history more broadly.

* * *

In a 1959 letter to a friend and colleague, Rabbi Elmer Berger, cofounder and leader of the anti-Zionist American Council for Judaism, reflected on the accomplishments and ambitions of his organization. Rabbi Berger's large ego no doubt colored his conclusions about the significance of the Council, and indeed he compared their efforts with the liberation work happening at that moment in Hungary and Tibet. "Remember," he urged his friend, "that before the Council, <u>nothing</u> was contributed in this field, in any orderly and systematic way since the 'non-Zionists' clammed-up and accepted 'synthetic Zionism' in 1929. . . . Tomorrow's Americans—in fact, today's Americans—have a whole new literature on a problem with which they are increasingly concerned. . . . More of these requests indicate a public interest—and a respect for us. . . . Tomorrow's Americans will not only know anti-Zionism exists," Rabbi Berger wrote, "but in reasoned and systematic fashion they will know why."[23] This book answers this "why" by studying the political lives of American Jews who criticized American Zionism. At the start of the twentieth century, Zionists, non-Zionists, and anti-Zionists engaged in at times contentious debates, and those debates only got more contentious—and the stakes higher—as the twentieth century wore on.

The Threshold of Dissent stretches across a century of history, beginning in the 1880s, when Jews in the United States, almost all of them immigrants from Europe and their descendants, sought to secure a place in the industrial economy in the midst of widespread xenophobia and white supremacy. It traces the creation and strengthening of American Jewish communal institutions, which coalesced around ideas about what elements of Jewish identity would be at the center of American Jewish communal life and would best serve the needs of Jewish security at home and abroad. Integral to the story is the response of American Jews to the rise of Nazism and the destruction wrought by the Holocaust, along with the profound fear that such immense loss could be possible again. An unconditional loyalty to Israel and to Israeli policies rose to the top of American Jewish priorities in large part because American Jews were told—and believed—that Israel offered assurance of Jewish safety from antisemitic terror, that it assured Jewish safety and survival after the horrors of the Holocaust. It rose to the top for other complicated reasons: among them that Jewish nationalism coexisted easily with American nationalism and especially with a budding American Cold War alliance with Israel.

The Threshold of Dissent examines one thread of the complex and tangled relationship between the United States and Israel by looking at the criticism of Israel and American Zionism by a select group of self-identified American Jews. It does not explore religious anti-Zionism,[24] or Zionism within the Jewish left, and as such it is far from comprehensive in its examinations of the critics of American Zionism. Instead it focuses largely on individuals whose criticisms of Zionism were bound up in mainstream American political ideas and who encountered opposition to their ideas within Jewish communal life. The subjects of this book are mostly absent from American Jewish history yet were essential contributors to conversations about American Jewish communal priorities. It's also important to note that given the patriarchal arrangements of American Jewish life through to the women's movement in the 1970s, the archival voices captured in this book's early chapters are almost all that of men.

This book alerts us to the lowering threshold of dissent on Zionism throughout twentieth-century US history. American Jewish Zionist leaders responded strongly to those who crossed this threshold of dissent, as those who criticized American Zionism and Israel were denied resources and faced harsh accusations. In that way, these leaders narrowed conversations about Jewish belonging. Their unwillingness to see these ideas as contested and subject to debate has been, in no small part, responsible for the growing generational divide among American Jews. An understanding of this history helps us understand some of the costs of the forced Zionist consensus.

The Threshold of Dissent suggests that opening up conversations on Zionism lends itself to greater pluralism, even democratization, within American Jewish life. Though many approach it with understandable trepidation, our moment makes clear that dissent from unqualified support for Zionism offers hope that more American Jews can align themselves with forces for liberation and freedom within the borders of the United States and throughout the world. In working for these forces within Jewish communal life, they would create a more stable foundation for young Jews seeking to connect Jewish belonging to campaigns for justice.

1

Jewish Anti- and Non-Zionism

The Reform Movement in the Early Twentieth Century

In the early nineteenth-century United States, Jewish leaders and lay-people sought to adapt Jewish traditions from their various nations of origin to their new lives.[1] Leaders of Reform Judaism, which was the religion's liberal branch, with origins in the European Enlightenment and the emancipation of Jews in Germany, spoke of the urgency of adapting Judaism, seeking to make it "compatible with science and reason, dynamic in its adaptation to modernity, and focused on social justice more than ritual practice."[2] In November 1885, a group of Reform rabbis met to adopt a set of principles that would set Reform Judaism apart from "a wholly nonsectarian universalism on the one hand and from more traditional expressions of Judaism on the other."[3] Scholars of American religion have long seen the Reform movement's Pittsburgh Platform of 1885, the document the rabbis authored, as a key symbol of this dynamism. And scholars have debated the significance of the Pittsburgh Platform's antinationalism, which was later regarded as a stand against Zionism, as the Reform movement leaders adapted to the modern United States.[4]

Rabbi Isaac Mayer Wise, an immigrant from Bohemia (now part of the Czech Republic) and the father of Reform Judaism in the United States, and Rabbi Kaufmann Kohler, an immigrant from Bavaria and a leader in radical Reform, met with other Reform rabbis in Pittsburgh. They were there to write a manifesto that answered the major questions emerging from Judaism's encounters with modernity. The Pittsburgh Platform asserted that the Bible was the product of ancient times, reflecting the "primitive ideas of its own age," and that its ideas were "not antagonistic" to modern history and science. It declared that all traditions that served to "obstruct" rather than to "further" Jewish adaptation to modernity, including the dietary laws of kashrut, or keeping kosher, no longer needed to be observed. The Pittsburgh Platform recognized both Christianity and Islam as what they called "daughter religions of Judaism" and as sharing a "providential mission" in the "spreading of monotheistic and moral truth." The document made clear that Reform Jews in the United States would identify as a religious community only, adapting their religion to preserve their Jewish identities but removing any barriers that kept them separate from other religions in working toward progress in the modern age.[5]

Reform leaders in the United States saw Jewish nationalism as one of these barriers and insisted that the return to the land of Zion embedded in the Jewish liturgy was a spiritual and not a literal journey. As the Pittsburgh Platform read, "We recognize, in the modern era of universal culture of heart and intellect, the approaching of the realization of Israel's great Messianic hope for the establishment of the kingdom of truth, justice, and peace among all men. We consider ourselves no longer a nation, but a religious community, and therefore expect neither a return to Palestine, nor a sacrificial worship under the sons of Aaron, nor the restoration of any of the laws concerning the Jewish state."[6] Reform Jewish leaders feared that Jewish nationalism, which emerged in the next decade as the Zionist movement, threatened mainstream acceptance of Jews in the United States. Like members of the League of British Jews, founded after the Balfour Declaration of 1917, they felt that rejecting Zionism kept them true to their moral contract with the United States.

These leaders focused intently on secure and safe integration because of the antisemitism they witnessed in Europe and in the United States in that era. American Jews had faced exclusion and even hostility during the Civil War, during economic downturns, and across the years of massive Jewish immigration from Eastern Europe. This antisemitism largely grew from broader currents of xenophobia and old antisemitic tropes. Jewish quotas in colleges and universities, along with discrimination in housing, professions, and some services (such as hotels), were obstacles to Jewish safety and success. American Reform Jews believed that Jewish nationalism could present Jews as a "race apart" and thus could spark antisemitic accusations of dual loyalties, for as Earl Raab, scholar of American Jewry, observed, "The specter of 'dual loyalty' . . . has always been a staple of hard-core antisemitism."[7] This threat would imperil their safe integration into the United States, diminishing their provisional whiteness in the era of Jim Crow, the formal system of racial apartheid that began in the 1870s.[8] Pogroms in Russia and the Dreyfus affair in France, where a Jewish army captain was falsely accused of treason because of antisemitism, stood alongside other similar incidents worldwide to offer evidence of the destructive power of those forces. Reform Jewish leaders in Germany, where Reform Judaism largely began, came to see Zionism as "dangerous and pernicious" for these same reasons. Jewish leaders in Germany expressed fear that Zionism would drain money and leadership talent away from thriving Jewish communities outside of the future Jewish state, a concern that American Jewish non- and anti-Zionists soon articulated.[9]

Leaders of Reform Judaism in America were responding to global and local antisemitism as well as to other historical developments. First, they were keenly aware that secular, rationalist religions such as Ethical Culture, a humanist movement that rejected the ties of Jewish peoplehood and the existence of God, were making inroads into the American Jewish community. Felix Adler, the son of a prominent rabbi and an ordained rabbi himself, had founded Ethical Culture in 1876, and some Jews seeking a liberal, secular movement joined that community.

Reform leaders also responded to the Christian missionary movement in the United States. In the missionaries' vision of the Second Coming of Jesus, Jews had a central role to play. If enough Jews accepted Jesus as their savior, those who converted would serve as what historian Yaakov Ariel describes as "evangelists to their brethren" in the millennial kingdom of the world to come.[10] The rise of Jewish nationalism, missionaries believed, served as proof that this moment was near, as they saw Jews as "a nation that was in the process of recovering its position as God's chosen people and had a great future before it." Zionism, then, fit neatly within what missionaries saw as the beginning of the prophesy's fulfillment. In its rejection of Zionism, the Judaism of the Pittsburgh Platform removed the link to this prophesy, adhering instead to Jewish ethics to guide daily life. Perhaps Reform leaders hoped to diminish the threat that missionaries posed to American Jews.[11]

The modern, liberal, ethical monotheism of the Pittsburgh Platform, along with its rejection of Jewish nationalism, marked Reform leaders' attempts to navigate a path for the growth of Reform Judaism amid all of these developments. As American Jewish historian Hasia Diner writes, by "focusing on the ethical principles associated with the Hebrew Bible," Reform Jews could "further two projects." First was their own safe integration into America, as they sought "to integrate Jewish beliefs and culture into the larger culture in which they lived, combining their bourgeois American social culture and their identities as Jews." Reform Jews could, Diner writes, "connect present to past" through the prophetic teachings of ethical living, bringing ancient Jewish texts into relevance in daily modern life. Downplaying or rejecting nationhood and nationalism, they believed, would diminish the likelihood that Jews would be thought of as disloyal to the United States and in that way would hopefully protect them from racist antisemitism.[12]

Second, Diner notes that the ideas of the Pittsburgh Platform allowed Reform Jews to "take pride in their faith community." By grounding their civic contributions in Jewish teachings, American Jews could feel gratified by their achievements as Jews as well as Americans.[13] Downplaying their particularism and their separateness and accenting their good deeds would, they hoped, speed their integration into the broader society, for Reform Jews were also finding a place for themselves in white America during the savage inequality and violence of the Jim Crow years. They were entering various occupations, balancing new versions of Jewish belonging with whiteness and American identity, and often feared that antisemitism might threaten their full integration. Indeed, as historian Eric Goldstein notes, Rabbi Kohler and other anti-Zionists in the Reform movement feared that Zionism "would bring the Jews' whiteness into question." Their anxiety stemmed from Zionism's emphasis on Jewish separatism and the idea that settling in Palestine would "associate Jews with uncivilized lands."[14]

American Jews responded to modernity, to the breakdown of the traditional identity of Jews as a religiously unified group, by both criticizing and supporting Jewish nationalism. They all aimed to speed Jewish integration, to balance American and Jewish belonging amid the rise of antisemitism across the world. Antinationalists like the Reform leaders in Pittsburgh in 1885 rejected Jewish peoplehood and separateness, emphasizing Jewish religious unity, ultimately urging American Jews to reject Zionism for fear of being accused of dual loyalties. Part of the future anti-Zionist argument embedded in the Pittsburgh Platform, then, was that rejecting Zionism would normalize Jewish citizens everywhere, making them appear like the many groups of people who were searching out a secure place in the social and economic landscapes of their home nations.

At the same time, some Jews embraced Zionism and the Jewish state as a means to these same ends of balancing American and Jewish belonging. Zionism gave American Jews a private cause to champion, separating them out as a group while not threatening their Americanism. As modern Jewish historian Michael A. Meyer notes, the "Zionization of Reform Judaism" occurred as the "political Zionism of the American variety" evolved. This brand of Zionism, modeled by Louis Brandeis, attorney and later Supreme Court justice, "was more philanthropic than ideological" and did not require that "diaspora" Zionists move to Palestine/Israel to be true to Zionist ideology. Reform Jews could see Palestine as a beacon of Jewish prophetic teachings and still be both loyal Americans and good Zionists.[15]

As the leader of the American Zionist movement from 1914 to 1921, Brandeis urged philanthropic support of Zionism in order to make it, as he asserted, "entirely compatible with loyalty to America." Indeed, Brandeis wrote that "to be good Americans, we must become better Jews, and to become better Jews we must become Zionists."[16] Brandeis reimagined Zionism, locating it neatly within what some American Jews regarded as their place in the United States. Rabbi Abba Hillel Silver, ordained as a Reform rabbi in 1915, was an early champion of the Zionist movement in the United States in the 1910s and 1920s, and like Brandeis, he led American Zionist organizations.

By the mid-1930s, the Jewish refugee situation in Europe became increasingly desperate, and with Germany's annexation of Austria in March 1938, the number of Jews needing rescue from Nazi power grew by hundreds of thousands. At the Evian Conference in July 1938, leaders from thirty-two nations and many relief organizations lamented the situation, but they did not open their doors to Jewish refugees. Kristallnacht, the terrifying night when Nazis destroyed seven thousand Jewish businesses and more than nine hundred synagogues, occurred four months later.

The rise of Nazi power came to eclipse fears of dual loyalties that had, in part, formed the foundation of some non- and anti-Zionist thought in the United States. Eastern European Jews and their descendants now had substantial representation in Reform Judaism, and the movement shifted toward accepting more Jewish rituals in their congregations. In light of all these events and changes, leaders issued a new declaration of principles, the 1937 Columbus Platform of the Reform movement. In the Columbus Platform, leaders like Rabbi Silver voiced strong support for Jewish nationalism and the Zionist movement.[17] The distance between the Pittsburgh Platform of 1885 and the Columbus Platform of 1937 represented a "clear realignment on Zionism" in the Reform movement, once the movement most resistant to Zionism.[18]

Non-Zionism and the American Jewish Committee

Some Reform Jews continued to resist Zionism even as Eastern European Jewish immigrants and their descendants were forming Zionist organizations and building strong support for Zionism within American Jewry.[19] The American Jewish Committee is well known for its early objections to Zionism. Elites made up the bulk of the membership of the AJC, including towering figures in American life at the time, such as lawyer Louis Marshall, banker Jacob Schiff, and scholar Cyrus Adler. The organization had been founded in 1906 largely to lobby and raise funds for Jews in Eastern Europe in response to the Kishinev pogroms of 1903, which drew worldwide attention to the antisemitic violence in czarist Russia. The AJC was dedicated to defending Jewish religious and civil rights in the United States and abroad. Its members drew from the position of Reform Judaism as articulated in the Pittsburgh Platform, seeing themselves as part of a religious community with firm loyalty to their home nation. Naomi Cohen, historian of the AJC, writes that its members borrowed from "the anti-Zionist position enunciated by Reform Judaism" in embracing the idea that "America is our Palestine, Washington our Jerusalem."[20]

The AJC's non-Zionists opposed the Jewish nationalism of political Zionism but supported Palestine as a Jewish religious and cultural center. AJC leaders such as Jacob Schiff insisted that their organization's membership reflected and represented both Zionist and non-Zionist positions. Sensitive to the spectrum of members' approaches to Jewish nationalism, they navigated carefully before and after the Balfour Declaration of November 1917, which made clear Britain's commitment to a Jewish homeland in Palestine.[21] In their April 1918 statement on the Balfour Declaration, the AJC spoke of their faith in the vibrancy of Judaism in communities across the world as well as their own "unqualified allegiance to this country." They expressed their "whole-hearted sympathy" with "Jews who, moved by traditional sentiment, yearn for a Holy Land for the Jewish people." In Palestine, they supported "a center for Judaism, for the stimulation of our faith."[22]

In March 1919, a group composed largely of American Jewish Committee members presented a petition to President Woodrow Wilson to protest the idea of a Zionist state. The goal was to guide Wilson's approach to the Paris Peace Conference. The group of rabbis, business leaders, and attorneys took careful note of the fact that Jewish military service in World War I had, as they put it, "shattered the base aspersions of the anti-Semites which charged them with being aliens in every land," proving their loyalty and citizenship.[23]

Elements of this petition demonstrate the complex dimensions of its authors' reservations and resistance. They wrote about global politics, citing Sir George Adam Smith, "the greatest authority in the world" on the Palestine region, a biblical scholar who had traveled widely in the Middle East and had written of Muslim and Christian claims to the land of Palestine. "It is not true," the authors quote Smith as saying, "that Palestine is the national home of the Jewish people and no other people." Smith's observations made him see "bitter and sanguinary conflicts" as "inevitable" if Zionism were realized, and he added that these were "legitimate questions . . . stirred up by the claims of Zionism, but the Zionists have yet to answer them." Above all, the signers believed that Zionism was "utterly opposed to the principles of democracy" and that uniting "Church and State . . . would be a leap backward of 2,000 years." They advocated for a global movement to secure Jewish citizenship rights everywhere. Their hope for Palestine was that it be a "free and independent state, to be governed under a democratic form of government, recognizing no distinctions of creed or race or ethnic descent."[24]

The petition began by pleading that those attending the Paris Peace Conference consider the representativeness of American Jewish Zionist leadership. Its authors claimed that in their dissent from political Zionism, they, and not the Zionist leaders, were "voicing the opinion of the majority of American Jews who were born in this country and of those foreign born who have lived here long enough to thoroughly assimilate American political and social conditions."[25] These ideas proved important into the 1920s, when Zionists also feared that violence between Jews and Palestinians would convince Americans "to believe that Zionism was a cause that defied American principles" because it was inherently undemocratic.[26] Non-Zionists and Zionists alike feared that if Palestine were to develop into a violent and undemocratic nation, American Jews, seen as intimately linked to the Jews of Palestine, would face antisemitism at home.

* * *

The more elite and wealthy German Jewish membership of the American Jewish Committee was very different from the membership of the more populist American Jewish Congress (AJCongress), founded in 1918 by Eastern European, Jewish, Zionist-leaning American Jews.

Members of the AJCongress passed their own resolution supporting Jewish settlement in Palestine, one intended to guide the delegation that the AJCongress was sending to the Paris Peace Conference of 1919. Especially important to AJCongress members were the final lines of the Balfour Declaration, which emphasized the continued importance of the rights of Palestinian Arabs as well as the vibrancy of Jewish life around the world. AJCongress members quoted the Declaration in the concluding lines of their own resolution: "It being clearly understood that nothing shall be done which shall prejudice the civil and religious rights of existing non-Jewish communities in Palestine, or the rights and political status enjoyed by Jews in other countries."[27] Members of the AJCongress, like members of the AJC, sought to balance support for Jewish settlement in Palestine with respect for those (non-Jews) who lived in the region and also with support for other Jewish communities. Into the 1920s, even as Rabbi Stephen Wise, a Zionist leader who spoke on behalf of the Zionist movement at the Paris Peace Conference, came to head the AJCongress, the organization sponsored forums at which anti- and non-Zionist American Jews expressed similar concerns.[28]

In those early decades of the Zionist movement, some groups of American Zionists and non-Zionists alike saw the indigenous land claims of Palestinian Arabs as a "problem," an obstacle to presenting Zionism as compatible with—even an outgrowth of—American principles (ignoring the fact that the lands of the United States, too, were stolen from indigenous peoples). They believed that displacing the communities native to Palestine was unjust and feared that doing so would lead to violence between Palestinian Arabs and Jews that would ripple outward to create tension and strife in other regions. Gradually, however, leaders in the Zionist movement aimed to downplay these land claims in order to sustain faith in the idea of Zionism as bringing true democracy to the Middle East.

In 1929, as revolts led to bloodshed in Palestine, Rabbi Judah Magnes publicly aired his call for a binational state for Jews and Arabs in the *New York Times*. Zionist leaders panicked. Rabbi Magnes, who was born in San Francisco, was a Reform leader, one of the founders of the American Jewish Committee, and a pacifist during World War I who moved to Palestine and saw Jewish life there as contributing to the vibrancy of Jewish communities around the world; he advocated for Arab-Jewish cooperation until his death in 1948. Non-Zionist American Jewish Committee members continued to wrestle with these issues. Within the AJC's 1943 *Statement of Views* were references to Jewish-Arab cooperation, the need to "safeguard and protect the fundamental rights of all inhabitants [of Palestine]" and "to safeguard and protect the holy places of all faiths."[29] Drawing heated criticism from Zionists, the AJC began to take a wider view of the Zionist project in Palestine and, subsequently, articulate wider criticisms. Historian Geoffrey Levin finds that the non-Zionist and pro-Israel leaders of the AJC quietly drew attention to the plight of the Palestinian minority living under military law in Israel from 1948 to 1966.[30]

* * *

Both the AJC and the AJCongress made Jewish safety the greatest priority. The stakes were high, as these years before World War II were marked by a measurable rise of what Jewish communal leader Raab called "political anti-Semitism."[31] Through the 1910s and 1920s, many American Jews were advocating for liberal immigration reform to allow Jewish refugees to enter the United States; they needed only to listen to politicians' debates over immigration, which tapped into xenophobia, racism, nativism, and antisemitism. These sentiments were codified in the Immigration Act of 1924, which drastically cut immigration and effectively barred all immigrants from Asia. And so, as historian Maddalena Marinari writes, "all saw clearly that there was danger in drawing attention to specifically Jewish concerns."[32]

Both critics and supporters of Zionism claimed that true American ideals were aligned with their positions. From the Pittsburgh Platform through post–World War I international affairs, non- and anti-Zionists articulated two common themes. First, they drew attention to the fact that Zionist leaders were not answering questions raised by the Zionist movement, including questions about the fate of Palestine's indigenous population. Second, they insisted that Zionist leaders' views were not representative of and did not speak for all Jews in the United States. Several members of the American Council for Judaism, founded by Reform rabbis in 1942, with the Pittsburgh Platform as a key foundational document, continued to raise both of these issues.

The American Council for Judaism

Reform Judaism's skepticism toward Zionism in the late nineteenth century lived on in the American Jewish Committee. Then after the Reform movement's Columbus Platform in 1937, which expressed support for Zionism and the right of Jewish refugee settlement in Palestine, the mantle of Reform anti-Zionism was taken up by the American Council for Judaism, founded in 1942. Dismissed by some as "merely a nuisance both to the State Department and to the American Jewish community" and "a lost case," the Council's history offers us evidence of the contentious debates over Zionism and of the anti- and non-Zionist ideas held by American Jews. Its history also demonstrates how some Jewish leaders slowly began to marginalize those who dissented from an emerging Zionist consensus.[33]

The esteemed Rosenwald family offers one of many links between these two eras of Zionist critiques. In her biography of Sears and Roebuck leader and businessman Julius Rosenwald (1862–1932), historian Hasia Diner reminds us that the Rosenwald family's patriarch remained a committed anti-Zionist despite what he described as "avalanches of appeals" from some of his closest colleagues. These men, like him, were towering figures in American Jewish philanthropy and communal work in the early twentieth century.[34] "Rosenwald perceived that Zionism emphasized the separateness of the two populations and put Jews above Arabs," Diner writes, though he never said these words directly.[35] Rosenwald funded many Jewish cultural projects in Palestine, but only ones that he felt were divorced from Jewish nationalism.

Julius Rosenwald's anti-Zionism occasionally drew fire from Zionist leaders. One example of this involves his contributions to what was known as the Agro-Joint, a project of the American Jewish Joint Distribution Committee (JDC) that sought to settle Soviet Jews on collective farms in Crimea and Ukraine beginning in the late 1920s.[36] Fuming that Rosenwald funded a project outside of Palestine, Zionist leader Rabbi Stephen Wise wrote that "with one scratch of his pen on a check," he "blasts the hope of millions of Jews, living and dead."[37]

Many of the elite Reform Jews of the JDC, like Rosenwald, chose to align themselves with non- or anti-Zionism.[38] As historian Yehuda Bauer notes, leaders of the JDC, an organization founded in 1914 to aid Jews in dire circumstances, wrestled with "the problem of Zionism" until the mid-1930s, as the group competed with Zionist organizations for funds to aid European Jews. JDC leaders sought to build Jewish infrastructure in Germany and other countries and also emphasized that Palestine was not the only site for refugee resettlement. Because "many of the richer elements in Jewry . . . were more inclined toward" non- or anti-Zionism, the JDC's position served their cause. By 1937, given the dire situation of Jews in Germany, American Zionists and the JDC leaders began to work together more closely to aid Jewish refugee resettlement in Palestine and elsewhere.[39]

* * *

Lessing Rosenwald (1891–1979), one of five children of Julius and Augusta Nusbaum Rosenwald, took over the leadership of Sears Roebuck after his father's death in 1932. The son built on his father's legacies in multiple ways, becoming a philanthropist and an organizational leader. He served on the American Jewish Committee's executive council and, in 1943, became the first president of the American Council for Judaism.

The Council was founded in 1942, after leaders in Reform Judaism's Central Conference of American Rabbis had passed a pro-Zionist resolution that supported the formation of a Jewish army in Palestine. This small group of rabbis met for a two-day conference to protest what they saw as the caving of many Reform leaders to Zionist propagandizing, and it was there that they founded the Council. Rising to a leadership role in the Council was Rabbi Elmer Berger. In the paper Berger delivered at the founding conference, he told the story of the anti-Zionist work he did from the pulpit of his Temple Beth El in Flint, Michigan. He noted that he objected to Zionism for two reasons. He believed that Zionism betrayed the principles of Reform Judaism; he believed that, as Jewish resources increasingly flowed to Zionist organizations and to Palestine, Jewish community life in the United States would be neglected.[40]

With local chapters and regional offices in Richmond, Dallas, Chicago, and San Francisco, Council members were motivated by their fear that "a state would be a serious obstacle to Jewish integration in America."[41] This same theme had long been present in Reform Judaism's critiques of both Jewish nationalism and Zionism. Yet the name that members chose for their organization, the American Council for Judaism, along with the many documents, speeches, and articles they wrote about the Council across the decades, demonstrated their complex and multidimensional objections to Zionism. They thought of Judaism expressly as a religion, and so members of the Council "condemned all forms of Jewish separatism," including Zionism, because in their view it threatened to make Jews targets of antisemitism. Given their objections to Zionism, they took note of the increasingly Zionist leadership of mainstream American Jewish organizations and thus often "denied the right of any group to speak for all Jews." They also addressed concerns about the impact of Jewish statehood on those native to the Middle East, "rejecting the creation of an exclusively Jewish state as undemocratic and as a retreat from the universal vision of Judaism."[42]

Council members saw Zionism and the creation of an ethnocracy (in which state power is determined based on ethnic identity) in the Jewish state as antithetical to Judaism's true teachings. In the opinion of Council members, Judaism was a religion that taught universal lessons of justice and ethics, and Jews were destined to spread these lessons throughout the world. Council members were deeply invested in the survival of Reform Judaism. They underscored this idea in the name they chose for their organization, as they sought to "save American Judaism" from Zionist leaders and their ideas.[43]

* * *

Council leaders founded their organization as tragedy continued to unfold in Europe. Nazi power grew, millions of Jews and others were put to death, and the refugee crisis grew increasingly urgent. Council members responded to these tragedies and to two defining events in the history of Zionism that followed World War I and the Balfour Declaration: Britain's White Paper and the Biltmore Conference. The White Paper, which Britain issued in May 1939, set firm restrictions on Jewish immigration to Palestine under the British Mandate and struck many as representing a weakening of British support for a Jewish homeland there. The White Paper was issued following growing, popular Palestinian Arab resistance to the British Mandate and to Jewish settlement in Palestine, the Great Palestinian Revolt of 1936–39.

The issuing of the White Paper contributed to the immense crisis that faced Jewish refugees fleeing Nazism and the fear that Jews would have nowhere to escape. In response, American Zionists planned a world meeting at New York's Biltmore Hotel in May 1942. The six hundred delegates to the conference passed what came to be known as the Biltmore Program, rejecting the White Paper of 1939 and calling for the fulfillment of the original purpose of the Balfour Declaration and the British Mandate. American Jewish leaders largely endorsed the Biltmore Program and called for the Jewish Agency to have control over Jewish immigration; praying for "liberation" for Jews in "ghettos and concentration camps in Hitler-dominated Europe," they joined the call for a "Jewish commonwealth" to solve the Jewish problem and create a new entity in the democratic world order.[44] As historian Melvin I. Urofsky wrote, the Biltmore Conference "clearly indicated the new mood of American Zionism." Before the Biltmore Conference, he continued, "American Zionists saw Palestine as a refuge; after Biltmore they fought for a state."[45]

The Council's founding calls this unity, not its urgency, into question. Rabbi Morris Lazaron was one of the Reform rabbis who protested the Jewish army resolution that sparked the founding of the Council. He identified himself as a former member of the Zionist Organization of America, who "left the Organization because I could not accept its philosophy, its aims, and its methods."[46] At this founding meeting on June 1, 1942, Rabbi Lazaron read a moving speech. He spoke first of the immediate need to defeat the Axis powers and then to take on the challenge of restoring order and human rights to displaced people in Europe, which he called "work of reconstruction so complex and far reaching . . . in building a chastened world where men should have learned through suffering that the will and the power to do right are the only abiding sources of might."

Rabbi Lazaron rejected the idea that the demands of the World Zionist Congress were "the opinion of all American Jews." To the room full of rabbis, he said, "As men who have dedicated our lives to the faith of Israel, we have not only the right but the duty" to consider these demands because "we cannot by our silence seem to give consent to those things we reject." Lazaron felt that "recognition of Jewish sovereignty in Palestine" showed "inconsistencies which are hard to reconcile." He wondered how to balance "unreserved support for the United Nations" with "cooperation with the Arabs" and the Jewish Agency's "full control of immigration." How can Zionist leaders "deny diaspora nationalism for the Jews," he asked, but then call upon "Jews who are citizens of other countries to work for a political goal related to a land other than their own"?

Rabbi Lazaron and his fellow non- and anti-Zionist rabbis supported the building up of Palestine as a cultural center and "as a refuge." They made clear that they would not accept "secular Jewish nationalism" aligned with "international political pressure" because, they concluded, "a state based on race or creed [w]as fundamentally wrong and indeed is the antithesis of one of the principles for why this war is being fought."

Rabbi Lazaron ended his speech with a plea for an emphasis on Jewish philosophies of peace, "the banner held aloft for 30 centuries. . . . For all the reversion to the brutal which the present war indicates," he said, "the progress of man is forward." Lazaron saw Judaism as a "universal religion" and urged Jews to hold fast to its lessons in "human brotherhood." "The physical suffering of the Jews is not the only test of democratic civilization," he asserted, "but the example of Jewish faith under fire becomes the inspiration of world redemption."[47]

One year later into the horrors of the war years, in June 1943, Council president Lessing Rosenwald gave voice to the organization's perspective in his *Life* magazine piece, "Why Americans of Jewish Faith Are Opposed to the Establishment of a Jewish State." Edith G. Rosenwald, his wife and one of the few women whose voices can be found in the organization's files, recounted years later that the magazine had "carried an article by King Ibn Saud [first king of Saudi Arabia] and another by Zionist leader Dr. Stephen Wise on the Palestine problem," adding that Lessing "wanted to make clear that there was a third viewpoint." She saw this, her husband's column, as the Council's first "walk on the stage of history."[48]

Rosenwald acknowledged the "indescribable barbarism" of the Axis powers and noted that "unquestionably Palestine has contributed in a tangible way to the alleviation of the present catastrophe in Jewish life by providing refuge for some of Europe's Jews." Also present in his arguments were ideas reminiscent of Reform Judaism, that "nationalistic philosophies" have "caused untold suffering to the world, and particularly to the Jews." Further, though, he predicted that to set up "an autonomous religious state" in a land that "for centuries has been a Holy Land" to Christianity, Islam, and Judaism would create "turmoil and strife." He worried that Jews in Europe might be "forced" to immigrate to Palestine and so proposed that Palestine be "*one* of the countries selected for resettlement." Rosenwald concluded by expressing hope that Palestine would establish a democratic, autonomous government "in which Jews will be free Palestinians [here meaning inhabitants of Palestine of all backgrounds] whose religion is Judaism." Referencing American pluralism, he hoped "that Palestine might be another demonstration to the world that men of all faiths can live together in mutual respect for one another, and that such high regard of man for man is the cornerstone of lasting peace."[49]

Rosenwald arrived at this position via a different route from that of the Council's Reform rabbis. He saw himself as a patriotic American and before 1941 was a member of the isolationist and antiwar America First Committee. In September of that year, Charles Lindbergh accepted an invitation from this committee to speak in Des Moines, and in it he identified Jews as one of the pressure groups, alongside British leaders and the Roosevelt administration, pushing the United States into the war. Relying on antisemitic tropes, Lindbergh also cited the profound influence of Jews on movies, press, radio, and government. Rosenwald resigned from the America First Committee in protest. After the bombing of Pearl Harbor on December 7, 1941, with other members of the Council, Rosenwald urged President Truman to liberalize American immigration laws in order to bring more displaced persons (those displaced by the war) to the United States. One scholar suggests that Rosenwald and other Council members hoped to demonstrate that they did not all want to go to Palestine; another scholar notes that this work "demonstrates that, contrary to Zionist claims, he [Rosenwald] was not indifferent to the needs of his fellow Jews."[50]

The Holocaust fundamentally reshaped debates over Zionism in the 1940s. As historian Maddalena Marinari notes, a growing number of "exasperated" American Jews, "including non-Zionists, called for the creation of an autonomous Jewish state as the only solution to the refugee crisis."[51] As news of Nazi atrocities spread, American antisemitism soon "seemed stripped of any respectability."[52] Protestant leaders, too, had come to see Palestine as "an enduring solution to the problem of Jewish statelessness" during the Holocaust. Even though many had ties to the Arab Christian communities of Palestine, Protestant support for Zionism grew stronger and more visible.[53]

Yet the historical currents that led to the anti-Zionist sentiments of Reform Judaism's leadership did not fade away. In the decades that followed, many German American Jews, including Reform rabbis and Council members, moved from anti-Zionist to non-Zionist positions, from active opposition to some degree of support. Anti-Zionists continued to voice concerns about the Zionist project. As historian Rafael Medoff notes, the position statements of the American Council for Judaism kept the rights of Palestinians still in the public eye in the 1940s,[54] and several members of the Council continued that work in the decades that followed.

In 1946, a few years after Lessing Rosenwald gave voice to the Council's anti-Zionist position in *Life* magazine, the radio journalist Tex McCrary interviewed him on New York City's WEAF radio station. McCrary introduced Rosenwald, welcoming him as president of the Council, as a spokesperson of an organization "concerned with the solution of the Palestine problem." McCrary asked Rosenwald to present the positions of the Council. Rosenwald first thanked McCrary for allowing Americans "to hear all sides" of the issue and "make up their own minds." He then articulated his organization's platform with these words: "[The Council] affirms that Jews are nationals of their respective countries and are Jews in religion only; are not a nation, race, or a people. It believes that integration, not segregation, marks the road to equality, security, and happiness. It seeks for all Jews everywhere equal rights and responsibilities with other citizens." While these statements drew neatly from the Reform tradition, McCrary's follow-up questions prompted Rosenwald to explore more of his anti-Zionist position. Rosenwald asserted that Palestine should be a "state where Jews, Moslems, and Christians can worship as they see fit and are accorded equal rights and responsibilities."[55]

Rosenwald also affirmed that Council members opposed a Jewish state in Palestine and that they agreed with the 1946 recommendations of the Anglo-American Committee of Inquiry, composed of American and British representatives tasked with proposing solutions to the political conflicts in Palestine and the many displaced Jews in Europe.[56] In April, the Committee of Inquiry proposed continuing the British Mandate over Palestine and recommended that one hundred thousand displaced European Jews be allowed entry. The committee wrote that only Palestine sought to give homes to Europe's displaced Jewish populations but that Palestine alone could not meet Europe's emigration needs and that the United States and Britain needed to find places for other displaced persons to live. Its members recommended that Palestine should be "neither a Jewish state nor an Arab state"; because it is a "Holy Land, sacred to Christian, to Jew, and to Moslem alike . . . it is not, and can never become, a land which any race or religion can justly claim as its very own."[57]

Rosenwald asserted that Council members, like the members of the Anglo-American Committee, "reject the claim that Palestine has been given to the Jews of the world and that all Jews therefore have special rights in regard to Palestine." When McCrary pressed Rosenwald on the Jewish "right to Palestine and a state of their own to assure security," Rosenwald countered that "there is no more assurance that Jews will be secure with a Jewish State than without one." He insisted that the "political problem of Palestine" be divorced from the "humanitarian" problem of displaced European Jews of the Holocaust. First, he said, "peace must be established . . . in Palestine. The warlike atmosphere of Palestine is no place for men, women, and children who already may have suffered more than human beings should endure. No, Mr. McCrary, Palestine alone cannot solve the problem; the nations of the world *can* and *must*."

Just as Zionists linked the language of Americanism to Zionism, so too did Rosenwald's language draw from American ideals. When McCrary

asked if "the American people favor creation of a Jewish State," Rosenwald highlighted what he saw as the unrepresentativeness of Jewish leadership and the Americanness of anti-Zionism:

> I don't know what the majority believe; nor does anyone else, despite their
> claims. I am confident, however, that possessed of the facts, the American
> people would uphold the stand taken by the Anglo-American Committee
> in favor of a Palestinian state for all nationals and against a Jewish State
> for Jews alone. All Americans have a stake in Palestine because it is a key
> to the peace of the world. Let them study the proposals for a Jewish State
> in light of democratic principles for which they stand as a people. They
> believe in equal rights for all citizens without regard to race or creed.
> They believe in the separation of church and government. They believe
> that one group shall not dominate the others. They believe in the right
> of self-determination. The Jewish State cannot be reconciled with these
> principles.[58]

Lazaron, Rosenwald, and other anti-Zionists claimed that their ideas
were in line with American "democratic principles." Rosenwald's statements fit neatly alongside other Jewish responses to modern American life
and also within the Council's early, evolving platform, which shifted from
a religious mission to save Reform Judaism to a more explicitly political
opposition to Zionism. The name of the organization harkened back to its
founding ideas, and a few years later, members argued over whether the
organization needed to adopt "a permanent program of religious development" alongside the anti-Zionist work.[59] This need was perhaps more
acute given the Council's strong position that Jews were defined as a religious community, not a race or a nation entitled to sovereignty as the
Zionists argued.[60] Council members such as journalist Leonard Sussman
later took on this religious outreach work in designing curricula for Jewish
religious schools that had no references to Zionism or Israel.

To be sure, the Council concerned itself with Israel, with the impact
of Zionism on American Jews and Judaism and on the rise of antisemitism in the Middle East. Council leaders advocated strongly to bring
displaced persons to the United States after the war and to liberalize
American immigration laws. These stances disproved the idea that anti-
Zionists cared little for victims of antisemitism.[61]

In these same years, Isidore Feinstein "I. F." Stone (1907–89), a secular American Jewish journalist who strongly identified as a Jew and a Zionist, coupled profound sympathy for Jewish refugees with deep concern for the implications of the Zionist project. He warned that the campaign to gain support for Israel among American Jews was based "on half-truths." In 1946, at the invitation of the Haganah, the underground Jewish defense forces in Mandatory Palestine, he traveled with Holocaust refugees to Palestine for his reporting. One year earlier, he expressed strong misgivings that without any agreements with Palestine's Arab citizens, Palestinian Jewry was being led into a "blind alley." Like Council members, Stone hoped that the United Nations or the Anglo-American Committee would lead Jews and Arabs to a "bi-national settlement."[62]

But it was the Council's anti-Zionism that sounded the alarm of mainstream Jewish groups. In 1944, leaders of the Zionist Organization of America formed a group originally called the Committee to Combat the American Council for Judaism, later the Committee on Unity for Palestine, with 112 local branches that kept watch on the Council and wrote "hundreds of thousands of pieces of pro-Zionist literature." For four years, the Committee on Unity for Palestine "battled" the Council. They put their arguments on display in the hearings over the Congressional resolution that urged the United States to support free Jewish immigration to Palestine as the terms of the 1939 White Paper, which restricted Jewish immigration to Palestine, were set to expire.[63]

These efforts aligned closely with the massive drive to "Zionize" the American Jewish community in the name of unity and, ultimately, to generate the appearance of an imagined consensus through sustained efforts to marginalize dissenting positions with regard to Zionism. The Council launched a zealous public relations campaign to match the energy of Zionist leaders, releasing statements to the press that sought to expose what it described as "Zionism's Real Aims." This was a subheading in a copy of a 1947 speech by Council leader Rabbi Irving Reichert of San Francisco, which was then published as publicity material.

In his speech, Rabbi Reichert asserted that the Zionists' aims were not related to the "undeniable . . . urgency" of Nazism's refugees. When Zionists "recruit members and solicit financial support," he continued, "the appeal is always made in terms of human suffering." Reichert saw Zionism's real aim not as humanitarian but as nationalist, the building of a nation-state in Palestine, which he argued would not solve "the Jewish problem." It was "an infamous libel" and a "slander," Rabbi Reichert asserted, "to accuse us [anti- and non-Zionists] of indifference to Jewish suffering because we will not accept Zionism as the solution to the Jewish tragedy in Europe." He pointed out that "non-Zionist generosity" was "in no small measure responsible for the miracle of modern Palestine." These were funds from Jews who saw Palestine as "*a* homeland," not "*the* homeland," a "sanctuary for the oppressed."

Reichert centered Jewish thought and belonging in Jewish religion. He quoted the Pittsburgh Platform and David Philipson's 1908 history of Reform Judaism to explain that above all, he feared that an exclusive focus on Zionism would "drive the Jew . . . further and further from his religion and leave him [*sic*] spiritually bankrupt." With "threats and reprisals," Reichert noted, leaders were "browbeaten" into adopting Zionist planks in their organizations. He saw this "as desperate and unwise as it was un-Jewish and un-American."[64]

A few years earlier, in his 1943 sermon on the eve of Yom Kippur, the holiest day in the Jewish calendar, Reichert had spoken of the Council's vision as one of "Jews and Arabs working harmoniously together in Palestine, under a democratic form of government." Council leaders advocated for the United Nations to "liberalize the opportunities for all" refugees to find homes wherever they wanted. Rabbi Reichert quoted the words of journalist William Zukerman on the courageous resistance of Jews in the Warsaw Ghetto, who fought against the idea that they were outsiders and thus homeless or in exile. He ended his sermon with a question. If his congregation believed that Jews were homeless, that nationality and race were the "determining and unique features of Judaism," and that only a Jewish state in Palestine would solve the Jewish problem, they should join the Zionist cause. If, instead, they believed that religious principles define Judaism, that the Jewish problem was part of the "world problem," solvable only through democratic means, and that Jews and Arabs needed to work together in Palestine, then they should join the American Council for Judaism.[65]

Rabbi Reichert's phrasing reads as mild compared to other, more strident Council publications. One mailing had the words "CHOOSE NOW" in bold, two-inch-high capital letters atop each page, with questions underneath such as "Will you accept Zionist domination of all Jewish activities?" and "Do you believe that because you are a Jew you must be a Zionist?" For each passage by the Council on the left side, the opposite page featured the counter argument in the form of a Zionist leader's published statement. The first left-side page, interestingly, featured the words of President Woodrow Wilson with the header "Democracy says": "You cannot become true Americans if you think of yourselves in groups. A man who thinks of himself as belonging to a particular national group in America has not yet become an American."

Opposite this was a quote from Daniel Frisch of the Zionist Organization of America about sending American Jews to Israel, those who are, as he put it, "American-bred young people who want to live as Jews—minus the hyphen—under the smiling skies of the reborn Israel." The Council relied on this quote to show that Zionism posed a direct threat to the *American* citizenship and patriotism of American Jews. The Council saw Zionism as an obstacle to true American belonging, and they used President Wilson's nativist quote to support their points.

The Council's publicity document contained statements about Judaism being a religion and Zionists claiming falsely to speak for all American Jews. The final page urged readers to "CHOOSE NOW OR THE CHOICE WILL BE MADE FOR YOU" by joining the American Council for Judaism.[66] With this mailing, Council leaders claimed that their positions aligned most closely with American ideas about integration, democracy, and patriotism.

Many Jews saw Jewish unity as paramount in the face of the Holocaust, and Zionist Reform rabbis accused the Council of creating schisms in American Jewry beginning with its founding in 1942. Rabbi Berger, however, asserted that "the nationalist tendencies in Jewish life are deleterious to the best interests of American Jewry, world Jewry, even Palestine Jewry," and thus "if a split occurs, it can hardly be charged to our side."[67] This rhetoric of unity, Council leaders later contended, served as a "restraint" used to "curtail some of our rights of freedom of speech." It was the "Zionist-nationalists," Berger argued, "who have broken the unity" because they have "compelled the choice" between working for the future of all Jews in all nations or making Palestine central and of foremost importance to Jews throughout the world. Any unity or consensus on Zionism, said the Council, was "nothing more than conformity."[68]

Jewish groups passed resolutions protesting the Council's public statements and urging national Jewish leaders to speak out against its work.
The Los Angeles Community Relations Committee, an umbrella group
for the city's mainstream Jewish organizations, for example, passed a
resolution in September 1947 stating that "the natural consequences" of
the Council's "continued activities [are] to supply material support and
comfort and comfort for known and active anti-Semites."[69] Richard Gutstadt, national director for the Anti-Defamation League, consulted with
Isaiah Minkoff of the National Community Relations Advisory Council
about the American Council for Judaism. Gutstadt found "culpability on
both sides," in both Rabbi Berger's ideas and what he termed the "very extreme statements that have been made by ardent Zionist leadership." Ever
conscious of American perceptions of the Jewish community, Gutstadt
worried that ricocheting public statements would "alienate the friends we
have" and "did not further Jewish dignity before the general community."[70]

Jewish leaders continued to express their fear of the Council's public
statements internally. David Petegorsky, executive director of the American Jewish Congress, relayed to his members that their organization had
considered a similar anti-Council resolution one year earlier. Congress
members had voted it down, fearful of the impact of a publicly aired,
intracommunal debate. Congress members instead opted to engage in
private correspondence with the Council. Petegorsky found the results
"wholly unsatisfactory." He wrote that he would have preferred "a strong
public statement by . . . the major national Jewish agencies," seeing this
as "more effective in discrediting . . . the Council."[71] Even before Israel's
statehood, then, two interconnected dynamics emerged. Zionist Jewish
leaders continued to feel the precariousness of their American belonging, ever conscious of how "Americans" perceived Jews in their everyday
lives. And these leaders began to link criticism of American Zionism to
aiding enemies of Jews.[72]

* * *

Through the 1940s, as the American Jewish Committee sought to become
more of a mass-membership organization, its leaders moved closer to the
Zionism of the American Jewish Congress. Consequently, by 1946, its
leaders were longer sympathetic to the American Council for Judaism.[73]
Though AJC members "recognized the positive impact of a Jewish state

on Diaspora Jewry," they continued to reject some tenets of Zionism in that they "held firmly to . . . [a] belief in the viability of a Jewish community outside a Jewish state."[74] Yet AJC and Council members continued to clash. This was not surprising, given that at that moment, the Council saw its mission as tied to fighting the influence of Zionism on American Jews.

The widening gap between the American Jewish Committee and the American Council for Judaism was apparent in a 1949 document titled "Rosenwald Explains ACJ to AJC[ommittee]." One year after the creation of the State of Israel, Lessing Rosenwald protested the equation of "Judaism with Israeli projects and problems." He questioned the representativeness of Zionist leadership and their ability to speak for all American Jews and too feared that the AJC, and Zionists in general, were trying to silence discussion and dissent among American Jews. Rosenwald concluded that "the impression that all Jews think alike on Israeli matters" was far more dangerous than what he saw as an exchange of ideas. Rosenwald's hope was that all publicity, for or against Zionism, would be aired in public discussions. And he insisted that subscribers to all views must have access to "the same media. . . . Otherwise Jewish nationalists will succeed in their objective to convince fellow Americans that what they say and do is representative of all Jews."[75]

By 1950, as historian Zvi Ganin writes, "anger on the part of the organized Jewish community at the Council's publicity policy finally reached the boiling point." Ganin's observation mistakenly excludes Council members from the "organized Jewish community."[76] Still, Ganin points to an important moment, when anti-Zionists and non-Zionists tried but failed to find common ground in their opposition to Jewish nationalism.

Many American Jews continued to think of themselves as non-Zionists, or perhaps just uninterested in Israel.[77] Though AJC leaders increasingly found the Council "extreme" in its "anti-Israel policy," over the course of many years they tried to broker an understanding with the Council, motivated, to be sure, by anxiety about a public airing of any intracommunal feud. Rosenwald's confidence in the usefulness of a public exchange of ideas was a rare find, as Cold War anti-communism and mainstream antisemitism fed longtime anxieties about accusations of double loyalties among American Jews.

The Blaustein–Ben-Gurion understanding of 1950 is central to the story of the growing mainstream acceptance and respectability of

Zionism in the United States. The American Jewish Committee's leader, Jacob Blaustein, met Israel's prime minister David Ben-Gurion in Jerusalem in 1950 to discuss, in effect, the moral contract of American Jews with the United States.[78] Israel's leader affirmed the autonomy of Jewish communities outside of Israel and noted that American Jews were not exiles who should immigrate to Israel.

This, Blaustein noted in his press release, would "put an end to any idea or allegation that there is any such thing as 'dual loyalty' on the part of American Jewry."[79] Blaustein asserted that he was "confident that the vast majority of American Jewry will continue to recognize the necessity and desirability of helping to make Israel a strong, viable, self-supporting state and will do its full part in that objective." He chose his phrasing carefully, stating that most American Jews already supported Zionism while using the future tense to suggest their potential financial and political contributions. He spoke glowingly of the growth of industry in what he described as the region's "newest democracy."[80]

The American Jewish Committee and other organizational leaders worked hard to keep Israel in the minds (and fundraising campaigns) of American Jews. A few weeks after the press release about the Blaustein / Prime Minister Ben-Gurion meeting, the AJC collected a "Summary of Press Reaction on Ben-Gurion-Blaustein Statements." The report relayed that most Jewish presses "warmly welcomed both statements as a much-needed clarification." Only "a few of the more extreme Zionist publications were somewhat limited in their praise and expressed hurt surprise that such a significant statement had been issued not to a Zionist body, but to the AJC." They noted the fact that Prime Minister Ben-Gurion had chosen to elevate the non-Zionist Committee to a new level of importance in relations between American Jewry and Israel.

The AJC's press summary recorded the dissenting responses of others who resisted the pressures of a slowly evolving, painstakingly enforced American Jewish consensus on Zionism and Israel. William Zukerman, editor of the *Jewish Newsletter*, which was highly critical of Israel and American Zionism, saw Prime Minister Ben-Gurion's choice of the AJC as deeply important, symbolic of the end of "militant Zionism" in the United States. Members of the American Council for Judaism were also pleased that "fanatical American supporters" of American Zionism could no longer justify encouraging a "mass exodus of our fellow

Jews to Israel." Indeed, Council members pushed further and "claimed a share of the credit for the pronouncement." It was important to Zukerman and Council members that the non-Zionist AJC had taken a lead role in this negotiation. For their part, AJC members were pleased that "the great weight of Jewish public opinion recognizes the achievement of the American Jewish Committee." They concluded that their work offered a "welcome release from tensions heretofore prevailing."[81]

These tensions emerged from contests over the role of Zionism and Israel in the future of American Jewish communal life. This 1950 meeting between Blaustein and Ben-Gurion is significant not only because Israel's leadership lent support for an American brand of Zionism but also because they wanted to keep non-Zionists engaged with Israel even after the creation of a state and to limit or even eliminate the role American Zionist Jewish leaders might play in shaping Israel's growth. American Jews were tasked mainly with providing financial and political support to this effort. This was affirmation, then, that American Jews were not in exile and that Zionism did not require them to move to Israel. In exchange, American Jews were to give money and support to Israel but only on "nonideological grounds."[82]

This arrangement may have contributed to the role of American Jewish leaders in marginalizing any Jewish dissent from American Zionism. As non-Zionism faded and Zionism gained support, American Jewish leaders understood that all money flowing to Israel was to have no strings attached, no expectations that American Jewish opinions on Israeli policies would be heard. American Jewish criticism of Israel and Zionism was seen not only as potentially injurious to American Jews but also as unwelcome in Israel.

Into the 1950s: Anti-Zionism

In 1953, Council members celebrated the organization's tenth year with a conference in San Francisco. There they spoke of their original founding ideas, their new campaigns, their current successes and challenges. Rabbi Morris Lazaron's anti-Zionism had by now put him in conflict with his Reform congregation's board in Baltimore. In 1946 he retired after thirty-one years of service and was elected rabbi emeritus; in 1949, when his congregational leaders insisted that he no longer speak about

Zionism, a testament to Zionism's growing respectability and mainstream acceptance, and in line with the increasingly Zionistic priorities of the Reform movement, he resigned as rabbi emeritus in protest.[83]

Then four years later, still with the Council, Rabbi Lazaron spoke of the continuing pressure from "the Government of Israel and the Zionist Organization of America . . . to use the American Jewish community as a pressure block for Israeli interests."[84] He began by noting that the US needed to "regain the confidence of the Arab and Moslem world" by ceasing to "play favorites" with Israel. He believed that "Israeli and Zionist policy . . . played into their [Soviet] hands," as it was being used by the Soviets to "embarrass the United States." Lazaron saw this as dangerous for the United States and the Cold War world at large.[85]

He then focused on what he described as Zionist and Israeli "attempts to capture [Jewish] communities, to dominate Jewish education and all our institutions and give to American Jewish life an Israeli orientation." He used the terms "infiltration," "domination," "intimidation," and "censorship" when speaking of the Zionist influence on American Jewish life. Most profoundly, he asked fundamental questions about the direction of American Jewish life: "Have we lost our capacity for indignation at wrong? . . . What Jewish organization has lifted its voice on behalf of the Arab refugees numbering some 800,000 people? . . . Does Jewish nationalism crowd out every feeling of sympathy for any other group than Jews?"[86]

Rabbi Lazaron was quick to point out the "extremists" and "fanatics" among all populations in the Middle East, to condemn murderous behavior among all groups and leadership regimes. But he also spoke of how Palestinians live on "bare hills" where they "gaze daily on wooded lands and farms which were their homes." Locally and globally, he said, "an undercurrent of resentment is rising," and he wondered what that might mean. Instead of using its funds for good, he continued, Israel sought to "constantly justify itself," and he lamented the "excesses of Jewish nationalism" in using all its money to build up its defense. It was the world's "anti-Semitism which created Zionism," Lazaron wrote.[87] Now he feared that antisemitic sentiment was emerging as a response to Israel's actions.

Ten years into his dissenting career on Zionism, Lazaron likely had little fear of American antisemitism, as it had largely been delegitimized by the Holocaust. Rather, he feared for Jewish communal life and for the impact of Zionism on global Jewish communities, on the United States, and on the wider world. Lazaron proposed possible remedies. He called for what he described as a "revolt of individuals and community leaders . . . against Jewish nationalist dominance of American life." He called upon the United States and the United Nations to "urge Israel to make substantial gestures to the Arab and Moslem people." These gestures would include restitution for Palestinian refugees, full and equal rights for all citizens of Israel, and the internationalization of Jerusalem so that the holy sites of all faiths would be protected by the United Nations.[88]

Finally, Lazaron concluded, "Moslem, Christian, and Jew must show regard to the sanctities of our faiths, all of which proclaim 'justice, justice, thou shalt pursue.'" He ended his speech with these words of optimism and hope: "Israel in Palestine may well become the advance guard of an army that brings not division, but cooperation; not prejudice, but compassion; not conquest, but justice; not war, but peace."[89]

* * *

That same year, in October 1953, four years after Israel and Jordan signed an armistice agreement, Israel attacked the Jordanian town of Kibya (also spelled Qibya). The reprisal raid followed an Arab attack in which a Jewish mother and her two children had been killed in Yehud. An independent special forces section of the Israeli Defense Forces, Unit 101, led by Colonel Ariel Sharon (who later served as Israel's prime minister), destroyed fifty homes, killing sixty-nine Palestinian civilians, at least two-thirds of them women and children who were hiding inside their homes. Although Sharon claimed that he did not know the houses were occupied, the event nonetheless shocked and embarrassed Prime Minister David Ben-Gurion. *Time* magazine covered the gruesome attack; its article on the event concluded with these words: "To survive, Israel needs peace. Last week, in defiance of the U.N. and in the slaughter of Kibya, Israel made peace harder than ever to obtain."[90]

US secretary of state John Foster Dulles also strongly condemned the attack, and Council members expressed "appreciation" to Dulles for assuming a stance of "impartiality." "We have consistently urged an American policy which would eliminate the impression that the United

States is 'the backer of expansionist Zionism,'" Council leaders wrote to Dulles. They acknowledged that America's efforts "to deal with the Palestine problem have been made difficult and complicated by special pleading [and] domestic pressure groups" and offered their support for his work.

Above all, the group's members conveyed to Dulles that "the very existence of our group is concrete proof that neither on the Palestine matter nor on any other is there any individual Jew or organization of Jews empowered to speak for all Americans of Jewish faith."[91] Rabbi Berger felt that Dulles's openness to the Council's platform represented "the first, hopeful sign of an American policy which would be some corrective to the one-dimensional kind of support which [President Harry] Truman ended up providing for Zionism/Israel."[92] The Blaustein–Ben-Gurion understanding meant that the Council could no longer attack American Zionism solely because it dismissed Jewish life outside of Israel. Yet Council leaders continued to challenge the representativeness of American Zionist communal leaders—and also the idea that Israel would make the world safer for both Jews and democracy across the world.

Rabbi Berger used the incident to reflect on what he saw as strong Zionist propagandizing, the attempts to win over American Jewry for Zionism's goals. When the United States joined in the introduction of a UN resolution condemning Israel, American Zionist leaders were shocked. Prominent Zionist rabbis in the Reform movement spoke out on the "one-sided attitude in the current Arab-Israeli controversy" and asked if the attention paid to the "assault on Kibya" indicated that "Jewish lives were held cheaper than the lives of other people."[93] Rabbi Berger expressed his own surprise that American Jews did not echo their government's "moral outrage" over the Kibya massacre, describing their reaction as evidence of American Jews' "brainwash[ing]" and their willingness to support the Israeli government no matter its actions.[94]

Several other Jewish leaders spoke up in the wake of the attack. Henry Hurwitz, a friend and supporter of the Council, wrote an essay titled "Israel, What Now?" in the *Menorah Journal*, a publication he edited, in which he called Kibya a "pogrom" and asked how Ben-Gurion, whose people faced pogroms, could "defend pogroms by his own people against their neighbors."[95] Reform Rabbi Arthur B. Lebowitz of the Jewish Community Center in Palm Springs, Florida, denounced the attack in a sermon accusing Israel of "cold-blooded murder," and he stated that the "Arab infiltrators into Israel 'were human beings who want to come home.'" Rabbi Lebowitz said that the Jewish community "prohibits criticism of Israel," terming it "censorship," and he spoke against what he described as Israel's "chauvinism, entirely dominated by military considerations." The *B'nai B'rith Messenger*, which covered his sermon, asserted that though Rabbi Lebowitz was entitled to say whatever he wanted, he had nonetheless done damage by spreading "biased, one-sided expositions."[96]

Rabbi Berger and the Council had long articulated fear of this "one-sided" dynamic among American Zionists and expressed dismay over American Jews' unconditional support of Israeli policies. Some scholars see the Kibya massacre as the event that catalyzed a more forceful lobby to champion Zionism and marginalize all dissent among American Jews and in American politics broadly. Historian Doug Rossinow notes that the American Zionist Committee for Public Affairs, later renamed the American Israel Public Affairs Committee or AIPAC, was founded in this moment.[97] Others note that in these years, support for Israel emerged out of a romance with Israel as a Cold War model of "responsible militarism."[98] The Council's close relationship with the Eisenhower administration engendered anxiety in some Zionist leaders because they feared diminished support for American Zionism and Israel.[99]

Though the Council did not have a huge membership, it played a decisive role in both the Eisenhower administration's foreign policy and the formation of the American Israel lobby as a counterforce. These narratives contradict the idea that anti- and non-Zionism had no relevant presence in the 1950s and had to await anticolonialist movements of the 1960s to light their spark once again.

One example of this new, outwardly focused Jewish anti-Zionism lies in Council writings after the Bandung Conference of nonaligned nations in April 1955, a conference heralded for bringing together independent Asian and African states (many just free from colonial rule) in hopes of development and peaceful cooperation. The powerful association of Israel with Western colonialism on the left prevented Israel from receiving an invitation to the conference.[100]

In the June 1955 *Council News*, a Council contributor with the initials LRS, almost certainly Leonard R. Sussman, explained the "Meaning of Bandung" to the anti-Zionist audience. Sussman directed the Council's religious education program from 1953 to 1955, after Israel's statehood, when the Council again devoted energy to Reform Judaism by creating religious education materials with no references to Israel or Zionism.[101] Not only was the Bandung conference significant because of the emerging power of newly independent Asian and African citizens, but Bandung was also important to observe for "the role that Zionism played" as an obstacle to peaceful cooperation on the world stage. Sussman described Zionism as a "big-time problem" given that all twenty-nine nations voted to "support the Arab position as against Israel's" and because these leaders spoke of Zionism as "the worst offspring of imperialism." Sussman quoted one official at the Bandung conference who called Zionism "the last chapter in the book of old colonialism." He drew attention to a periodical titled the *American Zionist*, which ran an article under the headline "Bandung Action Shows a Grave Moral Relapse." American Zionists saw Bandung as reinforcing the need for the United States to ally with Israel.[102]

Sussman asked his readers to see the conference from a different vantage point: as forcing the United States to think critically about its unconditional support of Israel, arguing that the millions of world citizens represented at the conference "cannot be ignored." "Bandung proved that Jews can no longer regard Zionism as a matter of purely Jewish concern," he wrote. "They cannot consider themselves unaffected bystanders while Zionism acts as their 'spokesman' on all manner of public issues."[103]

Sussman helps us understand how anti-Zionist advocacy lined up with other political commitments and how the anti-Zionism of these early organizations aligned with later anticolonialist and anti-imperialist critiques of Zionism. Sussman himself used this language in 1955. In addition to his leadership of religious education, he took over much of the leadership of the American Council for Judaism from Berger as executive vice president in 1949 and served in that position until right before the 1967 war in Israel.[104]

Sussman was a product of Reform Judaism's non-Zionism, a loyal member of what he called the "cathedral" of world Reform Judaism, Manhattan's Temple Emanu-El.[105] As a youth director for the temple in 1951, Sussman was shocked to see Holocaust teachings linked with support for the State of Israel in commemorations of Tisha B'Av, Judaism's day of mourning for the destruction of the ancient biblical Temple. When he wrote about this experience in the *Council News*, a "serious uproar" ensued in the Reform movement.[106] He later described this as the pivotal experience that led him to take more prominent roles in anti-Zionist advocacy.

In later years, Sussman wrote that he saw what he termed the "End of Judaism" as "largely in the hands of the Jews themselves." Taking aim at Jewish leaders' near-apocalyptic warnings about Jews' marriages with non-Jews, he wrote that "not only intermarriage reduces the number of practicing Jews," adding that "too many others restrict their 'Jewishness' solely to providing financial support or political aid to the state of Israel and weighing their personal acceptances as Jews by the scale of America's momentary support for Israel's geopolitics."[107]

Sussman deeply valued Judaism's "obligations of ethical practice and social justice." Going "beyond the family and the fellowship of Jews . . . commits Jews to the uplifting of oppressed human beings whatever their religious belief. . . . It calls on Jews to understand the travail of Palestinians as well as Israelis." It was this commitment he found most sustaining for his own Jewishness, and after leaving the Council, he became the leader of Freedom House, a US government–funded watchdog organization for democracy and human rights, for twenty-one years.[108]

* * *

The criticism of American Zionism by Council members began in the Reform movement, springing from efforts to balance American and Jewish belonging. Some Council members feared that Zionism could serve as a "racializing force," separating them as a people and preventing them from the security of full integration. Yet most Jewish leaders increasingly came to see Zionism as an acceptable, even integral, part of American Jewish identity. Supporting Zionism, they believed, could maintain unity among American Jews, preventing them from complete integration while also allowing them access to the privileges of whiteness.

Yet by the late 1950s, concerns about Zionism and Israel among some Council members grew broader. Some expressed concerns about Palestinian refugees, for example, and other Jewish organizational leaders used the Council as a reference when questions arose on the issue.[109] Rabbi Berger spoke at Arab Student League meetings as Arab American young people mobilized politically. In 1956, the National Community Relations Advisory Council passed resolutions indicting the Council and the American Friends of the Middle East for the "tone and content" of their "Arab propaganda," which they saw as "becoming increasingly anti-Semitic." The Advisory Council even accused them of "maintaining active liaison with native anti-Semitic groups and movements."[110] This was another example of Jewish leaders discrediting American Jews' criticisms of Israel and Zionism by labeling it antisemitic and by linking these critics' ideas to the "propaganda" of those outside of American Jewry.

A strong religious indictment of the American Council for Judaism came in June 1956, when the Orthodox American Board of Rabbis issued a press release announcing that the "Beth Din of America" (a rabbinical court of Judaism) resolved that its anti-Zionism was analogous to other, ancient "idolatrous" incidents in which "dissident fractional factions such as the Essenes and the Karaites . . . promulgated abortive doctrines that were incongruous with the true realities of our Toraic heritage and Divinely-ordained historic continuity." The Bet Din concluded that like these ancient examples, Council members would be "doomed to oblivion" for their "divisive deflections from the . . . universal solidarity of historic Israel."[111]

* * *

Founded in 1913 as a Jewish defense agency, the Anti-Defamation League kept a careful watch over American Jewish unity and on the emerging importance of Zionism in the projection of that unity. Though the Council had its headquarters in New York, Anti-Defamation League offices all over the country, including the one in New England, monitored local American Council for Judaism activity and sent out national alerts as early as 1949. That year, a Michigan member of the Council sent out a questionnaire on the relationship between American Jews and Israel. Leaders of the Anti-Defamation League sent preemptive warning letters to their regional offices identifying the author of the questionnaire as a "close friend of the American Council for Judaism and one of the leaders in the extreme Reform Judaism movement" and warning that the "tenor of the questions [in the questionnaire] was not favorable." Anti-Defamation League leaders echoed the Zionist Emergency Council, which had been "advising its people to ignore" the questionnaire.[112]

The Anti-Defamation League and other communal Jewish lead-ers viewed intensifying criticism of Israel more urgently in the 1950s. When a Council leader was to visit a local radio talk show, they feared that his appearance might negatively impact the local Jewish fundrais-ing campaign. They applied pressure so that the Council leader's ap-pearance would not occur while the "CJA [Combined Jewish Appeal] campaign" was "in progress."[113] The distribution of material related to Rabbi Berger's book, *Who Knows Better Must Say So!*, a collection of es-says about Berger's CIA-sponsored trip to the Middle East in 1955, also sparked concern and surveillance.[114] These incidents show just how abiding the fear of the Council among the Anti-Defamation League and other Jewish communal institutions was in these years—and also how these organizations' leaders sought to limit access to critical views of Zionism and Israel.

* * *

Despite accusations of antisemitism and disunity, Council members continued their advocacy. In addition to keeping the issue of Palestinian rights in public conversations, Council leaders spoke about how Ameri-can Jewish life had become increasingly tied to Israel and Zionism in attempts to win over the majority of American Jews.

In July 1952, Council members wrote a document titled "An Interim Recommended Religious School Curriculum" in response to what they called "growing demand." "There is a tragic deficiency," the au-thors noted, "of teaching materials devoted not to nationalistic, racist, self-segregated, secular, or otherwise non-American 'Jewishness' but rather to the religion, history, ideals and practice of Judaism." To this end, the Council published several Jewish texts and also completed a "Religious School Textbook Analysis" to take stock of what books anti-Zionists might find appropriate for Jewish schooling.[115] One year later, at a Council conference, "40 young adults from eight states got together for a special 'youth brunch'" to discuss Zionism in the programming of Jewish youth groups. "Miss Eleanor Ann Lipkin, acting chairman of the New York youth section . . . told how the major Jewish youth movements were virtually all conducted in a manner to promote Zionism."[116]

With that in mind, in 1953 Council members wrote an advisory pam-phlet for parents on how trips to Israel alienated American Jewish youth from their families by urging them to move to Israel as part of their responsibilities as Jews. Here members drew from the organization's early concerns about dual loyalties and the teachings of Judaism, combining those with a vision of modern Jewish life without Zionism. After these Jewish organizational trips to Israel, Council members wrote, "Young people return home disturbed over whether they are fully satisfying their responsibilities as Jews if they remain in the United States, or as Americans if they consider seriously the values they have learned abroad." Further, members asserted, "We are deeply concerned about organized Zionist efforts to encourage the immigration of young people on the basis of false claims and 'duties' falsely associated with the religion of Judaism." Into the 1960s, Council members criticized the "strong indoctrination" of these youth trips to Israel, which they believed would serve as leverage for fundraising for Israel and for furthering the Zionist content of American Jewish life.[117] They saw the campaign to "nationalize all Jewish summer camp children" as another piece of the "youth indoctrination program" of Zionist leaders.[118]

In 1956, Sussman wrote to a colleague concluding that "every social, political, religious, and educational aspect of the lives of Jews is now under some Zionist control as a result of the Jewish Agency's domination over the channels of financing."[119] Tied to this assertion of Zionist "control" was the Council's concern, beginning even before 1948, that American Zionists were stifling free expression among American Jews by marginalizing or silencing those who rejected Zionism. The Council wrote of Judaism as a religion, of their rejection of Zionism, and of their firm belief that American Jews did not speak with one voice. So it was that a concern about agreeing over Zionism became, or overlapped with, a concern about creating space for a plurality of voices and positions in the American Jewish world.

This was a concern of the Council throughout the decades. A Council Publicity Department campaign in the early 1960s specifically tried to push against what Rabbi Berger, leader of the Council, had long criticized as too few outlets for those who were not supportive of American Zionism or Israel. Around that same time, the Council sent a form letter to newspaper editors, columnists, and others "to protest the use of Zionist or pro-Zionist spokesmen without suitable balance on _____ [a subject to be filled in by the person individualizing this form letter]."[120]

The attempts of Council members to present a balance of perspectives on Zionism joined with anxiety about how Zionist leaders framed current events only to serve Zionist agendas. And at a National Executive Committee Meeting of the Council in June 1960, the group's members expressed their fears about the trial of Adolf Eichmann, the Nazi leader who had been captured in Argentina and brought to Israel for his trial. "The trial will be used by Israel to advance its [Israel's] claims as a spokesman for all Jews," Council leaders observed. They knew that "in the Eichmann case the Zionists have attained a major propaganda issue on which to advance their claims and goals."[121] Sussman wrote that their anger over the Eichmann case emerged from Israel's claim of "sovereign authority in Jewry." This was, he wrote, "Zionist exploitation of the Eichmann trial."[122]

Sussman's anti-Zionist work at the Council broadened as the years passed, and it led him to a career in human rights. Like Sussman, Rabbi Berger began in the Reform movement and moved to the Council. His own passionate anti-Zionism led him to focus exclusively on pro-Palestinian activism. His 1955 trip to Lebanon, Syria, and Jordan familiarized him with the plight of Palestinian refugees, the horrors of the refugee camps. The American Friends of the Middle East, a CIA-funded Protestant organization whose goal was to build pro-Arab sentiment in the United States, sponsored his trip.[123]

In April 1959, in a letter to his Council colleague and friend Clarence Coleman Jr., Rabbi Berger took stock of all that he and the Council had done. He also included some broader observations. He considered past campaigns, Sussman's religious school curriculum, and the role of the Council's anti-Zionism in providing a singular "liaison between religiously liberal Christians and religiously liberal Jews." Berger underscored the global significance of the Council's ideas. "Were it not for the Council," he wrote, "there would be no knowledge—none at all—not only in the Arab world, but in the Afro-Asian complex of nations, of the existence of an anti-Zionist position."[124]

Yet it was always a very small group. A few years later, *Time* magazine estimated the Council's membership at twenty thousand and identified the organization dismissively as allied with "Arabs" who "distribute Rabbi Berger's anti-Zionist pronouncements."[125] Sussman credited Berger and the Council for building on anti-Zionism's roots in Reform Judaism. In his autobiography, Sussman presented Rabbi Berger as a difficult man who treated people with disdain; "cajoled, even browbeat his staff"; had a "fiery temper"; and chose "denigrating nicknames for executives and then insisted they join him daily for lunch at Schrafft's."[126] These were the reasons Sussman felt that he was asked to replace Rabbi Berger as leader of the organization.

Even with that honest appraisal of Rabbi Berger's personality, Sussman insisted that Berger's analysis of the Middle East was important, smart, and indeed prescient. Sussman arrived at these conclusions about Rabbi Berger's activism even as Berger left the Council in October 1969, splitting off from the American Council for Judaism to found the American Jewish Alternatives to Zionism.[127] In his platform for that organization, Rabbi Berger candidly articulated the links between his own anti-Zionism and world events. As he put it, "The refusal of the 'establishment' to recognize that the [anti-Zionist] principles for which the Council has stood for more than twenty-five years are directly involved in the deepening crisis in the Middle East."[128] Largely a "one-man organization" with backing from a few of Berger's former supporters from the Council, American Jewish Alternatives to Zionism was to be "exclusively for educational and religious purposes" and would be "dedicated . . . to applying Judaism's values of justice and knowledge to the Arab-Israel Zionist conflict."[129] In his study, historian Geoffrey Levin calls Berger "American's most single recognizable Jewish critic of Israel" from the 1940s to the 1960s who was "deeply aligned with the Palestinian cause."[130]

Drawing from the Pittsburgh Platform, the American Jewish Committee's early years, and the original mission of the Council, American Jewish Alternatives to Zionism pledged that "Americans of whatever religious faith or national origin owe exclusive national allegiance to the United States." Further, Berger's organization vehemently "repudiate[d]" any attempts to link Jews with "any nationality claims or national interests." He went on to argue that Judaism "demands that justice receive primary consideration in the settlement of controversy" and so argued that Jews were "obligated by the revered moralities of Jewish tradition" to "apply principles of justice and truth" to Israel.[131] Rabbi Berger consistently cited the Pittsburgh Platform's antinationalism as the basis for the Council's anti-Zionism, and later, in the 1950s and 1960s, Palestinian scholars and activists used the Pittsburgh Platform's and Berger's positions in the Council as they "made their case against Zionism."[132]

* * *

Though many objected to Berger's leadership style and personality, to dismiss him as a "fanatic anti-Israel activist" is to underplay the significance of his anti-Zionism and its connections to other political currents. Since Berger's death in 1996, various scholars have read his critiques and concluded that "they tell us much more about Berger's neuroses than anything else."[133] But Sussman writes of the importance of Berger's ideas during the Second Intifada in 2000–2001, when "both American and Israeli Jews were painfully reexamining their relationship." Experts were debating, "What does it mean to be a Jew in the modern world?" Sussman writes. "That is the question Elmer Berger addressed when no one else would."[134] By the late 1960s, when Rabbi Berger founded the American Jewish Alternatives to Zionism, journalists took note of the fact that he met with Arab leaders when no other Jewish leaders would. In the British *Guardian*, journalist Geoffrey Moorhouse referred to Berger as "the Rabbi with more friends in Islam."[135]

Remembering the Council: Looking Back to Its Origins and Forward to Its Legacies

The American Council for Judaism rose to prominence when there was still room for criticism of Zionism in American Jewish life. In his 1990 history of the Council, historian Thomas Kolsky described this criticism as "the final and perhaps the most vocal assertion of a long tradition of opposition to Zionism by Reform Judaism." Importantly, Kolsky concluded that "the Holocaust, which ultimately made the establishment of Israel possible, destroyed any realistic chances for the Council's success."[136] Further, he added, "At the end of World War II, the Palestine issue had become an emotional, not an academic, question."[137] He analyzed the Council only up through Israel's statehood in 1948, observing the organization's failure but also the relevance of its "ominous predictions." Israel, he wrote in 1990, did not become a "light to the nations" but instead assumed the stature of a "garrison-state."[138]

Reviewing Kolsky's book in the *New York Times Book Review*, writer and editor Murray Polner took the analysis of the Council seriously. Polner drew attention to Kolsky's emphasis on the Council's work on behalf of displaced Holocaust survivors and its loyalty to a vision of a democratic Jewish state in which Jews, Muslims, and Christians would all have equal representation and rights. Though Polner noted that "few people remember the ACJ," he credited the group for predicting that Israel would become "the dominant issue in American Jewish life." He also wondered about the meaning of Zionism in the late twentieth-century United States: "The old-line Zionist organizations with their aging and shrinking memberships are fast becoming as irrelevant as the American Council for Judaism once was."[139] Polner here might have written about the fierce conservative backlash in the United States and Israel that was unfolding even as he wrote, backlash that would have significant implications for the forced Zionist consensus among American Jews.

* * *

Though he is dismissed by many historians of the American Jewish experience, Rabbi Berger fiercely propagated ideas that continue to have relevance today. In his autobiography, Sussman concluded the chapter on the Council by quoting the 1990 thesis of a Reform rabbinical student named Mark Glickman. In his thesis, titled "One Voice against Many: A Biographical Study of Elmer Berger, 1948–1968," Glickman wrote that he began his research "very sympathetic to Zionism and actually quite hostile to Berger and his views." Upon its completion, Glickman wrote that he had "come to believe that Berger's vision of a democratic, de-Zionized Israel is one that carries a great deal of merit."

This vision would end "legalized discrimination against Arabs" and strengthen global Jewish communities. Despite the Blaustein–Ben-Gurion understanding of 1950, which confirmed that the first loyalty of American Jews was to the United States, Glickman wrote that Jews were still encouraged to feel less at home in the "diaspora," an idea he saw as damaging to both Israel and the United States. Glickman also asserted that the Law of Return, which grants automatic Israeli citizenship to Jews, should be made obsolete. He described his vision as a "dream." Sussman, clearly sympathetic to Glickman's dream, called it the product of "a young rabbi's discovery of Elmer Berger's inflammatory ideas."[140]

The anti-Zionism of Rabbi Berger can be seen as a bridge between Reform Judaism's objections to Jewish nationalism and Zionism, which lived on for a time in the American Jewish Committee and then in the Council, and the positions of some left-leaning American Jews through the 1940s and 1950s. Notably, some of these American Jews allied themselves with Berger and built on his ideas. Berger's own journey into public conversations about Zionism and Israel took him from the confines of the Reform movement's community outward, to a robust, visible pro-Palestinian position, one that lay far outside of mainstream American Jewish communal life. In the decades that followed, other individuals would build on the early critiques of Jewish nationalism and criticize the lack of democracy and self-determination in the ethnocracy of Israel, the "problem" of Palestinian refugees, Israel as an imperialist project, and the role of Zionism in American Jewish life.

Conclusion: Anti-Zionism's Legacies

Reform Jewish anti-Zionists had diverse worldviews and political commitments. Not all followed the path of Sussman, to human rights, or of Rabbi Berger, to Palestinian advocacy. Indeed, in a 2019 article, Kyle Stanton wrote about how Beth Israel synagogue in Houston, Texas, under the leadership of Rabbi Hyman Judah Schachtel, a Council member, in the 1940s adopted a "Basic Principles" platform. It stipulated that no Zionists or adherents of kashrut (the dietary laws of keeping kosher, likely Eastern European Jews and their descendants) could be members of the congregation. "Additionally," Stanton wrote, "the document affirmed that the race of Jews in Houston was Caucasian."[141]

Stanton made clear that Council-led congregations often voiced opposition to civil rights because members felt that both Zionism and integrationist sentiments "brought into question southern Jewish allegiance to the Solid South."[142] For these American Jews, nativism and racist exclusion paired with anti-Zionism as they sought out a path to patriotic Americanism and southern belonging, which was built on Black oppression. Political scientist Matthew Berkman found that "the Council represented a conservative racial politics that ran counter to nascent postwar efforts to rearticulate American national identity around an ideal of cultural pluralism."[143]

Yet the presence of American Council for Judaism statements in the Black press of the 1950s speaks to a concurrent historical development. Black leaders were growing sympathetic to anticolonialist critiques of Zionism and sometimes turned to Council members and other non- and anti-Zionists to help explain American Jewish Zionism. For instance, in 1957, the Black newspaper *Atlanta Daily World* cited Council president Clarence L. Coleman Jr., who called out the "tragedy" of American Jews' "myopia," bemoaning the loss of their "normal capacity for healthy skepticism" where Israel was concerned. Coleman asserted that "authentic Zionism is kept from public view" because, given its strident and shrill insistence on Jews' residence in Israel, it "will not receive the enthusiastic endorsement of American Jews."[144] In 1958, the *Chicago Defender* covered the debate over whether Jews were a "race, religion, or nationality."[145] As with others of his colleagues writing for the Black press, journalist Louis Cassels turned to Council members to explain the dangers of nationalism for Jewish identity. Though the ideals of some, perhaps most, Council members were tied to racist tropes and all were tied to strivings for whiteness, the Council provided one of the few spaces open to discussion about how unconditional Zionism was becoming increasingly central in American Jewish life.

* * *

The actions of Marjorie Arsht (1914–2008), Reform Jewish leader, teacher, and Texas Republican Party activist, provide another good example of the diverse political commitments of anti-Zionist Council members. In early 1961, after hearing Prime Minister Ben-Gurion's speech disparaging all non-Israeli Jewish communities as "in exile" and "godless," Arsht wrote to Ben-Gurion. In a pointed exchange with Syd Appelbaum, an aide to the prime minister, she identified their arguments as "the age-old conflict between Orthodoxy and Reform Judaism—between particularism and universalism." Arsht's anti-Zionism hung on the question of what she called the "Political Allegiances" of American Jews. She recorded her horror upon attending a Zionist meeting in Texas and witnessing that at the end of the meeting, under the Israeli flag, the meeting attendees sang Hatikvah, the Israeli national anthem.[146]

All this she saw as a "major setback in the civic condition of American Jewry." For Israel to be true to Jewish tradition, Arsht said, it must become a "light unto the nations," a "blessing . . . to all mankind."[147] An ally of the Council, an heir to the anti-Zionism of the Reform movement, Arsht never mentioned the plight of Palestinian refugees; she never spoke of the politics of the Middle East at all. Arsht was one of the founders of the modern Republican Party in Texas, and she held many leadership positions within the party in the 1980s and 1990s.[148] The trajectory of her life did not parallel those of Berger or Sussman, yet all three drew from the early Reform movement's anti-Zionism.

With their efforts to safely integrate into white America, some Reform Jews responded to antisemitism and nativism by rejecting Jewish nationalism and Zionism, which they felt drew attention to American Jews as a separate and distinct people and made them less safe and appear less invested in the United States. They believed that Zionism did not fit into the worldview of Reform Judaism, for they saw Zionism as asking American Jews to work on behalf of the needs of another nation, thus encouraging accusations of dual loyalties. Finally, Reform Jewish leaders heard in Zionism the denigration of Jewish life outside of Israel. Their Judaism emphasized universalist teachings, which they saw as their unique contribution to American life and culture. Rosenwald, Berger, and Sussman were part of a group who for various reasons viewed Zionism with grave concern. Even as they sought to articulate their diverse perspectives, they found themselves pushing against a more unified set of efforts to enforce an American Jewish consensus on Zionism by lowering the threshold of acceptable dissent.

2

The Jews in Revolt

William Zukerman, the Jewish Newsletter, *and Midcentury Critics of American Zionism*

American Jews with diverse experiences and worldviews contributed to the development of both Jewish non-Zionism, which meant opposition to the building of a Jewish state but support for a center of Jewish cultural and religious life and a safe haven for Jewish refugees in Palestine, and anti-Zionism, which meant opposition to Jewish nationalism and Israel as a Jewish state. Fearful that Jewish nationalism and Zionism would call their integration and whiteness into question by raising the specter of dual loyalty, many American Jews drew from Reform Judaism in embracing non- and anti-Zionism in the early twentieth century. Another thread within the tapestry of these ideas can be found in Jewish radicalism and the Yiddish left, from ideas that Jews brought with them from Eastern Europe or encountered in New York City and other urban areas with a strong Jewish working class. It was in Europe, in 1897, that two movements central to this history began: the Labor Bund and the Zionist movement.

The class- and ethnic-based Bund (translated fully as the General Union of Jewish Workers in Lithuania, Poland, and Russia), which was founded in Vilna by members of the Jewish working class and the intelligentsia, was profoundly influenced by Marxism and socialism and fought against antisemitism and for Jewish rights and revolution. The movement emphasized Jewish autonomy wherever Jews lived, and it rejected Zionism, insisting that Jews were united by history, culture, and language. Its members chose Yiddish for education and organizational purposes as they worked toward a socialist society.[1] Founded in Basel, Switzerland, with the First Zionist Congress, the Zionist movement sought to connect to religious liturgical longings for Zion and the establishment of a Jewish homeland in Palestine, working in Hebrew to make Jewish nationalism a reality.

Communist, anarchist, and socialist Jews in the United States, including members of the Bund, emerged as strong opponents of Zionism.[2] Some on the left regarded Zionism as an arm of British imperialism, as reproducing capitalist inequality and victimizing Palestinian laborers. The Council's Leonard Sussman had used this language, borrowed from anticolonialist activists in newly independent nations in Asia and Africa, after the Bandung Conference of 1955.[3] After 1948, some Jewish left-wing anti-Zionists believed that support for Israel distracted Jews from working for justice in their own countries. They worried about the diminishment of Jewish cultures outside of Israel, cultures that were denigrated and dismissed as "diaspora" communities, especially those centered on Yiddish language and culture.

Drawing from liberal and left ideologies as well as from Zionism, socialist Zionist Jewish immigrants were also integral to the history of support for Zionism beginning in the early twentieth century. After the Holocaust, many on the left grew sympathetic to Zionism. The Soviet Union's brief support for Jewish statehood in 1947 and 1948 contributed still more to the turn of communists toward Zionism. Though the Communist Party first rejected Zionism as "bourgeois nationalism," in 1947, the Soviet Union reversed its position and supported a Jewish state, alongside an Arab state, in Palestine. "The fight for Jewish statehood in Palestine," wrote Alexander Bittelman, American Jewish political activist and journalist, "can and must be carried on by Communists not as bourgeois nationalists but as working-class internationalists." This, Bittelman added, was an "anti-imperialist fight for peace because it aims to prevent Anglo-American imperialism from turning the Middle East and Israel into a strategic bridgehead for Wall Street's new world war." In this way, Zionism was "an organic part of the world struggle for peace and democracy."[4] Liberal and left Zionists saw in Israel the potential to build a communalist future for workers.

William Zukerman (1885–1961), a Yiddish- and English-language journalist, offered trenchant observations and criticisms that challenged American Jewish institutions and presented new ways of thinking about American Zionism, Israeli policies, and Jewish identity outside of Israel.[5] In his early career, like many American liberals of the 1920s and early 1930s, Zukerman was deeply influenced by the Stalinist left, and he listened keenly to raging debates over Zionism. Ultimately, he was both baffled by and angry with American Jews for their all-encompassing embrace of Zionism and unquestioning support of Israel's leaders.

Like members of the American Council for Judaism, Zukerman disputed the central role of Israel in Jewish life, insisting that Jews should remain loyal to their nation of origin, where he believed their own Jewish future would and should lie. He eschewed orthodoxy and rejected Zionism in that vein. He criticized Israel's policies, its treatment of Mizrahi Jews, with origins in the Middle East and North Africa, and the indigenous population of Palestinians. And he and some of his colleagues expanded their criticism of Zionism to rail against what they saw as American Zionism's negative impact on Jewish life, especially on Yiddish American culture.

In 1948 Zukerman founded and began editing the English-language *Jewish Newsletter.* In its pages, he kept readers apprised of developments in Jewish organizations and movements, especially those whose roots lay in the Jewish labor movement and the Left: the Bund, socialist Zionism, the Jewish Labor Committee, and the Territorialists, a group that aimed to create a Jewish homeland outside of Palestine and the Middle East. To be sure, not all those who supported Yiddish language and culture, as Zukerman did, rejected Zionism. Yet his critique of American Zionism, in particular, was grounded in his experiences in the Yiddish left.

Zukerman wrote pointedly about what he considered key and urgent concerns, including diminishing freedom of expression in the American Jewish world, the denigration of Yiddish in Israel,[6] and what he described as the "trend towards theocracy" there.[7] Perhaps most notably, from the 1930s forward, Zukerman wrote of the Palestinians. In his periodical, he consistently drew attention to the denial of justice and human rights to the members of the native Arab population of Palestine and then Israel. He was one of the few American Jews who kept this watch and issued warnings about human rights violations against Palestinians and the dire consequences of these violations not only for those who lived in that region but also for global politics.

Like others who greeted American Jewish social mobility and suburbanization with ambivalence, Zukerman mourned the loss of the Yiddish-language, working-class labor activism that he saw as central to American Jewish political culture. Many rabbis and communal leaders who saw in suburban American Judaism "corruption and decline" turned to Israel, where they saw strong, conventionally masculine, Jewish men leading the important struggle toward Jewish safety and liberation.[8]

Inspired in part by these ideas, American Jewish leaders worked diligently to turn back any perceived threats to a consensus on Israel and Zionism. The 1943 American Jewish Conference, organized by the leaders of thirty-two mainstream American Jewish organizations, tried to unify American Jewry on its postwar agenda. By this time, in the midst of the destruction of the Second World War, very few American Jewish organizational leaders opposed the growing role that American Zionism played in American Jewish life. While unity proved elusive with regard to an overall agenda, and while the Conference fell apart by 1949, the broad support for Zionism was clear, as was the fact that Jewish leaders tied their support of Palestine/Israel and Zionism to the rescue of Jews from Europe and to the safety and future of global Jewry.

Zukerman chose a different path. He mourned the fact that Zionism had come to dominate American Jewish life and indeed saw Zionism as furthering the corruption and decline of American Jewishness. Circulation of Zukerman's *Newsletter* hovered around five thousand, and it contained the voices of allies and supporters such as historian Hans Kohn, philosopher Hannah Arendt, journalist and communal leader Henry Hurwitz, and the American Council for Judaism's Rabbi Elmer Berger and Rabbi Morris Lazaron.[9] These academics, journalists, critics, and communal leaders arrived at their criticism of Zionism via diverse intellectual paths but were brought together by Zukerman, an occasionally bombastic critic who created an important space for independent voices. He witnessed and eloquently chronicled the Russian Revolution, two world wars, Israel's statehood, and the growth of modern Jewish life across the world. His insights reflect one of the clearest and most sustained articulations of non- and anti-Zionism during this period.

Scholars describe Israel as a polarizing issue among Jewish and non-Jewish anticolonialist activists beginning in the 1960s and 1970s, and many Jews later admitted that they felt forced to choose between their anticolonialist activism and their Jewishness precisely *because* of Israel. American Jews who departed Zionist *or* anticolonialist organizations in these decades talked about how they did so because of forces outside the Jewish community. Zukerman's critiques emerged immediately after the Holocaust and reflected debates over religion, Zionism, and class that were happening inside the Jewish community.[10]

Zukerman paid a high price for his position, as mainstream Jewish leaders took increasingly strong and unyielding stands against those who opposed the forced Zionist consensus. In the 1950s, Zionist Jewish leaders in the United States joined with Israeli diplomats to limit public discourse and deny funding and access to American Jews such as Zukerman, who stood in opposition to this consensus by criticizing Zionism and Israeli policies. Zukerman was a loyal anti-communist and was neither a radical nor a civil rights activist. Yet he linked the growing right-wing, revisionist politics in Israel with white supremacy and reactionary politics the world over in ways that mainstream Jewish leaders identified as a threat.

This analysis of Zukerman's writings from 1930 onward shows that, despite differences in background, various American Jewish critics of Israel and Zionism found common ground in the pages of Zukerman's *Jewish Newsletter*. Battling accusations of antisemitism, self-hatred, and even communist sympathies, Zukerman alongside his journalist colleague Hurwitz met with heated attacks for their criticism in the 1950s. Both died at the age of seventy-five in the fall of 1961, leaving behind records of their grief and horror over the Holocaust and their profound disappointment and disillusionment at Israel's founding, its policies, and the fealty the country inspired among American Jews.

William Zukerman: *The Jew in Revolt*

William Zukerman was born in 1885 near the Polish city of Bialystok, what his son, George, called "one of those gloried seats of Eastern European Jewry." His family was not wealthy. He once wrote a friend, "[My] parents were too poor to send me to Cheder; this is how I escaped that scourge, but I also missed my Hebrew."[11] In his unpublished memoir, George Zukerman describes how his father emigrated aboard the SS *Darmstadt* from Rotterdam, arriving in Baltimore in 1900. William, the son writes, "was accosted by a zealous group of older passengers who demanded to inspect his package of food." This was "a self-appointed rabbinical court" who "had taken it upon themselves to assure the purity of food consumed by all other Jewish passengers." William's "food was declared 'trefe' [not kosher, or prepared according to Jewish dietary laws] and thrown overboard." For William Zukerman, this "was an example of schoolyard bullying as much as an assertion of orthodoxy." According to his son, sixteen days of fear and extreme hunger "ignited in [his father] a flame of life-long hatred for orthodoxy. Even at age fifteen [William] had trouble reconciling the futility and frustration of the orthodox practices that surrounded him with the hope and promise of the new land."[12]

William Zukerman made his way to Chicago, where he began as a newspaper delivery boy. He worked in factories while studying philosophy at the University of Chicago and ultimately worked his way up to be a journalist for the Yiddish-language *Jewish Daily Forward*.[13] Between the world wars, he was based in London and served as chief European correspondent for the Yiddish-language *Morning Journal* and contributed to several other Yiddish publications. Zukerman moved back to the United States, to New York City, in 1940, and into the 1950s, he was the American correspondent for the *Jewish Chronicle* of London and other publications. George Zukerman recalls the Yiddish and English typewriters sitting side by side on his father's desk, with a "telex" in between them.[14]

Zukerman's exposure to antisemitism and radical movements as a poor Jew in Eastern Europe doubtless played a role in his embrace of left-wing political solutions to "the Jewish question." Zukerman idealized socialist Zionism, hoping for an equal partnership between Jews and Palestinians.[15] Yet he found Jewish nationalism an insufficient solution to the whole of the Jewish question. In 1934, in the pages of the *New York Times*, Zukerman contrasted Palestine, which strove to "solve the Jewish problem nationally," with the Soviet land of Birobidzhan, on the Soviet-Chinese border, which had just been declared a Jewish Autonomous Region and "was the first attempt of its kind to offer a solution to the Jewish problem on the basis of social and economic reconstruction." The mid-1930s saw the high point of interest in Birobidzhan as a Soviet Jewish homeland and cultural center, the product of Soviet efforts to invest in ethnic minorities. Zukerman noted that "non-Zionists, even anti-Zionists" as well as a "strong Jewish labor and radical element[s] naturally [were] gravitating toward the social experiments of Soviet Russia."[16] In 1932, he served as a spokesperson for the Birobidzhan colonization movement as the means of "Jewish regeneration."[17] Importantly, Birobidzhan's official language was Yiddish, and thus Zukerman and others were excited at the possibility of cultural experimentation there.

More than a decade before Zukerman founded the *Jewish Newsletter*, while based in London with a close view of Hitler's advances, he wrote a book titled *The Jew in Revolt*, which he described to his friend Henry Hurwitz as having "an avowed and outspoken Socialist appeal."[18] The title spoke to Zukerman's firm hopes, as he envisioned that "the Jew"—and here he indicated "no matter to what class he belongs"—was becoming a part of a "moral, as well as an economic, and social revolt."[19] The book is important both as a measure of Zukerman's early politics and worldview and as a set of visions and predictions of what some Jews thought might be possible for Jews in and outside of Palestine.

* * *

In Palestine Zukerman saw a chance for experimentation with socialism, and in *The Jew in Revolt*, he praised the pioneer Labor Zionists for building this utopia. To "work the land" in a "planned social economy," he wrote, was to "escape the ghetto" and to "make it [the land] their own by right of labour." But Zukerman also used the book to sound the alarm about how capitalism was wreaking havoc in Palestine, eclipsing the socialist vision of the pioneers. He laid the blame on the "petty Jewish bourgeoisie," their "rush and push, grab and keep" philosophy as they sought profit and state power.[20] And he tied this philosophy to the dehumanization of Palestinians native to the region, to their forced removal from Palestine. To capture his thoughts on these injustices, Zukerman quoted the person he identified as "the great Jewish philosopher, Dr. Chaim Zhitlowsky," a prominent socialist:

> [The Arabs] were considered just another physical obstacle in Palestine, to be overcome as part of the programme of upbuilding the National Home, like a marsh to be drained or a desert to be irrigated. That the Arabs, too, are human beings like themselves, who can have fears, hopes and aspirations; that they too can actually love the piece of desert ground which they call their home, and can fear, even if groundlessly, that it will be taken away from them; that they too have a moral right to a country where they and their ancestors have lived for eleven hundred years, and that they may refuse to be juxtaposed like inanimate objects,

never occurred to these great moralists, the alleged descendants of the Prophets.[21]

These sharp words demonstrated the depth of Zukerman's (and Zhitlowsky's) disappointment. Zukerman saw the global, universal Jewish mission as one with socialism. The growth of exploitative capitalism in Palestine, according to Zukerman, reflected a tragic, missed opportunity and showed how misguided the Jewish bourgeoisie were: "The Zionists had a wonderful chance then to gain even the political goodwill of the Arabs by cultivating ordinary social relationship[s] based on human equality and friendship, which incidentally would also be more in accord with the Jewish character and tradition. But the Jewish middle class chose to follow the road of its class interests rather than of its inherent national inclinations, and this road could not but lead to havoc and tragedy."[22]

As he was preparing his book for publication in 1937, Zukerman saw it as offering an essential lesson to "Jews of all classes" that "nationalism begets nationalism."[23] Without full recognition of the rights of Arabs, Zukerman presciently predicted, conflicts in the region would become only more frequent and more brutal, the rise of Arab nationalism creating still more tension in the region. "Jews must temper their nationalistic feelings with higher ideals of internationalism and social justice," he asserted. "It may be a hard road, a slow and even thorny road, but it is not a road which leads to eternal guerrilla warfare in Palestine and to a hopeless enmity between the Jews and the Arabs."[24]

Zukerman saw Jews as existing on a higher moral plane.[25] He also subscribed to what scholar Amy Kaplan terms "Orientalist progressivism," embedded in popular culture and much of Western scholarship alike in that era.[26] Using the racist language of his day, then, he praised Zionism insofar as the movement "brought Europe to the Arabs" and made them "civilized." Ultimately, Zukerman hoped that a "labour-minded intelligentsia" would emerge among Jews and Palestinians and defeat the narrow nationalism and chauvinism of middle-class Zionism.[27] Foreshadowing his own commitment to Jewish publishing and in a fleeting moment of optimism that soon abated, he wrote of the crucial role of the independent press in that defeat: "For the first time, perhaps, in its history the official popular Zionist Press publishes articles stating the Arab point of view with a lucidity and warmth which show clearly that the chauvinistic fog which for a time obscured the strong sense of justice of many Jews is lifting. Several years ago the authors of such articles would have been excommunicated as enemies of Zion and traitors to Israel. Even the intolerance of criticism, the most distressing feature of middle-class Zionism, seems to be passing; It is now almost possible to criticise Zionism and not be called an anti-Semite."[28]

In *The Jew in Revolt*, Zukerman drew from the intellectual discourses of the Jewish left. Many Jews on the left first rejected Zionism altogether, regarding it as British imperialism and bourgeois nationalism incompatible with the true class struggle. Many communists first saw Zionism as the abandonment of the class struggle and a betrayal of Jewish and Palestinian resistance to British imperialism in the Middle East. From this vantage point, Zionism stood for the provincial, opposing force to progressive and internationalist organizations such as the Bund.[29] In the 1910s and then after the savage destruction of the Holocaust, however, many came to see Zionism as compatible with their other political commitments, as linked to Jews' liberation. And the realization of a socialist utopian community in Palestine was for these Jews a vital part of workers' struggles for justice across the world.

In *The Jew in Revolt*, Zukerman presented his version of the reconciliation of nationalism with liberation as a non-Zionist. His work resonates with the historic contradictions of Jewish radicalism in that he dedicated himself to internationalism and universalism while also romanticizing the role of Jewish workers in bringing about a more just world.[30] The book was replete with observations and warnings that proved prescient. In his writing about "intolerance" toward criticism of Zionism and Israel, for example, he identified a force that later had a significant impact on his own life and career.

In correspondence with friends and colleagues, Zukerman predictably chose reviews of *The Jew in Revolt* that accented his own sense of the book's purpose. The Communist *Daily Worker* declared it "a socialist approach to the Jewish problem." The London *Jewish Chronicle* wrote that though Zukerman offered "correct analysis of some of the ills that afflict Jewry, one must profoundly disagree with his conclusions," adding, "Mr. Zukerman's eloquent indictment of Mammon does not prove that Judaism has failed, but that its teachings need to be more thoroughly applied."[31]

In a letter to Yiddish scholar Zalmen Reyzen, written in Yiddish, Zukerman expressed his happiness that his book earned good reviews in England. "As this is almost the first book in English which offers the non-Zionist Jewish perspective on Jewish questions," he explained, "it has been received with interest here. Soon the publishers will issue a second printing."[32] For Zukerman, Judaism's teachings were intricately tied to a very specific relationship to Mammon, to class struggles. These teachings were, he believed, the authentic Jewish contribution to the world.

The same year he published *The Jew in Revolt*, Zukerman authored a memorial for Peter Wiernik, a Yiddish journalist who had edited the *Jewish Morning Journal* for more than thirty years. Wiernik had been skeptical of both political Zionism and socialism, a "great lover of everything Jewish and of the laboring Yiddish-speaking masses." Zukerman praised Wiernik's "intellectual calm and tolerance," which made his newspaper "a free platform for various opinions." Zukerman noted that it was "paradoxical" that Wiernik, a Jew from Bialystok like himself, would be more American than US-born Jews or than "Americans of the oldest stock." But Zukerman believed Wiernik to be just so. The America defined by "Hollywood and Wall Street" was not Zukerman's America, and thus Jews who subscribed to the day's "narrow hysterical nationalism," which Zukerman often described as intricately tied to Hollywood and Wall Street, were not true to their Americanism or to their Jewishness.[33]

Embedded in Zukerman's memorial for Wiernik was a nostalgia for the Yiddish press's earnest debates over Zionism and other topics. A few years later, in a 1943 article in the English-language *Jewish Sentinel*, Zukerman observed the Yiddish press as "richer in talent, profound thought, and creative writing than any daily press in the United States, including the American." Yet he also blasted the Yiddish press for "intolerance," what he described as their "extermination of any unorthodox opinion which runs counter to the majority." He found them "liberal and even radical in their social and political outlook" but found their "liberalism and radicalism [as] limited to the non-Jewish world." Within the Jewish world, Zukerman asserted, the Yiddish press policed ideas, was full of "controversy and personal polemics," and was "steeped in hatred, bitterness, and strife."[34] Those criticisms and that lament ran through Zukerman's commentary as he cast a sharp eye on the events transforming the modern world around him. These observations remained central to his journalism, to his theme of revolt and rebellion and rejection, for the rest of his life.

Zukerman's *Jewish Newsletter*, the Free Jewish Club, and Midcentury Jewish Critics of American Zionism

The editorial advisory board of the *Jewish Newsletter*, including socialist Norman Thomas and Rabbi Morris Lazaron, a member of the American Council for Judaism, described the publication as Zukerman's "brain-child." Later, they reminisced that Zukerman "treated Jewish problems, even after 1948 [the founding year for the *Jewish Newsletter* and the first year of Israel's statehood], in universal rather than nationalist terms . . . from the standpoint of basic human values."[35] Zukerman considered the journal's "main service to liberal journalism dedicated to the principle of freedom of thought and of the press," especially with regard to Israel, which "was no more sacred than any modern state." And he added, "Lack of criticism has been one of Israel's great tragedies and . . . just criticism of its shortcomings can still save it from final disaster."[36]

Beginning in the very early days of his journal's publication, Zuker-man juxtaposed his fervent criticism of American Zionism and Israel with expressions of fervent hope for Jewish contributions to a more liberal, tolerant society, one guided by those "basic human values, in the U.S., Israel, and across the world." Zukerman's reporting of Menachem Begin's 1948 visit to New York City captured this well. Begin was the leader of the right-wing Zionist militant group Irgun and earned fame for his contributions to the fight against the British during the Mandate. He later led the right-wing Likud Party and was Israel's sixth prime minister. In 1948, Zukerman responded with horror to the celebration of Begin in New York by American Jewish Zionists, calling out the hypocrisy of heralding Begin as "the Man who defied an empire." Zukerman termed this the "flourish and sensationalism of Hollywood at its worst."[37] He labeled Begin a "terrorist" whose Irgun "introduced into Israel the most brutal of Nazi tactics—the killing of innocent hostages." He concluded with an observation that drew from the recent presidential election in the United States, in which southern Democrats had bolted from President Harry Truman's base of support to form the States' Rights Party, or the Dixie-crats, in opposition to civil rights. "The American people will not in one and the same month reject the Dixie-crats and the Ku-Klux-Klan crowd at home and take to their bosom an Israeli version of it even if it does come disguised by a clever showman," Zukerman wrote.[38]

With these words, Zukerman joined other liberals who drew attention to what they termed Begin's "terrorism." Scientist Albert Einstein and the prominent intellectuals Hannah Arendt and Sidney Hook signed a letter to the *New York Times* that, like Zukerman's column, was intended to educate readers as to the "discrepancies" between Begin's true actions and his "bold claims" of contributions to "constructive achievements in Palestine" and to "freedom, democracy, and anti-imperialism." As a corrective, they noted that "within the Jewish community they [Begin's party] have preached an admixture of ultranationalism, religious mysticism, and racial superiority." Einstein and his colleagues wrote of the "attack on an Arab Village," the massacre at Deir Yassin, where more than one hundred Palestinians were killed by Jewish militia groups,[39] which "exemplified the character and actions" of Begin's party. They urged American Jews and "those who oppose fascism throughout the world" to reject Begin's ideas.[40]

Zukerman noted how throughout his celebratory tour of New York City, Begin "railed against Albert Einstein for being among twenty-one academics accusing him of 'openly preaching the doctrine of the Fascist state,' and accused the American Council for Judaism of anti-Semitism for its criticism of him."[41] This put on display what Zukerman hoped was ending in 1937, the continued accusations of antisemitism for those who criticized Zionism—in this case, Council members and allies who publicly rejected the actions of Begin and his party colleagues. In Boston's *Jewish Advocate*, Zukerman reported that Begin's farewell address, "delivered in Yiddish" at the Manhattan Center on West Thirty-Fourth Street, was intended for "home consumption, not for the liberal outside American world." And home meant the Eastern European immigrant Jewish world. In the address, Zukerman reported, "all disguises of democracy were openly abandoned." Begin "thundered" that the partition plan, proposed by the United Nations to create two states, one Jewish and one Arab, was dead; that Palestinian refugees would not be allowed to return home; and that the Jewish state would exist on both sides of the Jordan River and all of Jerusalem would be in its possession. This was an aggressive, expansive vision that erased the rights of Palestinians. Begin devoted "most of his speech to a reply to the criticism leveled against him by Professor Einstein's group, by the American clergymen and by the liberal Jewish press." These were the individuals in whom Zukerman placed his faith. As Begin "compared himself and his Irgunists with the Maccabees of old who were denounced as fascists of their time," socialists and Labor Zionist organizations were "parading the streets in front of the hall." For Zukerman, it was they who exposed the "masquerade" at the heart of Begin's visit.[42]

While on the intellectual journey to these ideas, Zukerman was consistently willing to admit mistakes. That same year, the first of his *Jewish Newsletter* and of Israel's statehood, Zukerman wrote openly to his friend Henry Hurwitz of how his own political positions had evolved: "Only the dead do not change," he asserted. "I am not ashamed of the fact that I have changed considerably in my attitude toward pro-Sovietism [Stalinism] and Zionism."[43]

Soon after, Zukerman put his stand against both orthodoxies, communism and Zionism, into print and into his criticism. In a letter to the editor of the Boston *Jewish Advocate*, he drew attention to the denial of Jewish religious expression under Communist rule. Communist leaders often respond disingenuously, Zukerman wrote, that "Jews in those countries do not WANT their culture." He analogized this with the Orthodox leaders' denial of non-Orthodox religious expression in Israel. The more liberal denominations of Judaism were not allowed in Israel, Zukerman wrote, and Orthodox Zionists explained by saying that Jews in Israel "do not WANT them." For Zukerman, this demonstrated that "the state power acquired by the rabbinate" in Israel was designed "to force its own form of religion on all Jews in Israel."[44]

Although he had largely abandoned formal affiliations, Zukerman continued to admire and even build coalitions with members of the Jewish left. Into the early 1940s, he contributed coverage of the Holocaust to *Jewish Frontier*, the journal of the American Labor Zionists.[45] His publishing in that journal meant that there was still room for dissenting opinions on Zionism and Israel.

Never was Zukerman's faith in the Jewish labor movement more on display than when he joined the short-lived Free Jewish Club in October 1949. A group of individuals met on West Twenty-Seventh Street in Manhattan to craft a platform for the organization, united out of concern for the continuity and richness of diasporic Jewish life amid what they saw as its capture by Jewish nationalism. The ideas of club members emerged out of their own experiences in radical politics, labor organizing, and journalism, first in Europe and then in the United States. The members included Dr. Y. N. Shteynberg (1888–1957), who edited the Vilna journal *Fraye shriftn—farn yidishn sotsialistishn gedank* (*Free Papers—for Jewish Socialist Thought*) and was a member of the Freeland League, whose members sought territory for Jewish settlement outside of Palestine/Israel; Hayyim Solomon Kazdan (1883–1979), a member of the Bund who worked for and wrote about secular Yiddish schools; and Dr. Herman Frank (1893–1952), who edited the anarchist weekly *Freie Arbeiter Stimme* (*Free Voice of Labor*).[46]

The founding statements of the Free Jewish Club are notable as an expansive critique of Zionism, assessing its destructive impact on Jewish life around the world:

> The reigning Zionist viewpoint wishes to take over one space after another in Jewish institutional life. The Jewish press is being placed under a single spiritual-cultural leadership. It gives one-sided information and elucidations (even about Israel), and does not permit other Jewish viewpoints and ideas to take the stage. Freedom of opinion in the Jewish public sphere has all but vanished.
>
> The aforementioned viewpoint wants to toss all worthwhile Jewish institutions and foundations (religious and secular, social and culture) at the feet of one and only purpose: Israel. It reroutes away from them both material means and the interest of the Jewish people, and thereby undermines their further existence. Unfortunately, there have been several recent cases of Jewish communal institutions that had previously maintained a politically pluralistic character, but now find that they are too weak to stand up to this assaulting wave. Some of their leaders are ready to compromise their principles in significant ways, and they don't see that that will undermine the very foundations of their institutions.

Aggressive nationalism was, Free Jewish Club members believed, degrading the ethical foundations of Judaism. They termed it "self-annihilation" and linked the fight against "totalitarian nationalism" to the fight for the revitalization of Yiddish, the democratization and free exchange of ideas within Jewish life, and the valuing of Jewish life and culture outside of Israel. The sole mention of the Middle East in the group's manifesto connected American Jewish apathy toward the suffering of Palestinian refugees to this degradation.

Group member William Zukerman praised the Free Jewish Club in very early issues of his *Jewish Newsletter*, noting that it "united progressive Jews of all parties." He emphasized the fact that club members had been attacked in print but that no one would print the club's responses to the attacks. This he saw as "a graphic illustration of the 'freedom' of opinion that prevails in the Zionist press at present." In Yiddish and English, Jewish journalists—what the club members termed "journalists and patented spokespeople"—blasted the club members as "enemies of Israel."[47] Perhaps because of these strong criticisms, the club appears to have disbanded shortly after.

These brief collaborations reveal Zukerman's dedication to providing an outlet for what in his *Jewish Newsletter* he called "free opinion." They also reveal his high expectations for the Jewish labor movement, as he was sharply disappointed when its members failed to live up to this level of intellectual independence, which he equated with respect for dissent and especially with resisting pressure to support Zionism and Israel unconditionally.[48]

One example lies in his consideration of the Jewish Labor Committee, founded in 1934 by leaders and members of Jewish or Jewish-led trade unions and fraternal organizations, mainly to mobilize support for anti-Nazi and antifascist activities. As the Jewish Labor Committee moved toward supporting Zionism, Zukerman wrote of his disappointment that "at such a time, the official Jewish Socialist organization, whose basic principle has always been that the home of the Jews is the place of his birth or abode, throws its weight in favor of mass-emigration of Jews from the United States to Israel." Quoting the *Detroit Jewish Chronicle*, he called it "a threat to the well-being of American Jewry."[49]

This tenet emerged out of the idea that all "diaspora" Jews were exiles and that only what was called the "ingathering of the exiles," with all Jews moving to Israel, would realize Zionism in its fullest sense. About this, Zukerman wrote that "the entire non-Jewish world came to see in 1959 that Ingathering is not normal migration intended to relieve the legitimate economic and political needs of individuals who are forced to leave their homes, but an artificial movement created by propaganda for the upbuilding of a nationalistic state under the guise of legitimate immigration. As such it hurts not only the immigrants, but the countries of emigration as well; it also contributes powerfully to the tensions of the Cold War."[50]

For a time, Zukerman pinned his hopes on Labor Zionism, socialist Zionist pioneers who embraced the need for a Jewish homeland built by the Jewish working class.[51] But he lamented "the passing of Zionist labor in America," as he found that it had "lost . . . every spark of its old independence." This group was now a "full-fledged American branch of the State of Israel" and thus a contributor to the destabilization of the Cold War Middle East.[52]

Zukerman also expressed disappointment in Israel's rejection of Yiddish, as the language was "publically humiliated and systematically incited against in Israel."[53] He turned to Yiddish writers such as socialist and Zionist David Pinski to share his continued disenchantment with Israel's development. Living in Israel, Pinski wrote a story of Jews who moved into Palestinian homes and felt uneasy given the history of Jewish displacement and dispossession. Within this Yiddish story, Zukerman found hope for Israel's democracy, which lay in the new, Yiddish-speaking arrivals, many of them refugees, who were, he wrote,

> proof that noisy, bumptious chauvinism, military conquests and theocratic rule are not the only products of the new State. Israel's chief aspiration may be to be like other nations, even in conquest, and she may succeed in it. But behind all these likenesses with modern states in transient and inessential things, there are some fundamental spiritual values which rise above the State, its Knesseth [Israel's national governing body], its Religious Bloc, its party politics and power-diplomacy, because they stem from the experience of an old and sorely tried people with a high sense of morals. It is these people who have come from outside Israel, who are not only the physical, but also the moral mainstay of the new State, and they will not permit it to become just like other modern power-mad states which make of our world the nightmare that it now is.[54]

This was Zukerman's fervent hope. As Israel's power grew, he sketched visions of what might come to pass. "It is the larger question," he wrote, "of whether the Jews have come to Palestine as aggressors to grab everything that they need by their own will, decision, and power; or whether they have come to settle in peace and in understanding with others and to abide by the dictates of justice for all as interpreted by the majority of mankind." Dating back to his writing of *The Jew in Revolt* in 1937, Zukerman's abiding fear was that "Israel will go the way of 'all nations.'"[55] He saw the continued tragedy of violence against Palestinian refugees at the center of this question of Israel's position or character. He linked the refugee issue to peace in the Middle East region. "Why should they [Jewish leaders and laypeople]," he asked, "expect that the Arab refugees, who had lived in Palestine all their lives and who also have a historic connection with it, far more immediate than that of the Jews, will give up their claims to their homes for settlement in Iraq or Saudi Arabia, even if such a course were economically more attractive?" He continued, "So long as the Israelis fail to understand that they have no monopoly on love of country or justice, and that in this age there are no chosen people entitled to special privileges which are denied to others, there will be no real settlement of the Arab refugee problem and peace in the Middle East."[56]

Zukerman blasted American Jewry for its culpability in intensifying the refugee issue and "infuriating the Arab world." "American immigrant Jews who during the last generation, shed most of their social radicalism and turned moderate and conservative," he wrote, "have clung to extremism in nationalism and have formed the most radical wing of the World Zionist movement. Revisionism [the right-wing, expansionist movement within Zionism] has had its most vociferous adherents among American Jews." He indicted American Jews for their attitudes toward Israel: "American Jews have adopted an attitude of sheepish adoration and unqualified praise and support of everything the Israeli government did." He went further: "Nowhere have critics of Israel, either as individuals or groups, been more despised, vilified and hated as if they were traitors."[57]

Zukerman's disappointment regarding the increased presence of Jewish nationalism and the growing power of conservative religious leaders suffused all that he wrote. He responded with characteristic emotion, for example, when he heard news of American rabbis' boycott of the two remaining Yiddish-language daily newspapers, the *Day-Morning Journal* and the *Jewish Daily Forward*, "because they appear on Saturdays and thus desecrate the Jewish Sabbath." Zukerman believed the Yiddish press had only itself to blame for the rabbinical boycott. "One might also point to a curious paradox involved in this boycott," he wrote, "namely that both Yiddish dailies, which were started years ago as liberal and Social-ist publications, fighting clericalist and nationalist bigotry, have, under pressure of the advent of nationalism, turned into ardent supporters of nationalism and clericalism. It is they who are largely responsible for the fact that the rabbis have gained their present power and threaten to destroy their own creators."[58]

Just as Zukerman used the pages of his *Jewish Newsletter* to attack those who, he felt, had caved to mainstream, unconditional Zionism, he also used it to defend those who dissented from those ideas. Leaders of religiously liberal organizations and publications such as the *Recon-structionist*, the journal of the Reconstructionist movement in Judaism, earned a special degree of Zukerman's ire when they embraced uncon-ditional Zionism.[59] *Reconstructionist* editors rejected statistics on the number of "Arab refugees" that Zukerman cited as displaced by Israel's founding and its further expansions into Palestinian land: in his *Jew-ish Newsletter*, he cited this number as eight hundred thousand. *Recon-structionist* editors referred to Zukerman's data as "biased propaganda." Zukerman in turn lamented the fact that the journal had to "descend to the use of totalitarian hate propaganda in dealing with opponents, a practice which has become the accepted rule of the Zionist press of America."[60] He wrote in defense of his friends and also to conceptualize how future generations might think about, even judge, the years they lived through:

> It is almost despairing to see how the entire Zionist press of America and even publications such as *The Reconstructionist* has [sic] adopted the spirit and technique of totalitarianism in dealing with its opponents. I am sure that when the history of American Jewry of this period is written, the most shameful chapter of it will be the one dealing with the treatment by the victorious Zionists of their opponents, particularly of their organized opposition—the American Council for Judaism. The verdict of history will be that a dominant section of American Jewry was so much carried away by the hate propaganda of the age, of which the Jews were the most pitiful victims, that they, in their turn, became peddlers of hate and prejudice

against other Jews who did not share their views about the establishment of a Jewish political state. In a world drenched in hatred and shivering in cold wars, these Jews chose to add to the general tragic lot of mankind a bitterness and venom of their own which poisoned Jewish social life of the period, demoralized the Zionist movement itself and infected also large numbers of other Jews with the same poison.[61]

In his colorful and evocative writing, Zukerman expressed his continued confusion and anger that this "poison" simply did not fit with what he saw as the worldviews of Jewry—in other words, liberal and inclined toward social justice—and also with American pluralism. Indeed, he called the Jewish community's condemnation of the Council "undemocratic and un-American."[62] His hopes that the American Zionist movement might engage freely in debate were dashed. In his *Jewish Newsletter*, he captured his feelings about Jewish politics and state-sanctioned racism in Israel and the United States. First, in 1952, he joined with allies to criticize the racism embedded in Israel's citizenship law.

Zukerman on Jews and Racism in the United States and Israel, 1952–60

Israel's citizenship law of 1952 expanded upon the Law of Return passed by the Israeli Knesset in 1950 and furthered Israel's consolidation as a state.[63] The Law of Return gave Israeli citizenship to Jews around the world when they arrived in Israel and was intricately tied to the idea of the "ingathering of the exiles," as Israeli leaders intended that the law would boost the Jewish population of Israel.[64] The 1952 citizenship law deprived Palestinian refugees who lived in Palestine before 1948, under the British Mandate, the right to acquire citizenship or residence status in Israel. Palestinians Arabs who still lived in Israel had to demonstrate "uninterrupted presence" within the borders since 1948, which proved extremely difficult.[65] "Passage of the act had been deferred," reported the *New York Times*, "because of sharp differences among the legislators, mainly on two points—racial discrimination and the concept of dual citizenship."[66]

Minister, pacifist, and socialist leader Norman Thomas called the citizenship law an "outright discriminatory law creating one set of rules for Jews and another for the Arabs." Zukerman noted that "Jews, and American Jews in particular, have always been exceptionally sensitive on the point of discrimination. At the slightest infringement of equality, especially before the Law, they were the first to shout loudest, to organize the largest mass meetings." Of Thomas and others, regarding American Jewish support for the citizenship law, Zukerman wrote, "These people feel strongly let down by the Jews and their liberals."[67] Zukerman gave voice to his own disappointment that American Jews, vocal in protesting discrimination within American borders, did not protest what he felt was a racist law in Israel.

Thomas, Berger, and Zukerman joined philosophy professor Israel Knox in declaring their own protest statements in a Council-published pamphlet. Their responses to the act fell along predictable lines. Rabbi Berger drew from the Reform movement's antinationalism and spoke of American Jews' patriotism, asking, "How can Jews, who consider themselves 'indivisible' Americans, go along with an act admittedly legislating double nationality status for them?"[68]

Zukerman first expressed dismay because the act "limit[ed] the citizenship of Arabs."[69] He praised the protests of the law in Israel and berated American Zionist and non-Zionist organizations for their silence. He also identified what he saw as their hypocrisy, writing, "How can these organizations go on with their work for civil rights without defining their position on what is going on in Israel in the field of legal discrimination against a minority?" He questioned whether they had the "moral right to demand of the Arab countries or . . . of the countries behind the Iron curtain not to discriminate against Jewish nationals, while they remain silent on discrimination against a minority in Israel."[70]

The American context provided Zukerman with a pointed example of this hypocrisy in action. He drew parallels between the Israeli citizenship law and the US McCarran–Walter Act of 1952 (also known as the Immigration and Nationality Act of 1952), which upheld the nativist National Origins Quota System restrictions of 1924 and was passed over President Truman's veto. The act was the product of Cold War xenophobia, and the exclusions it mandated posed serious concerns to Jewish group leaders, who feared that the legislation allowed former Nazis to enter the United States while barring anyone with ties to radicalism. Seeking to aid as many Jewish refugees and immigrants as possible,

Jewish leaders also feared that immigration officials might use the act's anti-communist provisions to exclude Jews from Europe.

Zukerman then turned again to what he saw as contradictory in American Jewish worldviews by contrasting American Zionists' support for the Israeli citizenship law with their opposition to the McCarran–Walter Act.[71] The "principles underlying both laws," asserted Zukerman, were "essentially the same." "The Zionist press in America," he added, sounded "the loudest cries" against the US legislation. Jewish groups used all of their resources to draw attention to the injustice of the law. Under both the Israeli and American acts, Zukerman asserted, "minorities are legally discriminated against." In the protests by American Jews over the US act, alongside their silence over the Israeli law, Zukerman saw what he described as a "flagrant act of double morality," a "sacrifice of the principle of universal justice for reasons of nationalistic expediency." He concluded his observations by asking, "Who will take Jewish protests of any moral issue seriously after this?"[72]

At the invitation of the Council and Rabbi Berger, Norman Thomas also contributed to the pamphlet.[73] In an essay titled "A Menace to Fraternity," he focused almost exclusively on observations that people around the world had shared with him, specifically regarding what he described as "American favoritism to Israel and neglect of displaced Arabs." Thomas's travels had convinced him of the truth in this observation and also that "Arabs are at best second class citizens in the land where their forefathers have lived for centuries."

Thomas called the treatment of Palestinians in Israel "Hitlerism in reverse" and like Zukerman called out the "bad grace" of American Zionists who loudly criticized the McCarran–Walter Act (as he did) but "apologize[d] for Ben-Gurion's law of nationalism." Above all, Thomas wrote, the act was a "menace to the fraternity upon which world peace depends." He predicted that "the evil of Israeli chauvinism" would, through deprivation and discrimination, be "fanning the flames of Arabian chauvinism and Moslem fanaticism" and "play into the hands of the communists." Echoing Zukerman, Thomas observed that American Jewish silence on the Israeli act marked what he described as the "betrayal by Jews of the principle for which they have fought so valiantly through some many years." Like Zukerman, Thomas thought of Jews as "stalwart friends" of progressive movements and was baffled by what he saw as their departure from the "fight against the mood of reaction in America." The fight against conservativism grew "far more difficult," Thomas wrote, "when Jewish papers have to spend time apologizing [for] their double standard of national ethics: one for Israel, where the Jews are a majority, and another for America, where they are a minority."

Thomas concluded with words of praise for the American Jews who bore "testimony to the principles of liberalism and equality" in criticizing the citizenship law, including in that praise the Council's request for him to write on this issue. "By no means are all Jews lost to the principles of their own spiritual leaders down through the ages."[74] According to Thomas, the American Council for Judaism represented the truest heir to the long tradition of Jewish support for struggles for justice in rejecting policies such as Israel's 1952 citizenship law. Indeed, Lessing Rosenwald, president of the Council, wrote a letter attacking the law in the *New York Times*.[75] Coverage of resistance to the law in the *New York Times* came in the form of a one-paragraph report, buried on page 18, about Council members holding a meeting and voicing criticism.[76] By 1952, Zionist leaders had already long targeted Rabbi Berger, and now these protests over the law drew these leaders' attention to Thomas and Zukerman as well.

The protests over the law by Thomas, Berger, and Zukerman likely did not reach the mainstream. Indeed, Labor Zionist Shlomo Katz was relieved that the Council pamphlet "may pass almost unnoticed by the general public." Still, Katz sent a furious letter of protest to Thomas[77] and was already attacking Zukerman for his criticism of Zionism in the pages of his publication, the *Jewish Frontier*.[78]

The broader meaning of their observations, as articulated in this pamphlet, shone through clearly. Unconditional support for Zionism among American Jews was wreaking havoc on Jewish commitments to justice. In Israel, these men contended, American Jews saw only what they wanted to see.

By 1957, the United Jewish Appeal turned to American Jewish donors to help Israel in the Suez crisis. Egyptian president Gamal Abdel Nasser had nationalized the Suez Canal, seizing the British- and French-owned firm after the United States and Britain refused him economic aid. Britain and France colluded with Israel to attack Egypt, and the United States gradually brokered a cease-fire in November 1956, though UN troops remained in the Sinai early until 1967. The United States, ever fearful of communist expansion, became still more invested in intervention in the Middle East, and American Jewish fundraising campaigns furthered this investment. For its unqualified support of militarism abroad, in late 1957 Zukerman termed American Judaism "machine-gun Judaism."[79]

As Zukerman had expressed anger over American Jewish celebrations when Menachem Begin visited the United States in 1948, so too did he call out the hypocrisy of American Jews' aligning themselves with liberal causes such as civil rights in the United States while positioning themselves on the right wing of Zionist politics in Israel: "Above all . . . [the non-Jewish American] cannot understand his Jewish neighbors in America whom he has always known to be liberal and humanitarian on most social problems, and who are still very vociferous on questions of social justice affecting their own group, yet fail to realize that a wrong has been committed against the Palestine Arabs by the Israelis, and are placing their tribal emotions above universal justice."[80] Zukerman tapped into these ideas again after several local white supremacists bombed the Atlanta Hebrew Benevolent Congregation in the fall of 1958. The temple was targeted because its leader, Rabbi Jacob Rothschild, spoke often in favor of civil rights leaders' campaigns for racial integration.[81]

Zukerman began his article by giving voice to the positions of mainstream Jewish leaders. "American Jews as a minority ethnic group must take a strong stand against segregation because racial and religious bias is indivisible, there being no difference between anti-Negroism and antisemitism," he wrote. "If racial segregation is not defeated now, they argue, Jews will be the next victims. The bombing of the Atlanta synagogue should be considered a signal for a new and strong fight for civil rights in which the Jews are to play a leading role." Zukerman applauded this idea and then turned it on its head. "This position would have been unassailable had it not been advocated dishonestly by people who are themselves segregationists as far as Jews are concerned and advocate integration only for others," he wrote. He continued,

How can the American Jewish Congress and other outspoken Zionist organizations honestly fight segregation in the South if opposition to integration of Jews with non-Jews is the basic principle of Zionism? How can Orthodox Jewish religious leaders protest against segregation if Orthodox

Judaism fights for the 'purity' of its members in Israel and in this country no less fiercely than any segregationist? Is then religious and national
segregation better than racial segregation? . . . The obvious insincerity
and the double standard on civil rights of the Jewish advocates of integration for the South, but not for themselves, weakened and made their
position untenable.[82]

Here Zukerman drew parallels between the unequal human and citizenship rights of Palestinians and other non-Jews in Israel and the rights of
African Americans in the US.

Zukerman then turned his attention to Jews in the South who advised
Jewish leaders *not* to take a stand on integration, for fear that doing so
would cause what they described as "tension between Jews and non-
Jews in the South."[83] Predictably, these southern Jews rejected the idea
that organizations like the Anti-Defamation League represented all
American Jews in opposing American segregation. Zukerman latched
onto this idea for his own specific agenda: in their embrace of Zionism, he argued, national Jewish leaders also did not speak for all Jews.
In the pages of his *Jewish Newsletter*, Zukerman criticized the "cry of
anti-Semitism . . . kept alive and even exaggerated" by organizations
like the Anti-Defamation League in service of "Zionist propaganda."
He urged "a radical change . . . in the entire concept of anti-Semitism
in America." Above all he criticized these agencies for comparing anti-
Jewish sentiment to anti-Black racism, writing that to understate the
"problems faced by the Negroes in America . . . is to miss the point, to
exaggerate and even to help create the evil we want to fight."[84]

As Black-Jewish alliances encountered numerous challenges in the
1960s, including fraught neighborhood encounters between Black and
Jewish Americans in New York and other urban areas, Israel's alliance
with France in the Algerian War of Independence, and the growing alliance between Israel and apartheid South Africa, Zukerman's discomfort
proved to be prescient.

Zukerman was furious that Israeli journalists saw the bombing at the
Atlanta synagogue as confirmation that "American Jews were doomed
to go through the same experience that German Jewry did" and saw
it as just cause for a "mass exodus" to Israel.[85] The Israeli newspaper
Herut, he noted, spoke of the bombing as an opportunity "to deepen

the nationalistic conscience among the six million of our brethren in the United States and to show them what it means to lead a free life in an independent fatherland and not as a minority in a foreign country." For Zukerman, in light of Jewish suffering across the twentieth century, Jews had a special responsibility to fight for justice. The bombings, he wrote, "are part of a larger stream of hatred fostered by segregationist tensions which spilled over into anti-Semitic channels." Convinced that American antisemitism posed no serious threat to overall Jewish safety, he rejected the idea that Jewish leaders could exploit the Holocaust to instill unjustified fear and bolster the support for American Zionism. He called it "nationalistic propaganda at its worst, sacrificing truth and decency for the sake of ideological beliefs."[86]

A few months after this article appeared, the theme of the issue of the *Jewish Newsletter* was "Escape as a Philosophy," and the subjects of Zukerman's withering criticism were, again, Zionists and their policies. Zukerman observed the decline of Jewish populations in Eastern Europe as Jews and their resources traveled to Israel, something he saw as "harmful to the Jews all over the world, suicidal for Israel, and dangerous for peace in the Middle East and the world." He scolded Israeli officials for rewarding "escape" for world Jewry to Israel while punishing "the flight of Arab refugees" with "eternal banishment." He denied that Israel was any stronger "than when she was first established," adding that "antisemitism is now stronger and more widespread in the Muslim world than in the days of Hitler."

In a section of the *Jewish Newsletter* titled "Negroes and Jews," Zukerman began by excoriating the "Zionist propagandists" who "often speak of the Negroes and the Jews as being in a similar position of persecuted minorities." He considered this "demagogy," and he wrote, "There is no comparison between the heart-breaking tragedy of the Negro in the South or even in the North of the United States with that of the Jews in Rumania, Morocco or even in the Soviet Union." In the preceding few years, attempts at racial integration in Little Rock, Arkansas, and Birmingham, Alabama, had met state-sanctioned violent resistance. "It is this blend of love, tenacity, courage and faith in the final victory of right over wrong that is the driving force of the Negroes and of other underprivileged groups," he wrote, "fighting the eternal battle of many for progress."[87]

Here, too, Zukerman's praise served both to lift up one group and to rebuke another, as he worked in razor-sharp contrasts. African Americans know that they are "part of America" and that "a home is not a hotel which one changes as soon as it becomes inconvenient." "It has never occurred" to Black leaders, he noted, "to solve the Negro problem by mass-evacuation of all Negroes from the South, or to raise hundreds of millions of dollars for that purpose." He continued with even harsher criticism: "It is enough to compare the moral grandeur and nobility of the men of Birmingham and of the children of Little Rock, who fight for their rights, with the ostentatious vulgarity of the [Jewish Zionist] fund-raisers of Miami Beach and Madison Square Garden rallies, to realize what the philosophy of escape has done to the Jews."[88] Zukerman did not acknowledge the many American Jews who took part in the civil rights movement. Instead, he surveyed the turmoil of the United States, located many Jews outside of the struggle yet bound to Zionist fundraising, and then expressed his disappointment and shame. Zukerman continued to draw attention to the ways in which American Zionism, with its ties to Palestinian oppression, corrupted American Jewishness. As refracted through the lens of American Jewish fundraising and communal life, Zionism did not appear as an ideology of liberation.

As anticolonialist activists gained power and their critiques of Israel gained visibility, they sometimes turned to Zukerman as a source of dissent from what appeared an American Jewish Zionist consensus. The *New York Amsterdam News*, a Black newspaper, published Paul Hale's article detailing the "split" over Zionism among American Jews. The evidence for this split lay in the debate between William Zukerman in the *Jewish Newsletter* and the Zionist leaders of the *National Jewish Post*. In Hale's telling, Zukerman joined American Council for Judaism members as recipients of the "sharp words" of the Zionist leaders, and Zukerman pointed out the "unforgivable sin" of the plight of "Arab refugees."[89] The following week, a reader wrote a letter to the editor of the *Amsterdam News* identifying Hale's sources as "partial and partisan" and noted that the "overwhelming majority" of American Jews are "sympathetic to, and support, the State of Israel." Hale, she wrote, had "confused a scratch with a split."[90] Though Hale subtitled his piece "First of a Series," no additional articles on this topic appeared.

Zukerman also turned his analysis to the racism of Israeli policies toward Mizrahi Jews (those with origins in North Africa and the Middle East), which led to the "riots of the Oriental Jews in Israel." Beginning in the 1950s, Zukerman observed, the Israeli government encouraged Jewish emigration from these regions in order to enhance the Jewish population. Once in Israel, these immigrants were kept in camps and subjected to medical experimentation, and some parents had babies stolen and forcibly put up for adoption with Ashkenazic families (whose origin lay in Western Europe).[91] Zukerman drew attention to what he described as "the shameful physical conditions under which . . . thousands of Oriental and other immigrants lived in Israel for nearly ten years" and asserted that these conditions "were created by the ideology which places the building of the nationalistic state above the welfare of the immigrants."[92] He reported on what he termed the "race riots" in Israel of North African Jews, contrasting their treatment with the "white" Jews from Eastern Europe and noting that their "grievances must be remedied by far-reaching economic reforms."[93]

In addition to castigating Zionists for their chauvinism and hypocrisy and broadly for supporting racist policies in Israel, Zukerman examined the impact of Israel's policies, and he expressed fear about rising negative sentiment toward Israel on the world stage. In 1960, Zukerman wrote that Israel has "never been more isolated than during this year," noting that the isolation extended "from the Arab world to the Afro-Asian countries which seem to be solidly behind the Arab countries in their opposition to Israel despite the fact that Israel has made some successful attempts to form friendly economic relations with under-developed countries in Africa." The sum total of these observations was that Zionism and Israel's policies were contributing to a decline in safety not only for Jews but for all people in the world.[94]

In coming to these conclusions, Zukerman largely overlooked the fact that in his lifetime and until the late 1960s and early 1970s, especially after the 1967 and 1973 wars in Israel, many American Zionists did indeed work for civil rights. The rabbi of the Atlanta synagogue was one of many self-identified Jews, radicals and liberals, affiliated and unaffiliated with Jewish life, who worked for racial justice. As scholar Michael Staub notes, "During the fifties, as in earlier decades, American Zionism embraced a more fluid and internally diverse range of ideological commitments." What "bonded one American Zionist to another was Jewish pride," he writes. Zukerman's criticisms notwithstanding, it was not at all uncommon for American Zionists to link "justice and Judaism" and engage in American "antiracist activism" in those years.[95]

But beginning in the early 1960s, Staub charts the turn inward of American Jewry, the withdrawal of many Jewish organizations from such activism with a "redefinition of Jewish liberalism."[96] Israel was central to that redefinition, as perceptions of Israel's increased vulnerability emerged at the same moment that other developments in American Jewish life pulled many American Jews further from social justice work. In seeing the tensions between American Zionists' unquestioning embrace of Israeli policies and their stands on domestic civil rights, William Zukerman identified early the role that American Zionism might play in diminishing the commitments of American Jews to progressive coalitions.

Past the Threshold of Dissent: Zukerman, Hurwitz, and Free Speech on Israel and Zionism in the 1950s

From Zukerman's earliest writings in the 1930s through to the 1950s, American Jews allowed room for some degree of open discussion on Zionism and its role in American Jewish life. Criticism of Zukerman and his allies intensified, however, as the Zionist consensus took hold and as Zionist leaders built and policed unconditional support of Israel and centered American Jewish life around it.

Zukerman long knew there was a price to pay for the "independent thought" of his journalism. In 1949, the same year Zionist leaders accused him and his fellow members of the Free Jewish Club of being "enemies of Zion," he published an article in the *Jewish Newsletter* about rabbinical control over marriages in Israel. The article, he later recalled, suggested that this control, "in a sense, constituted the introduction of theocracy." Soon after, he lost his job on the *Jewish Morning Journal*, for which he had written for twenty-nine years, "on the ground[s] that [he] had publicly insulted the Jewish religion." Only after "protracted negotiations" with the Yiddish Writers Union, which agreed to take his case "in view of the fact that [his] dismissal from the *Journal* for publishing an article of opinion would have set a dangerous precedent for other members," did the newspaper agree to change his "dismissal . . . to . . . removal from the permanent position which [he] held on the editorial staff." His weekly pay dropped from ninety to twenty dollars.[97]

Zukerman wrote of this incident to the person who had published his first professional piece of journalism in the United States: Henry Hurwitz (1886–1961). Born in Lithuania, Hurwitz immigrated to the United States with his family in 1891. He grew up poor, in a Zionist family in Gloucester, Massachusetts. During his first year at Harvard University, Hurwitz founded the Harvard Zionist Society. He and a few of his peers there, including philosopher Horace Kallen, also founded the Harvard Menorah Society for the Advancement of Jewish Culture and Ideals in 1913. The organization fought discrimination, advanced Hebrew studies in the curriculum, and encouraged the study of Jewish history; eighty chapters, all modeled on Harvard, were present on college campuses by 1920, with Hurwitz serving as the organization's chancellor.[98] In 1915, Hurwitz founded the *Menorah Journal*, which published articles on Jewish culture and ideals as a means to promote Jewish humanism.[99]

The *Menorah Journal* founders included Hurwitz, Kallen, and Jewish studies scholar Harry Wolfson. Under the direction of what scholar Robert Alter called its "precocious managing editor" in the 1920s, Elliot Cohen, the *Menorah Journal* included acclaimed scholars and writers such as Salo Baron and Simon Dubnow, Reconstructionism's founder Rabbi Mordecai Kaplan, and reviewer Tess Slesinger. Hurwitz's dedication to frank and open-minded journalism and art remained steadfast through the long run of the magazine. According to Alter, "During its great period in the 20's the *Journal* managed very impressively to be specialized [according to Jewish interest] without being parochial."[100] Its editors, he added, "were always proud of the fact that they had never belonged to what they called the Jewish Establishment in America" and that freedom afforded them access to a variety of viewpoints. The *Menorah Journal* took a hard financial hit during the Great Depression, according to Alter: "Against the urgent claims on conscience of the radical movements, the *Journal*'s quest for high culture must have seemed like the most effete *fin-de-siècle* decadence and its insistence on Jewish identity a reactionary gesture of pathetic futility."[101] But it carried on into the 1960s with Hurwitz's leadership, as he clearly believed he had something to say to the world through his journalism.

The strongest criticisms running through Hurwitz's magazine in those decades were certainly focused on Zionism, Israel, American Jewish life, and the synergy among them. Indeed, Hurwitz's criticism of Zionism came to define his publication in its later decades.[102] Zukerman felt comfortable with the independent thought reflected in Hurwitz's journal. He recalled that Hurwitz "gave me my first chance in real self-expression," adding, "I remember always with gratitude my first contribution which I sent you (in 1929 . . .) I was not known to you nor to anyone in the United States."[103]

Hurwitz and Zukerman found common ground in their views of Zionism. Hurwitz's ideas aligned with those of the original members of the American Council for Judaism, as for him, "the pronouncements of the Reform movement's Pittsburgh Platform of 1885 constituted an *immediate* American heritage."[104] He viewed the prophetic teachings of Judaism as the religion's most valuable contribution to the world. In 1944 Hurwitz wrote to Max Epstein of Chicago that "if Zionism means the establishment of a Jewish Commonwealth or State, I am as anti-Zionist as you are." He first said he was a cultural Zionist in "wishing to see Palestine developed as a place of Jewish culture and as a refuge for Jews."[105] But to Zukerman, in 1946, Hurwitz wrote, "Though, in the matter of a Jewish state, I find myself surprisingly more 'left' (or left out) than even you. I don't believe any Jewish state at all can be 'viable' under present conditions."[106] In the spring of 1949, one year after Israel's statehood, Hurwitz was a guest at a chapter meeting of the American Council for Judaism, befriending its leadership and aligning himself with the Council's ideas.[107]

The *Menorah*, like Zukerman's *Jewish Newsletter*, met with strong criticism. According to Alter's "epitaph" for the *Menorah*, the journal's "hostility to the Jewish world" was "most clearly detectable" in Hurwitz's "hostility to Zionism." "After World War II," Alter writes, "the *Journal* takes a progressively critical stand on Zionism that will end as a flirtation with the militantly anti-Zionist American Council for Judaism. This final stage begins in 1945, notably enough with Hannah Arendt's essay 'Zionism Reconsidered,'" a "withering attack on the Zionist leadership and program."[108]

Arendt's perspectives on Jews and Israel drew tremendous controversy later, with the publication in 1963 of *Eichmann in Jerusalem*, when some interpreted her analysis of the "banality of evil" as harshly judging Jews for complicity with the Nazis. But in these earlier decades, her grim reflections on Israel's "romantic nationalism and militarism" meant that she found common ground with both Council members and Zukerman.[109] In her 1944 essay "New Leaders Arise in Europe," Arendt heralded Zukerman as "one lonely preacher in the wilderness" for his observations on the potential futures of Jews in Europe after the horrors of the Holocaust.[110] For his part, Zukerman quoted Arendt in the *Jewish Newsletter* through the 1950s and encouraged Arendt to comment on Israel's injustices for his publication.[111] Arendt's essay in the *Menorah* accompanied one by the *Jewish Newsletter*'s Zukerman in which he called for an affirmation of Judaism in all Jewish communities and also for a diverse Jewish leadership—outside of "Europe or New York."[112]

At the same moment as the two articles were being published, Hurwitz saw his funds decrease, and he turned to increased funding from the non-Zionist American Jewish Committee. But one year later, in 1945, the AJC also cut its funds to the *Menorah Journal*, likely because its content was critical of Israel. Hurwitz then turned to his friends at the Council seeking money so that the *Menorah Journal* could stay in business.

Hurwitz continued to publish essays extolling cultural Zionism and criticizing American Jewish philanthropies for their lack of transparency with regard to the millions of dollars they raised for "relief" and then sent to build up the Israeli military. "Throughout this period," writes scholar Lewis Fried, "subsidies and subscriptions to the *Menorah Journal* were being canceled." Hurwitz pointed to this as proof that the publication, like Zukerman's *Jewish Newsletter*, "suffered for its independent thought." In the final months of 1947, the Rosenwald Foundation offered the *Menorah Journal* a $10,000 donation.[113]

In a letter to a friend, Hurwitz narrated the life of his *Menorah Journal* with these words: "Through two World Wars and the Great Depression . . . we have kept our banner of independence flying, often torn but never sullied. When we published Zionist articles, our anti-Zionist friends would sometimes withdraw their financial support. When we published anti-Zionist articles, Zionists even more heftily withdrew their support." He confessed, "We could easily, more than once, have sold out, and could now be wallowing in money (like one or two other Jewish magazines) instead of constantly having to worry about how to pay the rent and the printers." He then put forward one of his main reasons for supporting the Council's ideas: he rejected the denigration of Judaism and Jewish communities outside of Israel.[114]

For Hurwitz, maintaining his journal's relevance and integrity also entailed addressing controversies in Jewish life. Hurwitz wrote an article titled "Israel, What Now?" in the wake of the 1953 Kibya massacre.[115] Bridging Zukerman's criticism of Zionism and the Council's emphasis on prophetic Judaism, in "Israel, What Now?," Hurwitz advised American Jews to replace what he called the "Cult of the State [of Israel]" with the "Religion of Judaism." Echoing Zukerman, he criticized American Jewish journalists as "subservient to the official Israeli or Jewish Agency line." Overall, he described American Jewish life as having a "pathological atmosphere, infected with elements of terrorism and totalitarianism," when those who criticize or reject Israel "are denounced as renegades or saboteurs."[116]

Hurwitz concluded the essay with an interjection: "What a paradox is here!" Jews in the West have been at "the forefront of liberalism. . . . Yet when Jews have gotten a chance to run a state of their own, look at it!" "We rub our eyes, some of us who were lifelong Zionists, and we hang our heads in shame," he continued. "This present Israel is not what we dreamed and hoped for and worked for—we who followed Herzl or Ahad Ha-am, Brandeis or Weizmann. . . . This century has witnessed many a tragic and fantastic spectacle, but perhaps none more bizarre than a Government of atheistic socialists combined with theocratic fundamentalists, maintained by American and British capitalists." He feared for Israel's stature on the world stage and recommended that leaders study suggestions offered by Council member Rabbi Morris Lazaron for a political solution to the "dangerous tension between Israel and the Arab States," including, among other items, the rejection of military aggression among all parties, compensation for stolen Palestinian land, the absorption of Palestinian refugees, the end of discrimination against non-Jews in Israel, the internationalization of Jerusalem, and an end to the "economic boycott" of Israel on the part of "the Arab states."[117]

In the 1950s, Hurwitz, like Zukerman, began to pay a high price for his independent thought. The boards of Jewish leaders in individual cities, long donors to national Jewish publications and organizations, stopped giving money to the Menorah Journal or reduced their allocation of funds. Hurwitz received less or no money from Baltimore, he confided in a friend, and also from Philadelphia, Seattle, Syracuse, and Worcester, Massachusetts.[118] In the 1955 spring/summer issue of the *Menorah Journal*, Hurwitz identified the publication of "Israel, What Now?" as the reason the board of directors of the Jewish Welfare Fund of Baltimore ended its relationship with the *Menorah Journal* altogether. The Menorah Association had been a member of the Jewish Welfare Fund of Baltimore and a beneficiary since its inception twelve years before. Hurwitz enumerated what he described as the "questions of communal policy and morality" raised by ending this relationship. His questions reflected the idea that the views of the members of the beneficiary agencies were required to align perfectly with those of the board of directors. Hurwitz questioned the "freedom of the Jewish press in America" and the equation of "Jewish Welfare" with Israel.[119]

Although his words lost him significant funding, Hurwitz remained undeterred. He continued to dissent from American Zionism with pointed criticism.[120] He predicted a third world war if Israel stood in the way of peacemaking and expressed hope that Israel would offer the United Nations, the United States, and "the Arab peoples" a "program of sound policy and high humanity" that "could appeal to liberal Christians and Muslims." This program included full equality for all citizens, full membership in the Histadrut for all workers, full compensation for confiscated Palestinian property, the return for a number of Palestinian refugees to be determined by the United Nations, a permanent home for Jewish refugees, and Israel's renunciation of any claims of what he termed "World Jewish Peoplehood."[121] He urged Israel to stay out of the Cold War, to place itself in the hands of the United Nations. He urged "all Arabs" not to condemn "all Jews" and vice versa. He celebrated Israel's aid to Jewish refugees while also drawing attention to Israel's role in forced Jewish immigration from other nations to increase its Jewish population.[122] For his dissent, both the Federation of Jewish Agencies of Greater Philadelphia and the Combined Jewish Appeal of Boston "expelled" the Menorah Association. Hurwitz was convinced that this expulsion resulted, above all, from his sympathetic presentation of the case for the anti-Zionist Council "with some courtesy and comprehension."[123]

"We here in Menorah have burned our bridges," he acknowledged to a friend. He knew that his criticisms of American Zionism, his disagreements with Israeli policies, lay past the threshold of acceptable dissent: "Whatever our enemies (mostly former 'friends') say about our 'selling out' to ACJ, I am sure it is understood in ACJ circles that this is not the case." He did hope to gain more support among American Jews. He also wanted to build new bridges, as he saw himself and his colleagues as "hav[ing] a job to do in the Moslem intellectual world," a vision that he hoped "[Fayez] Sayegh's coming article will advance."[124] Sayegh was a Protestant, Georgetown-educated Palestinian academic and activist and the head of the Arab Information Center in New York City in the mid-1950s. Hurwitz, Zukerman, and Council leaders were some of the only members of the Jewish community to meet with Sayegh, the "public face of the Arab cause in America," in the 1950s.[125]

Given his public statements and his relationship with Sayegh, Hurwitz was the target of still more criticism. Readers alleged that his articles rested on an "anti-Jewish and anti-semitic foundation."[126] But he also had his defenders. In a column titled "The Need for Dissent," Samuel B. Finkel, a columnist for Boston's *Jewish Advocate*, wrote that after the publication of one of his dissenting articles, he knew that "evil motives will once again be attributed to [Hurwitz]," adding, "It is high time that it be made clear that to criticize some of the ways and practices of the American Jewish community and of the State of Israel is not an act of treason to Jewry. It is high time that it be made clear that such criticism may stem from a deep concern for the welfare of our people." While acknowledging that some of Hurwitz's criticisms were "bitter and biting," Finkel cited Biblical prophets along with Spinoza, Galileo, "Jefferson, Holmes, Brandeis and Stephen Wise" as proof of the courage of "brave dissenters" because "dissent was the bulwark of progress." Only the freedom to dissent, he wrote, can keep a society "just and durable."[127]

This commitment was the foundation of Hurwitz's friendship with William Zukerman, whose sustained critique of American Zionism and Israel became increasingly intense and met with increasing criticism from Zionist leaders. In 1955, Zukerman's ire was raised as tensions rose in Egypt, Jordan annexed the West Bank and East Jerusalem, and Israeli leaders conducted what they called "reprisal raids" in Gaza as part of Operation Black Arrow in retaliation for Israeli Jewish lives and property lost to Palestinian raids sponsored by neighboring governments.

The fear of war in Israel, Zukerman asserted, corresponded to a rise of extreme thinking among American Jews. "Chauvinism is running high," he wrote. "Militancy and extremism are rising from day to day as the temperature of a sick person." And he added, "There is a fanatical certainty abroad that there is only one truth and that Israel is the sole custodian of it." Speaking broadly and surely encompassing his own experiences, Zukerman noted that "any American Jew who doubts the sincerity of the Israeli politicians' protestations of peace is denounced as a pro-Arab, a partner of feudal barons, or an antisemite." While Israel's "outburst of emotionalism . . . has a basis in reality," he wrote, "the American-Jewish brand of hysteria is entirely without roots in the realities of American Jewish life. It is completely artificial, manufactured by the Zionist leaders, and almost mechanically foisted on a people who have no cause for hysteria by an army of paid propagandists as a means of advancing a policy of avowed political pressure and of stimulating fund raising."[128] He called on American Jews, so frequently the sources of his hopes and disappointment, to speak out, writing, "Why does not a single one of the many American Jewish labor leaders, famous for their liberalism and socialism, do what the Bund did in Israel—remind the Jewish world that the present war crisis is, at least in part, due to the Ben Gurion-Sharett [Israel's first two prime ministers] 'activist' policies?" One way he claimed to ease the crisis would be for the Jewish world to disavow these policies of extremism. "Such a disavowal would not be tantamount to a repudiation of Israel," he reminded them, "or the right to its existence."[129]

* * *

By the early 1950s, Zukerman's positions earned him additional and more widespread condemnation, as they also crossed the threshold of what was acceptable dissent from American Zionism. In 1951, Shlomo Katz, editor of the Labor Zionist journal *Jewish Frontier*, attacked Zukerman for his anti-Zionism, his advocacy of Palestinian refugees, and his suggestion that only "fanatical parents" would protest the singing of Christmas carols in public schools. Katz suggested a link between Zukerman and the "capo" in Nazi death camps, the members of the Jewish concentration camp police.[130] Katz accused Zukerman, then, of doing work that destroyed Jewish life.

Increasingly, Zionist Jewish leaders used false accusations of anti-semitism or communism to delegitimize criticism of Zionism or support for Palestinian rights. Although Boston's *Jewish Advocate* still published Zukerman's columns, they also published letters to the editor in which community members claimed that Zukerman misinterpreted Labor Zionism and demonstrated "condescension" toward Israelis.[131] In 1955, Jewish journalist Nathan Ziprin recorded that Zukerman's "skill of hoaxing piety" emerged when he was caught "red-handed, or better yet, Arab handed."[132] By 1959, Ziprin saw Zukerman as "an old hand in the band of anti-Israel drummers."[133] During the Suez crisis, Ziprin wrote that "for a non-Arab, Zukerman shows rather unusual concern over the Canal issue." He accused Zukerman of leftist sympathies, of relying for a source on "an obscure Jewish monthly in Israel published by the Jewish Bund."[134] When Zukerman published the praise of Dr. Fayez Sayegh for the *Jewish Newsletter* in a fundraising appeal letter, American Zionist organizations accused him of "peddling some of the worst, although slickly coated features of Arab propaganda against American Jews."[135]

For his public positions, Zukerman, too, saw his funds decrease. But businessmen and philanthropists John D. Hertz of Chicago and Aaron Straus of Baltimore each donated thousands of dollars to the *Jewish Newsletter* in the late 1950s to make up for funds lost.[136] By 1960, he no longer had a column in the *B'nai B'rith Messenger*. An article there that designated him as "anti-Israel" also labeled him "Meshuga," the Yiddish word for crazy.[137]

For his strong criticisms, diplomats in Israel's Hasbara or public information office put Zukerman on their radar. Inside the William Zukerman File in the Israel State Archives are letters from the mid-1950s in which Israeli diplomats expressed alarm about Zukerman's writings. In one letter, they referred to him as "the man who wrote the famous article in *Harper's Magazine* about rule of theocracy in Israel"[138] (referring to an article published in November 1950). They feared the impact of his criticisms, noting, "His influence might be limited now, but he is going to cause us increasing trouble if we let him get away with it. We had better try to do something fundamental about him at this stage."[139] Embassy officials worked with American Jewish publications' editors, attempting "rigorous editing" of Zukerman's articles in order to limit the impact of his reporting.[140] Tzvi Zinder, a press officer at Israel's information office in New York, wrote to an Israel consul in Chicago that "no appeal to justice or fairness has any effect in changing Zuckerman's [sic] stance."[141] Diplomats reported that Zukerman "conceal[ed] his cancerous enmity in 'goody-goody' support and advice."[142] They proposed "hitting back at this gentleman who appear[ed] to be conducting a many-fronted vendetta against Israel."[143]

This pointed language suggests just how threatening Israeli diplomats found Zukerman's writings on Palestinian refugees and American Zionism to be, how they identified the origins of his dissent, and also what they feared its impact might be.[144] Zukerman provided "ammunition to our attackers," they wrote.[145] He was dangerous because "his insidious propaganda is providing material not only for anti-Zionists but is confusing Zionists."[146] They surmised that Zukerman's comparison between Israel's citizenship law and the US McCarran–Walter Act emerged from "communists" in Israel and would not be difficult to counter.[147] Indeed, when Jewish leaders planned to respond to Zukerman in order to refute his ideas, they relied on Israeli diplomats, even strategizing with them, before presenting their refutations.[148] Working together, Jewish leaders and Israeli diplomats began a concerted campaign to contact presses in the United States and Europe who published Zukerman's writings, advising the use of all contacts to prevent his writing from reaching these outlets.[149] They urged editors to "react each time" he published something; they pledged to "supply suitable replies" to local Zionists for submission to the papers. "By encouraging a constant attack on Zukerman," these officials wrote, "we might be able to diminish his 'prestige' and persuade Anglo-Jewish editors to drop his material on the grounds that subscribers object."[150]

Both Israeli diplomats and American Jewish Zionist leaders kept close tabs on him and indeed clearly tried to sabotage his career. As historian Geoffrey Levin writes, these pointed attacks succeeded. In the early 1950s, Zukerman lost his column in the *Jewish Advocate* and his position with the *Jewish Chronicle*, and other Jewish presses ceased publishing his work.[151]

In 1958, Zukerman counted the Council, the Jewish Labor Bund, and Freeland as "the organized opposition" to Zionism. He praised them, along with what he described as the "few individuals [who] had the courage to voice their opposition to the official Israeli Arab policy in the midst of the McCarthy-like hysteria." He was proud, he wrote, that "the *Jewish Newsletter* . . . was the only Jewish publication which provided the platform from which these 'voices in the wilderness' could be heard."[152] In his writings, Zukerman brought internal Jewish conflicts over Zionism and Israel into sharp relief, illustrating that some American Jews continued to criticize American Zionism and Israel even after Jewish leaders drew a firm threshold of acceptable dissent and policed it carefully. Attacks on Zukerman betrayed the high stakes of the forced consensus on Zionism, just as Zukerman's writings offer important insights about the connections between American Zionism and American Jewish commitments to justice.

Conclusion: A New Direction

A few years before he died in 1961, in a letter to Norman Thomas, Presbyterian minister, pacifist, social reformer, and six-time Socialist Party candidate for president beginning in 1928, Zukerman described his own background as "Socialistic." He drew parallels between his intellectual development and the growing strength of the Zionist movement:

> I grew up in the intellectual and spiritual climate of the Bund in White Russia, and when I came to this country, I was connected with the Jewish Labor movement and worked for ten years as the Chicago correspondent of the Jewish Daily Forward. I left the United States for Europe toward the end of World War I and stayed away, mostly in England, until 1940. When I came back, I found that the Jewish Labor movement had drifted away so far from the Socialism I knew in the direction of intense nationalism, that I felt like a stranger. That feeling never changed. I never feel more isolated than when I come to a meeting of my old branch of the Workmen's Circle or find myself, by accident, among a *Forward* crowd.[153]

Here Zukerman captured the shift "in the direction of intense nationalism" of American Jewry during his lifetime.

In a moving obituary for Zukerman published in the *B'nai B'rith Messenger* in 1961, Zionist leader Joseph Brainin wrote that "the number of his enemies grew with every issue of his publication." Though ideologically opposed to Zukerman, Brainin acknowledged that he was "sad that a brilliant talent was strangled as it were by the rigid, brutal sectarianism of Jewish organizational life."[154] At Zukerman's funeral, the Council's Rabbi Morris Lazaron described him as a "man of towering strength and moral courage" who "chose to walk the hard path of dissent." Lazaron also praised Zukerman's compassion. "The praise of his contemporaries meant nought to him," he wrote in verse, "if to win them meant sacrifice of integrity."[155]

Motivated by a concern for Jewish safety after the Holocaust and also by worry over what Jewish nationalism in the form of Zionism would do to American Jewish life and Judaism, Zukerman and other anti- and non-Zionists appeared in the pages of the *Jewish Newsletter*, sometimes speaking out about Palestinian refugees.[156] During Zukerman's life, American Jewish leaders positioned him as a fringe figure. Though his biting criticism of Israel and Zionism was just one segment of a broader, if small, non- and anti-Zionist element in American Jewish life, it helped these leaders identify the threshold of dissent in Israel's early years. In referring to Hurwitz, Zukerman, and the Council as fomenting anti-semitism, Jewish leaders demonstrated their belief that only unity on Israel could help Jews secure safety after the Holocaust. For this reason, they also carefully policed the information available about Israel and Palestine within American Jewish communal life. During the 1960s, this became an ever-consuming task as criticism of Israel, tied into anticolonialist movements across the world, grew stronger. American Jews who learned from these movements and came to embrace non- and anti-Zionist ideas would also pay a high price.

3

"Israel—Right or Wrong"

Anticolonialism, Freedom Movements, and American Jewish Life

Before his death in 1961, William Zukerman predicted that unconditional, overly generous support of Israel by American Jews would
make theirs an "emotionally and intellectually closed society."[1] Zukerman decried what he saw as the moral double standard of American
Jews' advocacy for minority rights in the United States, which he felt
sat incongruously alongside their utter disregard for the abrogation
of minority Palestinian rights in Israel. He also rejected—and was a
victim of—American Jewish Zionist campaigns that categorized any
critique of Zionism or Israel, any work on behalf of Palestinian rights, as
antisemitism.

In the 1960s, activists in global anticolonialist movements, including the civil rights, Black Power, and Arab American movements in the
United States, began to learn and teach about the origins of Israel's statehood and its continued treatment of Palestinians and Mizrahi Jews from
the Middle East and North Africa.[2] They included strong anti-Zionist
critiques in their campaigns. Calls by scholars and activists for Palestinian rights increasingly gained traction as anti-Zionism aligned with
other anticolonialist political commitments, including protests over the
increasingly unpopular war in Vietnam.[3]

In terms of the continued growth of support for Israel in the United
States, it is difficult to overstate the impact of the Six-Day War in 1967,
also called the June War or the Naksa, meaning setback or defeat.
Though contrasting sharply with Israeli intelligence reports, which made
clear that Israel was ready to defeat its enemies in war, media accounts
likened the threat posed to Israel by warring nations to another Jewish
genocide.[4] Jewish community leaders and laypeople felt immense relief,
even euphoria, when Israel was victorious. Drawing from the cultural
renaissance within the Black Power movement, American Jews came

to celebrate Zionism with renewed energy as a liberating and unifying force.[5]

Zionist Jewish activists across the political spectrum celebrated Israel's victory just as they closed ranks, many leaving behind progressive coalitions and dedicating (or rededicating) themselves to Jewish life. At the conclusion of the war, Israel had annexed East Jerusalem, captured the Golan Heights, and began its occupation of the West Bank and Gaza Strip. Some radical Jewish organizations rejected this occupation of Palestinian land; other Jewish activists pushed back against criticism of Israel's occupation from within left-wing organizations.[6] After days of pain and fear for many American Jews, unquestioning—and in some cases militant—loyalty to Israel led Zionists to level fierce accusations of antisemitism, even genocidal motives, against those who criticized Israel.[7] Because the debates were, at their core, over Jewish safety and survival, they were inextricably tied to the lessons of the Holocaust.

Millions of American Protestants, both mainline and evangelical, had been strong supporters of Israel and of American Zionism in response to the destruction of the Holocaust.[8] Support for Israel became a means to address the antisemitism within Protestantism, to foster interfaith cooperation and understanding. The 1967 war was, however, as historian Caitlin Carenen notes, "a high water mark for mainline Protestant confusion over Israel."[9] Evangelicals and fundamentalists, whose base grew tremendously in these years, remained steadfast in their unconditional support for Israel because of the role Jews would play in their vision of the Biblical prophecy. Yet by that time, mainline Protestants had already begun to question and draw away from support for Israel, citing Israel's illegal settlement building on the West Bank and Gaza and supporting Palestinian rights and nationalism.[10]

It would be equally difficult to overstate the role of the 1967 war in the growth of anti-Zionism. Historian Salim Yaqub notes that the war "accentuated the Cold War rivalry in the Middle East," and as the United States became Israel's main source of weapons, those who opposed Israel and its subsequent occupation directed their anger in part at the United States and at American Jews.[11] During the Vietnam War, these Cold War tensions placed some Jews in difficult positions: though Israel avoided taking a position on the war, the United States and Israel were clearly anti-Soviet partners. In 1967, the Soviet government aided Arab nations that battled Israel. The war between Israel, Egypt, and Syria in October 1973, known in Israel as the Yom Kippur War and also as the Ramadan War or the October War, put these tensions into even higher relief, as the United States supported Israel, and the Soviet Union supported Arab nations.

If the 1967 war proved a watershed for American Jewish support of Israel, the 1973 war proved central to American support for Israel overall. This war went on three times longer, resulted in three times as many dead, and caught Israeli intelligence entirely off guard. Supporting Israel in the war's aftermath became central to reinventing the United States as what historian Shaul Mitelpunkt calls a "benevolent diplomatic powerhouse."[12] Both Israeli and American public relations experts sought to crystallize this image and to obscure the displacement, dispossession, and oppressive inequality faced by Palestinians in Israel and in the occupied territories after 1967. In censuring Jewish critiques of Israel and maintaining a low threshold for dissent, American Jewish Zionist leaders played important roles in contributing to that mission. This made it extremely difficult for American Jews to balance commitments to anticolonialist movements and to Jewish life.

With an increasingly "closed" worldview with regard to American Zionism and Israel, many American Jews believed that only unconditional support of Israel kept Jews throughout the world safe. The emergence of the Cold War partnership between the United States and Israel only strengthened the Zionist consensus, and the enforcement of this consensus among American Jews aligned with the interests of American militarists.[13] US Cold War policy, especially under President Nixon, linked a "victory" in Vietnam to Israel. As historian Paul Thomas Chamberlain notes, "If [the US] failed in Southeast Asia, the U.S. public might become more isolationist and demand a reduction in American engagement with other nations, such as Israel." Israel was central to American Cold War strategies to prevent Arab nations from aligning with the Soviets.[14]

In 1968, the American-born Israeli and Orthodox Rabbi Meir Kahane founded the right-wing Jewish Defense League in New York. Also drawing from Black nationalism and focusing on ideas of Jewish "pride" and "defense," Kahane turned the anticolonialist logic on its head and created an agenda for Jewish safety and visibility that aligned with American Cold War priorities. He argued that the Vietnam War aided Jewish safety by preventing the spread of communism and antisemitism. He saw Palestinians as enemies of Jews and argued that Jewish participation in civil rights and Black nationalist movements would distract Jews from fighting for their own rights.[15] Indeed, Kahane saw liberalism broadly as a potential substitute for Judaism and thought it would "erase the Jewishness of the Jew."[16] In this way, as historian Shaul Magid observes, Kahane opposed the New Left for its antiwar stance, its embrace of civil rights, and especially its criticism of Israel and Zionism.[17]

In the midst of the antiwar and Black nationalist movements, the rise of the Jewish Defense League and American Cold War commitments, as well as the 1967 and 1973 wars in Israel, Zionist leaders spoke to wide audiences linking criticism of Zionism and Israel to antisemitism. They spoke of it as emerging from external factors, from so-called Black antisemitism and Arab propaganda. In doing this, Zionist leaders erased decades of intracommunal contests over the role of Israel and Zionism in American Jewish life. They also pushed back against Jewish support of the New Left, antiwar, and anticolonialist movements, especially among younger Jews who were increasingly engaged with these movements.

The result was to further align the mainstream Jewish community with whiteness and anti-communism, with American political structures of colonialism and militarism. Jewish leaders maintained a low threshold of dissent on Zionism and Israel, asserting the need for Jewish safety and security. While reinforcing a Zionist consensus, then, they also reinforced positions of power in American political life.

An understanding of American Jewish dissent on Zionism is essential to a fuller portrait of American Jewish life. As Jewish leaders began to enforce the threshold of unacceptable dissent, their language of consensus reflected not a true communal agreement but a concerted effort to marginalize criticism and alternative perspectives. Movement activists alerted some American Jews to the oppression and inequality in the United States, Vietnam, and Israel. Steeped in knowledge of these far-reaching social movements in the 1960s and 1970s, especially the civil rights and antiwar movements, and with connections to the political left in Israel, some American Jews became ardent critics of American Zionism. As they spoke out against Zionism, many tried to maintain their commitments to Jewish communal life and to anticolonialism. In the politically fraught Jewish world of post-1967, activists had to walk a fine line. Vocal critics of Israel and American Zionism faced virulent attacks, attacks that insulated American Jews from fully developed critiques of colonialism and militarism in the United States, Vietnam, and Israel.

American Jews and the Anticolonialism Critique of Israel

Although African American leaders and laypeople had expressed sympathy for Zionism and Israel beginning in the 1940s and early 1950s, this support began to ebb among some Black Americans in the mid-1950s.[18] The Bandung conference of 1955 played a prominent role in the growth of anticolonialist thinking among African Americans and Arab Americans. Though the conference did not specifically address the dispossession of Palestinian families with Israel's founding in 1948, its ideas contributed to the growing solidarity among Black and Arab anticolonialist struggles.[19] The Suez Canal crisis of 1956 further contributed to this solidarity.[20] Black Americans heralded Nasser at the first Arab summit in Cairo in 1964, and the *Chicago Daily Defender*, a historically Black newspaper, noted that Nasser emerged as a hero at the summit for his work toward "a comprehensive Arab unity." Arab representatives there also referred to the "principles" of the Bandung Conference, which represented the "fight[ers] against imperialism and racial discrimination," in an appeal to "extend their support to the Palestine cause."[21]

American Jewish critics of Zionism took note of these new alliances as Israel's position on the world stage began to shift. Louis Harap, a Jewish socialist journalist, reported in his journal, *Jewish Life*, that Asian leaders spoke of "Israel's *de facto* collaboration" with Britain and France, two imperialist powers, in the war against Algerian independence from 1954 to 1962 "as proof that she cannot be depended upon to act as a trustworthy member of the Asian community."[22] He took note of the fact that Israel "is allying itself with colonialist France, whose current bloody suppression of the Algerian independence movement makes her the most hated of all European powers."[23] In a letter to the *New York Times*, historian Hans Kohn, friend of Zukerman and Hurwitz, wrote that "the coincidence of Israel's move into Egypt with the Franco-British invasion of the country tends to lend some credence to the thesis of Israel's being an outpost of Western imperialism in Asia. Such an impression must rally all Asian and African peoples behind the Arabs."[24]

Reinforcing this impression was Israel's alliance with apartheid South Africa. This relationship grew in the 1970s, as the antiapartheid movement grew across the world. Though Israel had supported Black African nations as they emerged from colonialism in the 1950s and 1960s, the alliance with South Africa met with skepticism and condemnation throughout the world.[25]

* * *

The story of these global currents is central to the history of American Zionism and the politics of American Jewish life regarding criticism of Zionism after 1967. Before 1967, many mainstream American Jewish leaders supported Black nationalist and Black Power movements. Even Jewish leaders who did not fully support these liberation movements compared them to Zionism as they sought to make sense of Black Americans' struggles for autonomy and empowerment.[26] In 1966, for example, Boston's *Jewish Advocate* reported, "An [O]rthodox rabbinical leader warned that the slogan '[B]lack [P]ower' and the reported deterioration in Negro-Jewish relations should not discourage rabbis from encouraging support of civil rights programs." The article noted that Jewish community leaders expressed understanding of the need for Black Power, as they understood that "progress toward the goal of full equality must be accelerated dramatically." Still, these leaders hoped that white people would be included in these coalitions for change. Yet Rabbi Emanuel Rackman of Yeshiva University went on record as saying that Jews and other whites should not "exaggerate" the fact that Black people wanted to "run their own movements." "Such statements," he believed, were made "in the same voice as Zionists in Israel, who have complained that American Zionists are interfering in their affairs."[27]

In these same years, as some American Jewish Zionists compared Black nationalism to Zionism to better understand it, the rise in Palestinian solidarity among Black nationalists and civil rights activists only widened the gap between American Jews and African Americans.[28] This rise also contributed greatly to the distancing of American Jews from progressive coalitions, such as those fighting for civil rights.

Not all Black leaders took these positions. In the mid-1970s, A. Philip Randolph and Bayard Rustin led an organization called Black Americans to Support Israel Committee (BASIC), with the support of two dozen significant figures in its full-page advertisement in the *New York Times*.[29] Historian Brenda Gayle Plummer also writes that a "Black-Jewish Informational Center with headquarters in New York City . . . channeled favorable reports about Israel to the [B]lack press."[30] The Black-Jewish Information Center, which was managed by Richard Cohen Associates, a public relations firm that worked with major Jewish organizations, reprinted articles mostly from Jewish publications that celebrated moments of unity between Black and Jewish leaders. The agency focused mainly, and predictably, on Israel. It released a statement when the Histadrut, Israel's General Federation of Jewish Labor, honored Black civil rights and labor leader Robert Powell, for example.[31] It sought to smooth over tensions, downplaying Israel's economic ties to South Africa.[32] This was an uphill battle, however, as unqualified support for Israel diminished among Black activists amid Israel's shifting position on the world stage.

Indeed, in taking public positions of support for Palestinians in the 1960s and 1970s, many Black leaders passed the threshold of acceptable public dissent on Zionism and Israel. Zionist Jewish leaders increasingly saw African American criticism of Zionism as a threat, especially when some Black Americans spoke of the Palestine Liberation Organization (PLO) as representative of the Palestinian liberation struggle. Often Jewish leaders attributed Black solidarity with Palestinians to "Arab propaganda" and felt doubly targeted as white people in thinking of Black nationalism as antiwhite.[33] Alternately, Jewish leaders attributed Black solidarity with Palestinians to "Black antisemitism," a phrase identified by scholars as a pernicious, racist concept intended to distance white Jews from Black liberation.

Scholars write about the National Conference for New Politics, held in Chicago in September 1967, as a turning point for Jewish left activists. The conference tried to bring together antiwar liberals, New Left radicals, and African American activists.[34] At the conference, a group of Black radical organizations proposed thirteen resolutions, most of them focused on "white support for [B]lack self-determination and political power."[35] One resolution focused on condemnation of "the imperialistic Zionist war."[36] Many self-identified Jewish activists heard this strong language as a threat, perhaps even an ultimatum. Even were they critical of both Israel and Zionism, they now felt that they could not balance those ideas with commitments to the New Left and anticolonialist activism. The vision of Israel with which they lived, that they had been taught, did not align with the language of imperialism, and many walked out of the conference to demonstrate their rejection of the resolution's ideas.[37]

As Israel and Palestinian rights emerged as prominent issues among Black and Arab American activists, these issues complicated progressive coalitions between African Americans and American Jews. This was certainly true after the National Black Political Convention in March 1972, where a group of delegates described Israel as "expansionist," condemned its work with imperialist powers, and called on the United States to end its support for Israel.[38] Tensions rose still more in 1979 after President Carter appointed Andrew Young as America's first Black ambassador to the United Nations. After his meeting with representatives of the Palestine Liberation Organization, Young faced calls to resign from many mainstream Jewish leaders. That same year, when two hundred Black leaders of a diverse array of Black organizations, including the National Urban League, the National Association for the Advancement of Colored People, and the Southern Christian Leadership Conference, met to talk about calls for Andrew Young's resignation, they drew attention to Israel's close relationship with apartheid South Africa and voiced full support for efforts by Black leaders to support peace by talking to the PLO. Black leaders called this their "declaration of independence on the Middle East issue," and they aligned that sentiment with strong criticism of the positions of Jewish leaders that were increasingly "contrary to the best interests of the [B]lack community."

A draft of the document, one ultimately not released, named the Anti-Defamation League, the American Jewish Congress, and the American Jewish Committee as three Jewish organizations that had "opposed the interests of the [B]lack community" in court cases over affirmative action.[39] Black leaders also labeled Jewish contributions to civil rights "patronizing" because the contributions were made "pending clarification of how the beneficiaries, who solicit them, feel about them." After Black leaders announced that the Jewish Defense League had used "threats of physical violence" against them, Nathan Perlmutter, the Anti-Defamation League's national director, denounced the threats as "wrong" and meriting "condemnation." Perlmutter cited Jews' "open record in [sic] behalf of civil rights and the betterment of the human condition." He wrote,

"We apologize to no one." The headline on the front page of the *Michigan Chronicle*, a Black newspaper, was "Jewish Leader Tells Blacks: No Apologies."[40]

In sum, anti-Zionism in the American left grew out of a new global mindedness and global solidarity among Black, Palestinian, and Arab activists: opposition to state-sanctioned racism and oppression at home and Cold War allegiances abroad, including America's involvement in Southeast Asia and in Israel and Israel's involvement in Algeria and South Africa. These new Cold War alliances served as an opportunity for mainstream acceptance and even power for Jews, and strong support for Israel proved central to their gradual withdrawal from some aspects of the domestic civil rights agenda.

As political scientist Adolph L. Reed Jr. noted, the focus on "Black antisemitism" seemed distracting to those who felt strongly that the xenophobia, racism, and antisemitism from the Right (for example, from the Ku Klux Klan and other white supremacists) posed an actual and far more formidable threat to minority groups such as African Americans, immigrants, and Jews. Certainly there were examples of antisemitism within civil rights, Black Power, Arab American, and other movements. By focusing so powerfully on "Black antisemitism," though, American Jews gave themselves permission to withdraw support from positions that challenged the racist status quo and thus their own emerging, perhaps vulnerable positions as powerful figures in American life. Linking much of the criticism of Israel to antisemitism and to Black and Arab American anticolonialist critiques under the disingenuous categories of "Black antisemitism" and "Arab propaganda," American Jewish leaders also reinforced their whiteness and thus their political influence.[41]

Unwittingly or not, then, some Jewish leaders in this way contributed to the backlash against liberation movements. At a 1979 meeting, Black leaders took note of American Jews' new role, leaving behind their work for Black equality and joining others as "apologists for the racial status quo."[42] Jewish leaders' policing criticism of Zionism and Israel was one component of this new role. Historically, debates over Jewish non- and anti-Zionism took place across the political spectrum, as Zionist critiques had been leveled by elite Reform Jews through the 1940s and secular Jews on the left through the 1960s. After 1967, as American Jewish leaders gained power and stature, they conflated anti-Zionism with antisemitism and also the diverse historical, political, and intellectual strands of the Left as a singular threat and so some joined the broader attacks on the left in the culture wars. This stance allowed them to demonize the movements that were providing activists around the world with a critical view of Israel and other colonial powers.

The Jewish Counterculture, American Zionism, and the War in Vietnam

Perhaps the greatest dissonance for American Jews lay in the antiwar movement, as the escalation of the conflict in Vietnam to a full-scale war in 1965 prompted some activists and scholars to draw direct parallels between Vietnam and Israel. In both cases, they argued, Western colonialism had destroyed the lives of indigenous populations and created conditions for long-standing military conflicts. Moreover, the Soviet Union and the PLO, both "enemies of Israel," were said to be offering aid to North Vietnam.[43]

Some activists analogized resistance movements in Vietnam, Algeria, South Africa, and Israel/Palestine, where they saw revolutionaries opposing Western imperialism and colonialism. In 1974, Noam Chomsky, a one-time socialist Zionist, a prominent linguistics scholar at Massachusetts Institute of Technology, and an outspoken critic of the Vietnam War, described American support for Israel as a "sort of magic slate rewrite of American failure in Vietnam." As historian Paul Thomas Chamberlain wrote, Chomsky and other activists and scholars on the left argued that "once critical of Washington's support for the South Vietnamese government, [they] ought to denounce the analogous set of policies that formed the basis of the United States' relationship with Israel."[44] These activists encouraged American officials to negotiate with the PLO as a means to peacemaking in the Middle East, a position that drew the ire of increasingly well-established and powerful Jewish Zionist leaders.[45]

With continuing fears that damage to Israel or a loss of American support for Israel would threaten the safety of all Jews and with Jewish communal life largely devoid of information about Israel's policies toward Palestinians and Palestinian history, most American Jewish liberals stopped short of applying anticolonialist lessons to the Israeli context. Michael

Walzer and Martin Peretz's 1967 article, "Israel Is Not Vietnam," played an important role in carving out a space for American Jews to support an increasingly militarized Israel. It also demonstrated how to downplay the parallels of American support for Israel's occupation and militarism while opposing US involvement in the Vietnam War.

In their article, which was published in the New Left magazine *Ramparts*, Walzer and Peretz disputed comparisons between Israel and Vietnam by contesting the idea that the relation of Jew to Palestinian in Israel was of colonizer to colonized. Both Walzer and Peretz earned doctorates in government at Harvard. Walzer was a political theorist, active in the civil rights and antiwar movements; Peretz helped found *Ramparts* and later purchased and edited the *New Republic*, an essential voice of American liberalism—American Jewish liberalism and strident American Zionism, in particular. Israel, they wrote, was built on "cooperative and collectivist arrangements," not on the oppression of Palestinians. Palestinians would not "want to be integrated" into Israel, they argued, distancing Israel from any culpability for the "Arab refugees [whose] misery . . . has been positively cultivated by governments intent on exploiting them for political purposes." They expressed skepticism about cries for "the 'national liberation' of the Arabs." Israel itself, they believed, was a true site of national liberation for Jews. Walzer and Peretz "condemn[ed] intervention in Vietnam" along with those on the left—but they dismissed the Left's analysis of Israel as misguided at best.[46]

Notably, in that same issue of *Ramparts*, Jewish journalist I. F. Stone's essay "The Future of Israel" appeared. Stone's position on Israel had changed drastically since the 1940s, and he now urged Israel to recognize the plight of Palestinian refugees. As historian Amy Kaplan wrote, Stone argued that Israelis must reckon with their "long-slumbering moral crisis" now awakened by the world's awareness of its occupation.[47] The following month, Stone elaborated on his position in an essay for the *New York Review of Books* titled "Holy War." "How we act toward the Arabs," he wrote, "will determine what kind of people we become: either oppressors and racists in our turn like those from whom we have suffered, or a nobler race able to transcend the tribal xenophobias that afflict mankind."[48]

It was Walzer and Peretz's article, though, that gained the most attention. Scholar and Palestinian activist Edward Said described their article as "pioneering" in its effort to show how "Israel was not like France, the United States or Britain in its nasty colonial adventures." Walzer used what Said called his "left credentials" to tell a story, one that distanced Israel from its violent history.[49] According to this story, not only was Israel *not* Vietnam, but Israel was the victory that Vietnam was not, a liberal democracy that deserved unconditional support from American Jews and non-Jews. This narrative left room for American Jewish opposition to the war in Vietnam, leaving loyalty to American Zionism and Israel untouched.

Jewish leaders even kept the Jewish counterculture activists of the late 1960s and 1970s—fierce opponents of the war in Vietnam—within the threshold of acceptable dissent on Zionism and Israel. Jewish publications described radical Jewish organizations as "pro-Israel, pro-Judaism, anti-Jewish establishment, and sensitive (or at least trying to be) to every human being with whom they come in contact."[50] The *New York Times* noted a rise in the number of radical Jewish newspapers on college campuses, explaining, "Some papers arose partly because Jewish student radicals found non-Jewish radicals taking anti-Israel stances. The Jewish students divorced themselves from that, took pro-Israel positions, while continuing to emphasize radical views."[51]

Artifacts of some of the Jewish counterculture testify to these "pro-Israel" positions. *The First Jewish Catalog: A Do-It-Yourself Kit*, compiled and edited in 1973 by Richard Siegel, Michael Strassfeld, and Susan Strassfeld, was, as scholar Michael Staub wrote, the "runaway best seller . . . [that] self-consciously recapitulated the ethos of the Jewish counterculture for both its own benefit and as well as the benefit of a mainstream audience."[52] Amid the resources about keeping a Jewish home and following the Jewish holiday calendar are entries about visiting Israel and how to move to Israel permanently—all with romanticized visions of Israel's past and present, with almost no words on the occupation or Palestinian rights.

All three catalogs—the second and third published in 1976 and 1980, respectively, and edited by Susan Strassfeld and Michael Strassfeld—offer windows onto the Jewish counterculture's largely unconditional embrace of Zionism and Israel. Indeed, in the 1980 catalog's entry titled "Traditional Attitudes about Israel," written by scholar and feminist activist Trude Weiss-Rosmarin, the introductory paragraph noted, "The section

reads like a love story because that is precisely how Jews have tradition-
ally related to Israel. Romance, yearning, passion, this is not the major
attitude adopted by traditional Jews; it is the *only* attitude."[53] "Modern
Zionism," Weiss-Rosmarin wrote, "is . . . not a break with Jewish tradition but . . . its logical continuation." This third catalog includes a timeline and resources with exactly one mention of Palestinians, who appear
on the timeline with only two words: "Arabs riot."[54] The central tension
discussed in its pages is that between Israel and the "diaspora"—on *how*
American Jews can give their money and time to Israel and how they
can make Israel the cornerstone of their Jewishness without necessarily
feeling the pressure to move to Israel.

The single mention of American Jewish criticism of Zionism and Israel is in a paragraph that discusses why American Jews feel "unrea-
sonably insecure" and how they "see Israel as our lifeline when we feel
threatened." With this acknowledgment is recognition of how American
Jews "drown criticism" of Israel: "Whereas in Israel recognition of the
Palestinians can be debated, here such debate is labeled as self-hating
and anti-Israel." Readers were advised to weigh being "honest with
[their] own personal ideals" up against "every Jew's obligation and need
to stand united with the community. . . . In the mainstream American
Jewish community today the one factor that can instantly make you a
good Jew is loyalty to Israel. To criticize Israel is to risk being ostra-
cized and to risk the loss of all credibility."[55] With these words, the editors linked loyalty to Jewish community with Jewish safety and with a
consensus on Israel. Later pages advised readers about "combating Arab
propaganda" with these words: "A sympathetic portrayal of an Israeli is
worth more than a hundred letters about why Israel can't give back *x*
until *y* happens."[56]

Yet the writing of other Jewish counterculture, antiwar scholars and
activists testifies to their radical rethinking of Zionism, deeply influenced by the era's liberation movements and in some ways challenging
the Zionist consensus with an emphasis on socialism and peace rather
than muscular, militarist defense, occupation, and settlement building. For example, in an era of radical liberation movements, a group
of young Jews met in 1970 as the Radical Jewish Alliance, authoring a
document called the "Radical Zionist Manifesto." In it, they expressed
their shared vision of "Israel as central to the liberation of the Jewish

people." Holding fast to Labor Zionism's vision of a "socialist society in Israel," they also drew from the era's anticolonialist movements in calling for recognition of the rights of "Palestinian Arabs."[57] The Jewish Liberation Project, founded in New York City, linked its commitment to socialist Zionism to its opposition to the war in Vietnam. In the pages of its *Jewish Liberation Journal*, edited by Aviva Cantor and published from 1969 to 1972, young Jews made clear their positions. They opposed the "lack of democracy in the government of the American Jewish community perpetrated by the federations" and demanded resources for vibrant educational programs to enhance Jewish life. They supported socialist Zionism and the freedom of Jews and Palestinians in Israel. And they opposed the "Jew in SDS [Students for a Democratic Society] who fail[ed]to see the incongruity between his whole-hearted support of Black, Vietnamese, and Palestinian nationalisms and his complete refusal to recognize equally valid Jewish nationalism."[58] For these young Jewish counterculture leaders, Zionism was about Jewish identity and pride, a collective consciousness that worked for the freedom of Jews and all other people.

In a 1971 book with the evocative title *The Bush Is Burning! Radical Judaism Faces the Pharaohs of the Modern Superstate*, civil rights and antiwar activist Arthur Waskow also urged American Jews to work toward a socialist society with a new Judaism as a guide. He drew explicit connections between the current, static state of American Jewish life and the forced Zionist consensus: the low threshold of dissent. "Among the Jewish people in America a generation ago," he wrote, "there was a wide range of feelings toward Zionism—and if the Jewish People in the United States had been wholly free, this diversity would probably have continued." The "Jewish Establishment" was to blame, he continued, for its members "acted in concert with American Empire to assert that the only 'possible' choices are 1) migration to Israel, 2) total support for Israeli government policy, or 3) dropping out of the Jewish community."[59] These established Jewish leaders "transformed American Zionism from a movement led by labor unionists and kibbutz-oriented socialists to one dominated by wealthy businessmen." Because unconditional support for Israel was of the utmost importance, American Jewish leaders "put great pressure on Jewish groups and organizations not to take anti-Imperial stands on issues of great importance in America—for example, not to oppose the Vietnam War—lest such stands endanger the Empire's commitments to the Israeli government."[60] He pointed to the successful efforts of the Anti-Defamation League to discourage American Jewish groups from allowing Uri Avnery, an Israeli peace activist and politician, to speak; he noted that the "Bundist movement—a Jewish socialist anti-Zionist movement that had great strength in the Jewish communities in Eastern Europe and America before 1940—has been systematically opposed, excluded, and where possible smashed so thoroughly that not even its history is taught to most young Jews, nor its existence mentioned."[61] Waskow offered an alternative to this conservative agenda, including the building of American Jewish political alliances with members of the Israeli left and Palestinian nationalist movements. Waskow saw American Jews as "the victim" of the Jewish establishment. He had faith that Jews could maintain their deep connection to Israel while working for peaceful self-determination for both Jews and Palestinians.[62]

Radical antiwar Zionists were visible in their protests against what Waskow saw as Jewish establishment organizations that did the bidding of the American empire. The Jewish Liberation Project protested outside of the headquarters of the Zionist Organization of America when its president, Jacques Torczyner, expressed support "for President Nixon's Vietnam War policies"[63] and called on American Jews for their support because "a communist victory in Far Asia will encourage enemies of Israel."[64] Jewish Liberation Project leaders called Torczyner's position "a betrayal of Jewish and Zionist ideals."[65] Members held up signs that read, "Zionism is not the tool of Nixon."[66] Drawing heavily from Black nationalists, they identified theirs as a "militantly Jewish, militantly left-wing organization that can work for socialism as Jews and take our proper place in the campus left," noting that they planned to become involved in "the struggle against ROTC, corporate recruiting and all the other issues of concern to the left . . . [but] with a Jewish perspective."[67] The Jewish Liberation Project was anticapitalist and feared that Israel and thus Jews would "be so allied to the West that we become symbols of its imperialism." American Jews' "security obsession," its "uptightness," led the community to "keep down protest . . . against a pro-Israel organization." When they occupied the offices of the Jewish Federation of New York in April 1970 demanding the Federation be more responsive to Jewish needs, especially to young people's Jewish educations, they counted theirs as the "first [demonstration] by one Zionist organization against another in the history of American Jewish life."[68]

Like others whose criticism of Zionism fell beyond the threshold of acceptable dissent, members of the Jewish Liberation Project wanted more diverse voices in Jewish organizational life. They rejected unconditional Zionism and how its proponents and supporters dominated Jewish organizations. They wanted money to be dedicated to Jewish education in Jewish communities outside of Israel. They urged "dialogue[s] . . . between the Jewish community and the Puerto Rican community, the Chicano community, and all the oppressed and dispossessed minority groups in this country." Taking "concerted and united action" would make clear, they believed, that "Socialist-Zionism is not only the self-liberation movement of the Jewish people but part of the liberation struggle of all people." Urging solidarity among Black and Jewish Americans, they condemned antisemitism within the Black Panther Party and saw antisemitism and "anti-[B]lack views" as "the two sides of blind ethnic chauvinism."[69]

With their loyalty to socialist Zionism, the members of the Jewish Liberation Project feared Israel would become a colonial power. In the pages of the journal, young authors asked if "it is possible that the Zionists . . . can survive only by completely denying the rights of others and becoming bedfellows of U.S. imperialism."[70] The more Zionism was captured by "the bureaucracy," group members believed, the more it was run by elites and *not* the Jewish masses; in the final months of the journal's publication, one headline about the pace of this capture read, "Zionism Betrayed."[71]

Also deeply influenced by anticolonialist movements, the Jewish organization Brooklyn Bridge Collective was "non-Zionist." Like the Jewish Liberation Project, its members took issue with American Jewish Zionist leadership: they "openly criticized some of the radical Zionists for being too close to the JDL" and rejected the priorities of mainstream Jewish communal life even as they felt Jewish pride and solidarity with nonwhite people.[72] Their first newsletter reflected their countercultural positioning: "Jewish, because that is what we are; because our Jewishness plays an important part in shaping our total selves . . . because we have learned—as have women, and [B]lacks, and gay people—that unless we look out for ourselves, we are just as likely to be the victims of oppression in a revolutionary society as we are in this one. Our struggle begins at home, with the oppression we face as Jewish people in America. We have been trapped in the buffer-zone between other oppressed peoples and the ruling class; shunted into the bureaucracies of the military-industrial-education complex."[73]

Firsthand accounts make clear that the women's group that organized within the Brooklyn Bridge Collective, which met from 1970 to 1972, struggled to take a position on Zionism and Israel—on the left broadly but also inside their organization. One member, Phyllis Bloom, recalled events that happened within the women's group. Bloom noted that the group helped her speak out to staff members of *Rat*, an underground women's liberation paper in New York. When an article appeared calling Zionism an "imperialist movement," she and her colleagues called out the *Rat* staff for not allowing for the possibility that some Jews, Zionists or not, "support the Palestinian right to exist."[74]

Another woman wrote under a pseudonym to the Jewish women's magazine *Lilith* to talk about her experiences with the Brooklyn Bridge women's group. She recorded moments of connection and solidarity among them as women and as Jews. Yet even in what she saw as a nurturing feminist environment, she grew frustrated with the group's wariness of even invoking Israel for fear of controversy:

> The Brooklyn Bridge men encouraged the women to start a women's group in 1970, early 1971. We invited women we knew from the feminist community and left-wing circles. The women who were three months into being Jewish were like the rabbis of the group. Most had never given much thought to being Jewish. Almost every woman reported that, when asked where she was going that evening, she had said, "to a (mumble) women's group," unable to admit it was a *Jewish* women's group because that was like joining Hadassah. After an agonizing hour, we hit upon the idea of talking about our mothers and how they had led more Jewish lives than we and how we'd ignored the way we're connected to that kind of life. That opened up a lot of excitement that continued for a year. I had become more and more dissatisfied with Brooklyn Bridge because they refused to deal at all with Israel, fearing it would split the group down the middle. I took a job in a Habonim [Labor Zionist youth movement] summer camp and was turned on by everything there.[75]

Brooklyn Bridge women's group members struggled to envision what an explicitly Jewish women's group would look like outside of a conventionally gendered Zionist organization like Hadassah. They were carving out space for other, more critical brands of Zionism; for feminism; and for anticolonialist criticisms that encompassed both Vietnam and Israel.

They struggled mightily because some American Jewish leaders conflated unquestioning American Jewish support for Israel with unquestioning American Jewish loyalty to the United States. These leaders insisted that American Jews had to support the war in Vietnam or the US would not continue to support Israel, and Jews around the world would be at risk.

But as support for the war in Vietnam waned, Walzer, Peretz, and others pushed back against those who refined their worldview of colonialism to include Israel. They rejected the idea of "America—right or wrong," and they continued to celebrate Israel, minimizing or ignoring those who drew attention to the "wrongs" that the country had inflicted. Endorsing Israel exceptionalism, they retained their blind spots to Israel's atrocities. Decades of limiting dissent on American Zionism on the part of American Jewish leaders meant that American Jews supported Israel while knowing little of the balance of Israel's policies, measuring what they knew of Israel's policies only up against the perils of Jewish destruction.[76]

While some liberal Jews, especially younger Jews, inspired by the zeitgeist, censured what they thought of as the "Jewish establishment" for its complicity in American racism, sexism, and (later) homophobia, and while they joined the antiwar movement in significant numbers, distancing themselves from the more powerful Jewish elites in political life, many continued to see Israel as Walzer and Peretz did: solely through the lens of Jewish liberation. Radical and socialist Zionists such as Arthur Waskow and members of the Jewish Liberation Project held fast to a hopeful vision of Israel as the realization of collectivist living in which Palestinian and Jewish laborers could work as equals, first to defeat British colonialism and then to create a thriving democracy.

Voices of dissent on Israel and Zionism continued to be heard. One year after the 1973 October or Yom Kippur War, Irene Gendzier, political science professor at Boston University, wrote a foreword to Noam Chomsky's *Peace in the Middle East? Reflections on Justice and Nationhood*. For herself, Chomsky, and others on the left, Gendzier wrote, the horrors of World War II "confirmed the intensity of anti-Semitism and the fundamental amorality of nations, whose interests at all times took precedence over a concern for humanity."[77] She identified antisemitism as "the motor force for the movement of modern Jewish nationalism."[78] Gendzier acknowledged that the Israeli government had long "sanctioned the discrimination against the Arab population."[79]

In his own introduction to the book, Chomsky explored the role of the threshold of dissent in the 1973 war. He noted that Israeli leaders' delusions of infallibility were fueled in part by "racist arrogance." "It cannot be stressed too often," he wrote, "that American Zionists who have supported these delusions and, with their cries of anti-Semitism and other hysterical abuse, quite successfully suppressed any discussion of the dangers and alternatives, bear a measure of responsibility for the events of October 1973."[80]

Chomsky analyzed what he saw as the agenda of American Jewish Zionist leaders in policing all criticism of Israel. "Left-liberal criticism of Israeli government policy since 1967 has evoked hysterical accusations and outright lies," he wrote. "Anyone associated with the peace movement or the American left who has opposed expansionist or exclusivist tendencies within Israel has been reviled, without documentary evidence, as a supporter of terrorism and reactionary Arab states, An opponent of democracy, an anti-Semite, or, if Jewish, a traitor afflicted with self-hatred."[81] Because these leaders conflated anti-Zionism with antisemitism, he observed, "any criticism of the policies of the state can be dismissed at once." For Chomsky, the massive opposition to the Vietnam War posed a tremendous threat to state power. Rallying behind Israel and American aid to Israel, he observed, left-liberals could reinforce confidence in state power. He wrote, "I think that Israel has suffered, and continues to suffer, from efforts in the United States to stifle discussion, slander critics, and exploit Israel's problems cynically for domestic political purposes, as it suffers from the general tendency in the United States to support the more chauvinistic and militaristic elements in Israeli society."[82]

Scholar and activist Edward Said's first opinion piece for the *New York Times*, "Arab and Jew: 'Each Is the Other,'" was published on October 14, 1973, during the October War, and he wrote pointedly of American aid to Israel, American Jewish support of Israel, and the brutal acts committed against Palestinians in the name of Zionism.[83] In an academic article one year later, Said noted that Chomsky established credentials and earned enmity as "an American Jew with an actual history of engagement in left-wing Zionism." Said wrote of Chomsky's "unified" political positions because Chomsky's criticism of liberalism, colonialism, and Cold War militarism included no exceptionalism for Israel, no room for the "liberal admiration for Israeli democracy" that accompanies the "'bomb-them-into-the-stone-age' attitudes towards the Arabs."[84] Those with this liberal admiration committed themselves, Said asserted, to "extraordinary moral acrobatics proving that the main thing to be remembered is that the present Middle East should not be misinterpreted by liberals as another possible Vietnam." Said took note of the furious response to Chomsky's criticisms among American Jewish Zionists. He identified Chomsky's courage in asserting that "the problems of the contemporary Middle East are not all reducible to memories of Jewish suffering in World War II." These were, Said noted, "scarcely allowable thoughts" when Zionist leaders equated Jewish safety with a forced consensus on Zionism.[85]

One of the most severe critics of Chomsky's *Peace in the Middle East?* was Michael Walzer, who published his review in the *New York Times*. Walzer was then a Harvard professor of government, formulating his theory of "just war," which was published a few years later. Walzer mockingly took note of Chomsky's "socialist values" and the fact that he "had been an internationalist for 30 years, come hell or high water," yet one "with a special interest in the Jews." According to Walzer, Chomsky held Israel to a higher standard than other nations because Israel was the "only state whose independence would have to be surrendered or radically compromised to make way for the new socialist commonwealth." Walzer asserted, "I do not believe that Israel can be a homeland unless it is a state." Chomsky, who supported a binational state for Jews and Palestinians, rejected the idea that any state could be both "Jewish" and "democratic." Walzer argued that such an arrangement would not be a homeland for Jews.[86] When Chomsky responded to Walzer's review by citing "systematic patterns of expulsion and expropriation of [Palestinian] lands for pure Jewish settlement, legal segregation, [and] repression of Arab intellectuals," a list he said was "by no means comprehensive," Walzer denied the existence of these "systematic patterns" and said there "is nothing in Israel comparable to the sort of thing" that the phrase "segregation . . . will call to mind among American readers." Walzer's final attack on Chomsky appeared in his last sentence, when he labeled Chomsky's binationalism a "socialist camouflage" for the main focus of his work: "an attack on Israel."[87]

Critics of Zionism such as Chomsky never made up more than a small minority of American Jewry. In part, their small numbers reflected the powerful force of Holocaust memory, the narrative that only unqualified support of Israel would keep Jews safe and thus was central to Jewish survival. In part, their small numbers reflected mainstream Jews' low threshold for dissent from American Zionism, supported by accusations of antisemitism and the betrayal of the Jewish community. These accusations were part of campaigns to delegitimize dissent, and they came from both individuals, such as Walzer, and organizations, perhaps none more visible than the Anti-Defamation League. The success of these campaigns can be measured by the intensity of the negative responses that followed when Jewish criticism of Zionism and Israel spilled into public debate. As the anticolonialist critiques of Israel gained more traction and as American Jews rose to greater positions of American political power, these negative responses grew still more intense.

The Anti-Defamation League and the "New Antisemitism"

In response to the growth and momentum of anticolonialist organizing and to widely held perceptions about the growth of antisemitism in the movement, Jewish organizational leaders stepped up their watch of Jewish and non-Jewish critics of Zionism and Israel. Inside the Jewish world, criticism of Zionism and Israel had long been equated with betrayal, even antisemitism, as the exchange with Chomsky and Walzer vividly illustrated. In the 1960s and 1970s, Jewish organizations feared the rise of criticism of Israel around the world and came to link that criticism with antisemitism—and with currents of thought that originated outside of Jewish communities.

Above all other organizations, the Anti-Defamation League (ADL) defined this work. Founded in 1913 as a Jewish defense agency, the Anti-Defamation League joined many other organizations in collaborating in the 1950s with the House Un-American Activities Committee in naming and persecuting alleged American Communists as well as monitoring the Ku Klux Klan and other hate groups.[88] Policing American Jewish organizations for communist influence was the agency's line of defense against persistent accusations of disloyalty, even treason, for American Jews associated with the left. For the Anti-Defamation League, then, the policing of Zionism's critics emerged out of its long history of anti-communism. They were already surveilling American Jewish anticolonialist activists as communists; from the 1960s forward, the Anti-Defamation League surveilled them as anticolonialists who were also non- or anti-Zionist and therefore, according to some, antisemites.[89]

Predictably, the Anti-Defamation League rejected Chomsky's analyses and indeed policed him, sometimes with great zeal. The organization's leaders sent representatives to Chomsky's lectures and filed reports with officials such as Irwin Suall, national director of fact-finding, an expert on neo-Nazis, the Ku Klux Klan, and other extremist organizations. ADL leaders categorized Chomsky as someone "incapable of finding anything good about Israel, American Jews, or anyone but Arab spokesmen and the Third World."[90] They saw him as a potential danger internal to the Jewish community but one who drew on currents of thought that were only available outside of it.

In the 1960s, New England Anti-Defamation League leaders read dozens of daily newspapers, searching for information on anyone whose statements they interpreted as favorable to "Arabs." They placed these articles in a file labeled "Israel and the Middle East, Anti-Zionism and Arab Propaganda Organizations."[91] In this file were articles on organizations such as the Peace Corps and Students for a Democratic Society. Records show that ADL leaders attended any organizational meeting when they heard a speaker was to present a "pro-Arab viewpoint." Increasingly, they surveyed liberal and left organizations, suspecting and searching out what they termed the "new antisemitism."[92]

In 1974, two national ADL leaders, Arnold Forster and Benjamin R. Epstein, published a book with this very title, *The New Anti-Semitism*. Rendering invisible the long-standing Jewish contests over Israel and Zionism, Forster and Epstein claimed that this new form of Jew hatred originated almost entirely from the left and could be heard in statements critical of Israel.

Overall, the book's arguments rested on three foundational ideas. First is Holocaust consciousness and Jewish persecution, and its dedication reads, "For those who have died because they were Jews." Second was the era's fervent anti-communism. The "radical Left," the authors contended, stood in contrast to the "liberal left, whose members, such as Norman Thomas, support Israel." Radical leftists, however, Forster and Epstein asserted, took their cues from China and from the Soviets, who saw Israel as a "redoubt of Western imperialism while the Arabs were an authentic third-world people struggling for their independence."[93]

Finally, the book's arguments rested on a comparative victimology with Black Americans. Though admitting that liberalism largely failed to free Black Americans from oppression, the authors asserted that Jews suffered from this new antisemitism because Americans are now "so preoccupied with the problems of [B]lacks in America that they no longer considered anti-Semitism a problem at all but rather a phenomenon of the past."[94] Jews, they noted, are "history's favorite victim."[95] But in allowing Black Americans to adopt anti-Israel ideas, which they equated with antisemitism, Black leaders were "isolating the [B]lack community from its real and historic allies"[96] because Jews were the "oldest and most consistent friends of [B]lack people."[97] In their telling, Black Americans and others convinced American Jews and other whites that their welfare was bound up in anticolonialism and peace work but that, in truth, that work threatened the Jewish people because it threatened Israel. Reaching back through the history of anti-Zionism, Forster and Epstein drove their point home by citing the Council's Rabbi Elmer Berger as one of those "paraded by the Arabs as examples of right-thinking Jews."[98]

Forster and Epstein did not question Israel's existence in the text, as it is "right and just and inevitable that there should be a Jewish state in the Middle East."[99] Nor are Israel's policies toward Palestinians marked as a concern, as Jews are "just as indigenous to the Middle East as Arabs."[100] The authors' "shattering conclusion" was that "there is abroad in our land [the US] a large measure of indifference to the most profound apprehensions of the Jewish people; a blandness and apathy in dealing with anti-Jewish behavior; a widespread incapacity or unwillingness to comprehend the necessity of Israel to Jewish safety and survival throughout the world." "This," they found, was "the heart of the new anti-Semitism."[101]

In left-wing organizations, the authors noted, those who defend Israel are seen as "obstacles to revolutionary goals."[102]

In such an environment, Forster and Epstein concluded, American Jews had no choice but to dismiss the idea that the left had anything to offer them. Although in the book's conclusion, the authors acknowledge that anti-Black racism and antisemitism lived side by side in the world-views of the Ku Klux Klan, for example, they focused far more intently on anti-Zionism as antisemitism on the left and the need for unqualified loyalty to Israel. The publication of *The New Anti-Semitism* contributed to the equation of anti- or non-Zionism with antisemitism and thus insulated American Jews from criticism for departing civil rights and other progressive coalitions. It also cast deeper suspicion over the loyalty of Jewish critics of Israel and American Zionism.[103]

Morris Schappes, Non-Zionism, and *Jewish Currents*: Peace, Justice, and an "Unnecessary Choice"

In this era, then, it often proved difficult for American Jews to balance Jewish affiliation with commitments to the struggle for civil rights. Yet some individual Jews worked—on the margins and with varying degrees of success—to maintain commitments both to Black liberation and to Jewish life. Morris Schappes, a scholar and journalist, is one example. He was a non-Zionist who supported the idea of a Jewish cultural homeland but not Jewish state-building. Bridging the Old and New Left, Schappes criticized Israel, American Zionism, and the Black Power and peace movements. He remained distant from accusations of antisemitism because his activities as a radical were largely off the radar of main-stream Zionist Jewish life.

Perhaps best known for his editorial leadership of the formerly Communist-affiliated *Jewish Life* (today known as *Jewish Currents*), Schappes offers an instructive example of allegiance to non-Zionism, Jewish communal concerns, and post-1967 Black liberation. Looking back, Lawrence Bush, who edited *Jewish Currents* for sixteen years, de-scribed its writers and readers as "in their own orbit," beholden to no one and largely ignored by mainstream Jewish organizations.[104] In part because of his radical credentials and in part because he was a non- and not an anti-Zionist, Schappes faced very little criticism from Zionist

Jewish leaders. Schappes maintained this balance into the 1970s, when he articulated a clear rebuke to those who made Jewish activists feel as if they had to choose between commitments to Jewish life and commitments to the civil rights and antiwar movements. Schappes was a critic of Israel and Zionism, a radical whose sophisticated understanding of Black nationalism and other anticolonialist movements never earned or merited accusations of a "new anti-Semitism."

Morris Schappes was born in Ukraine in 1907 and grew up in New York City. He joined the Communist Party in 1934. Six years later, while teaching at City College, Schappes was convicted of perjury during an investigation that attempted to purge Communists from New York's public education system and served over a year in prison. There he learned Hebrew and studied "Jewish history and culture within an internationalist framework."[105]

He wrote and edited several books on Jewish history and culture, including *The Jews in the United States: A Pictorial History 1654 to the Present* and *Emma Lazarus: Selections from Her Poetry and Prose*. In November 1946, he joined the editorial board of *Jewish Life*, written by Communists but independent of party affiliation beginning in 1956. He became its managing editor in 1958, when its name changed to *Jewish Currents*. Schappes noted that because of its Communist affiliation and worldview, from 1946 to 1956, *Jewish Life* existed on the margins of Jewish life: "We were considered outsiders," he said in an oral history interview.[106]

These were the early years of Schappes's faith in Israel as an anti-imperialist force. This position was expressed in his "It Happened in Israel" column, which he authored for *Jewish Life* throughout the 1950s. He drew content for the column from Israeli news clips, writing about the Histadrut's inclusion of Jewish housewives but exclusion of all Palestinian workers, the right wing's anti-Yiddish "chauvinism" in Israel. In December 1956, Schappes sharply criticized "Menahem Begin [*sic*], head of the Herut movement" (the conservative nationalist party) for proposing "expansion of Israel's borders" to "all of Jordan and parts of Syria and Lebanon."[107] His topics demonstrated his firm commitment to the realization of a socialist vision in Israel as well as his sharp disappointment when he felt that Israel stumbled on its way to that vision.

Though Schappes understood that many saw Israel as keeping Jews safe, he rejected the idea that Israel insulated American Jews from having to participate in broader struggles for liberation. "It was a conscious aim of Zionism," he wrote, "to divert the Jewish masses from the struggle against reaction in alliance with non-Jewish masses oppressed by reaction." The struggle against antisemitism had to be connected to struggles for justice for all groups, Schappes asserted, and only then would Jewish interests best be served. "Normalcy and equality themselves can be won by the Jews in our country only by fighting for equality," he wrote, "by organizing the Jewish masses and allies from progressive elements in the working class and the Negro people and the immigrant groups for the struggle against anti-Semitism and racism."[108]

Schappes also criticized both American Zionist and Israeli leaders for prioritizing Jewish life *only* in Israel. "The center of American Jewish life has to be in our country and not elsewhere," he wrote. "Only such an orientation can develop a proper relationship between American Jews and Israel, to whose existence, independence, welfare and peace they are all devoted, without reference to the confusing issue of 'centrality of Israel' or the dangerous foreign policy of the Ben-Gurion government."[109]

For his leftist views, after his release from jail, Schappes noted that "the ADL preceded me with my record" everywhere he went to speak about his books. After Michigan passed a law allowing victims of Red Scare tactics access to their police records, Schappes obtained the files about book talks he had given in Michigan: "Every place I had spoken in Detroit"—mainly synagogues and Jewish community centers—"the police were there taking down the numbers of every car parked within a two block radius."[110] They kept watch on Jewish programming that included lectures by Schappes.[111] More often, however, Jewish newspapers mentioned the publication of Schappes's history books with no mention of his politics.[112] His work appeared to be precisely "in its own orbit." His criticism of American Zionism and Israel, while closely monitored, did not cross the threshold of dissent—because he was a non- and not an anti-Zionist and perhaps because his radicalism prevented mainstream Jewish leaders from paying him heed.

Schappes reinforced these ideas when he narrated his own history and that of his colleagues at *Jewish Currents*. From 1956 to 1970, he noted, *Currents'* staff's "relations with the American Jewish community was that it was hesitant about us, there was continuation of old hostility based upon old perception" that the journal was anti-Zionist.[113] Studies of American antisemitism cited his works on Jewish life, categorizing him as holding the "orthodox 'Marxist'" position.[114]

In 1967 *Jewish Currents* split with the Communist Party's position to support Israel during the war.[115] Within the party, Schappes's prona-tionalist stand created great controversy. Schappes's obituary in the *New York Times* reported that because of his stance on Israel, the Communist Party warned him "that *Jewish Currents* was slipping into a 'blind avenue of Jewish nationalism.'"[116]

As a testament to the growing force of a Zionist consensus, *Jew-ish Currents*' "pro-Israel" position proved essential to Schappes's ac-ceptance in mainstream Jewish life after 1967. As scholar Alan Wald notes, Schappes's "espousal of the need for Jewish culture and for Jews as a people to survive" gave him "new entry" into the Jewish com-munity.[117] Once Schappes publicly equated Zionism and Israel with Jews' survival, doors previously closed began to open. Morris Abram, president of the American Jewish Committee, invited him to share his thoughts about "what . . . their program should be for the Jews of the USA in the 1970s."[118] "The fact that they were interested in what I said and asked me to speak to them," Schappes noted in a later interview, "I think signals the change." *Jewish Currents* had by then "formal group relations," he told his interviewer, with "every Jewish organization," including the American Jewish Committee, the Anti-Defamation League, the American Jewish Congress, and the National Council of Jewish Women.[119] He went on to say, "Since 1970 I would say we [at *Jewish Currents*] are the acknowledged left wing of the American Jewish community." When asked, "What makes you a left wing at this point?" Schappes answered, "Well our position on Israel. We are pro-Israel but non-Zionists and critical of the Israeli Foreign Policy since 1953 [as the US/Israel Cold War alliance grew stronger]."[120] Schappes and his colleagues "supported Israel's foreign policy from 1948 to 1953." Though since 1953, they "disagree[d] with its orientation on reliance on the USA."[121] He elaborated, "Israel should steer a course . . . between the two super powers instead of aligning with one." *Jewish Currents*, he said, maintained an "independent position, independent of all Zionists except the Socialist Zionists." He maintained faith in Israel's experimentation with socialism, its collectivist living on kibbutzim, and its strong labor federation, Histadrut. In Schappes's formulation, only the Cold War would draw Israel into imperialistic battles for oil and land.[122]

Schappes struck a balance in his pro-Israel non-Zionism, and that proved essential to his unique ability to maintain simultaneous commitments to anticolonialist movements and the Jewish world in the late 1960s and early 1970s. Instead of blaming forces exclusively outside of American Jewish communal life for the rise of antisemitism, Schappes saw a rise in reactionary forces among all communities. In October 1967, Schappes published two cartoons in *Jewish Currents* that clearly demonstrated his attempts to hold his commitments to Jewish life and anticolonialism in balance. One cartoon featured crass, antisemitic stereotypes of materialistic greed, as the force of "Jew-money power" attempted to strangle the "Arab world," represented by images of Egyptian president Gamal Abdel Nasser and boxing champion Muhammad Ali. This cartoon was first published in the newsletter of the Student Nonviolent Coordinating Committee (SNCC) and received much criticism. The second cartoon, juxtaposed with the first, was published by a Yiddish daily and featured viciously racist caricatures of Arab and Black individuals joining together to plot "anti-Israel propaganda." As historian Jennifer Young observed, "*Jewish Currents* editors explained that the cartoon demonstrates that SNCC was 'learning Jew-baiting from the Arabs.' They issued a call to all the Jews who had denounced SNCC's antisemitism to equally condemn the white racism of the Yiddish press."[123] Jewish progressives did this, notes Young, by "evaluating the incommensurability of Jewish privilege and Black oppression in the United States, and criticizing Jewish racism."[124] In the pages of *Jewish Currents*, Schappes simultaneously criticized antisemitism in one civil rights organization and racism and insensitivity to Black and Palestinian rights in the Jewish community. His worldview allowed him to draw pointed connections among these kinds of oppression.

In February 1971, *Jewish Currents* published a pamphlet that further illuminated these connections. It was titled "The Black Panthers, Jews, and Israel," and its authors addressed the fact that "Black Power's Palestine had achieved a broad currency" among activists.[125] In the pamphlet, Schappes and other Jewish leaders made two points that rarely appeared together: progressive Jews had an obligation to support the

Black Panthers, and Israel was not a creation of Western imperialism but, in effect, an antidote to it, as it was created by socialist forces' victory over British imperialism. Schappes hoped that these forces would again rule Israel and return the occupied territories to Palestinians.

In the pamphlet, Schappes urged Black Panther cofounder Huey Newton to publicly repudiate antisemitism, identifying it as intricately bound up in white supremacy and other conservative forces. He wrote, "To fail to do so for any reason is to play into the hands of reactionaries and to weaken ties with white, including Jewish, supporters, friends and allies: We trust that Huey Newton will implement his declaration that his Party 'is not anti·Semitic' by public activity against anti-Semitism wherever he finds it, as part of his continuing struggle against reactionary ideology of all sorts. And anti-Semitism, like white racism, is part of reactionary ideology." Holding fast to his view of Israel as aligned with forces for justice and supporting a binational state, Schappes asserted that "progressive Jews . . . support unreservedly Israel's right to exist and the Palestinian Arab right of self-determination. We invite Huey Newton to consider *this* as his program. Then we can discuss how peace in the Middle East can be achieved, with freedom, equality and guaranteed rights and states for both peoples."[126]

As early as 1966, Schappes wrote that he believed American Jews also had an obligation to work for justice in Southeast Asia. President Johnson had criticized American Jewish opposition to the Vietnam War using Israel as leverage. Indeed, Johnson hoped to "change the thinking on Vietnam of American Jews" by pledging arms to Israel. Schappes condemned this move as one that would only heighten Cold War tensions between "Israel and the Arab States."[127]

In December 1967, Schappes wrote an article in *Jewish Currents* that directly addressed the idea that liberal and left Jews felt "forced to choose" between their activism in antiwar and other left movements and their belonging to Jewish communal life. Schappes scolded the American peace movement for weakening its own base by forcing Jewish supporters to "choose between working on the Middle East front or on the Vietnam front." He quoted an SNCC memo that he interpreted to mean that "no Jew can meaningfully fight to end the war in Vietnam unless he [*sic*] denies Israel's right to exist!" Schappes likewise assigned responsibility to American Zionists, who "reject Arab anti-Israelism" and thus "fail to see the forward historical thrust of Arab anti-imperialism." These Zionists, he believed, "with the best of intentions, weaken Israel's position by isolating it from the international left."[128]

Critical of mainstream Zionists and the antiwar movement, Schappes praised the "progressive Jewish movement" in the United States, which "weds a progressive Jewish consciousness to an internationalist outlook." He respected that Jewish progressives called first for the region to be "free from the tentacles of oil-colonialism and the Cold War." He urged attention to "burning problems" such as "Arab refugees, equal rights for Arabs within Israel, and border issues." To unite the peace movement and the Middle East progressive movement, Schappes suggested, would mean that Jews who were "alienated from the peace movement" would not have to face an "unnecessary choice." Schappes urged them to join "fronts." American Jews could work for peace and anti-imperialism in Southeast Asia and the Middle East simultaneously. He saw this as the American peace movement's greatest challenge.[129]

While the Anti-Defamation League and other organizational leaders broadly saw the New Left as a site of ferment for what they termed the new antisemitism, Schappes drew from Old and New Left ideology to create an expansive space, one in which American Jews could hold fast to faith in progressive currents in Israel and in the United States and count themselves as contributors to broader struggles for liberation of groups in both nations. This approach, he believed, would contribute to Jewish safety and continuity.

Schappes largely escaped the surveillance and marginalization from mainstream Zionist groups such as the Anti-Defamation League. Communal leaders largely ignored him because of his political radicalism and for his positioning as a non- and not an anti-Zionist. Yet he remains important to the history of the threshold of dissent. His work demonstrates that there remained in the 1960s and early 1970s a small but vanishing space for a vision of broad coalitions working for justice against imperialism, racism, and antisemitism, whose members were critical of Israel, Vietnam, American Zionism, and American racism.

Injustice in Vietnam and Israel: Martin Blatt and Zionism
Reconsidered at Tufts University

Far more visible than Schappes's balancing act and the internal struggles of the Brooklyn Bridge Collective women's group were mainstream
Jewish leaders' unconditional endorsements of Israel as the forced consensus on Zionism and Israel gained strength. All of these historical
developments were intricately tied to the growing unpopularity of the
Vietnam War. Though they worried about alienating antiwar Jewish
youth, historian Amy Weiss notes, mainstream Jewish leaders felt that
a broad communal antiwar statement would "risk alienating President
Johnson and thus potentially jeopardize military aid to Israel."[130] Political insiders attested to the fact that President Nixon actively cultivated
support for the war in Vietnam among American Jewish leaders and
that he implied, "not always subtly, that this country could not sustain
its commitments to Israel if it did not sustain its commitment to the
regime in Saigon."[131] In 1970, one antiwar Zionist Jewish rabbi, Rabbi
Balfour Brickner (whose parents had named him for the Balfour Declaration of 1917, which declared Britain's commitment to creating a Jewish
homeland) echoed Schappes's sentiments when he wrote that "the Vietnam war was being used as a club with which to beat into silence those
in the American Jewish community. . . . Instead of realizing that the
right to protest is the one option remaining by which to protect Israel,
unfortunately the majority of American Jews and the preponderance
of American Jewish organizations have seen the situation in just the
opposite way, accepting the logic that a moratorium on American Jewish criticism of our government's conduct of the Vietnam war is good
for Israel."[132] Brickner carefully denied analogies between Vietnam
and Israel, asserting instead that the former was a "civil war" with an
"unstable, unpopular government" and the latter a "stable democratic
government" with the "full support of the populace." He wrote that Jews'
refusal to speak out against the war meant that they "implicitly accede
to those who suggest that a valid analogy obtains [sic] between the situation in Israel and that in Vietnam."[133]

Brickner declared the need for American Jews to exercise their "right
to dissent from our government's policies when we feel dissent is war-
ranted." But he also acknowledged just how difficult it was to balance

commitments to the antiwar movement and to Israel. "Such independence," he wrote, "requires that we become sophisticated, critical political acrobats."[134] Balfour later protested Israel's building of settlements in
the occupied West Bank, joining voices with the Jewish peace organization Breira.[135]

Other Jewish leaders took antiwar stands but refrained from talking
about Israel and human rights. Modern Orthodox Rabbi Irving (Yitz)
Greenberg testified to the Senate Foreign Relations Committee in 1970
about Vietnam three days after Ohio National Guard soldiers killed four
unarmed students during an antiwar demonstration at Kent State University. Rabbi Greenberg called out US presidents for escalating the war.
"The inability to admit error out of a misguided sense of pride," he said,
"was the ultimate failure of moral leadership."[136] A few months later,
Rabbi Greenberg invoked the Holocaust and Jewish unity on Israel with
no mention of Israel's occupation.[137] In 1980, historian Paula Hyman
wrote in the *New York Times* that Rabbi Greenberg identified American
Jewish fundraising for Israel in United Jewish Appeal as "a profound, if
secularized, theological response to the Holocaust."[138] Addressing the
United Jewish Appeal-Federation in 1982, Rabbi Greenberg said that "for
19 centuries . . . Jews have shown the dignity of powerlessness, how we
can suffer, be sinned against, and not inflict sins on others." Israel's statehood meant "the taking of power for a living space," and he acknowledged the "responsibility" that came with taking power: "You are bound
to do some wrong things along the way. It's racism to think that Jews
are incapable of such actions. . . . The Torah never claimed that Jews are
perfect people."[139]

Many American Jewish Zionist activists continued to defend Israel
even as protests over Israel's occupation grew across the world. If, as
Rabbi Brickner claimed, acrobatics were required of Zionists or non-
Zionists to remain in the peace movement, what room was there in
American Jewry for American Jews who dissented from *both* American Zionism and American militarism, for anti-Zionists who were also
antiwar?

The teaching experience of Marty Blatt at Tufts University in Medford, Massachusetts, a few miles from Boston, during the early 1970s offers an illuminating example of the mainstream Jewish community's low
threshold for this form of dissent. His story sheds light on how political

commitments to the antiwar movement aligned with anti-Zionism. Together with Uriel "Uri" Davis, an Israeli human rights activist and academic, Blatt mobilized the Zionist Jewish leaders of a major American city. And so this story also speaks to how much these leaders believed was at stake in carefully maintaining the threshold of dissent.

Blatt was born in Brooklyn in 1951 and raised by his Jewish parents. His father's family had emigrated from Poland; his mother had been born in Heidelberg, Germany. Blatt's mother left Germany in the summer of 1938. Her father died in a Nazi labor camp, and this loss proved central to Blatt's life, his political consciousness, and his sensibilities.[140] Blatt's parents were devoted liberal Democrats and liberal Zionists. He himself worked for John Kennedy's presidential campaign in 1960. Blatt hoped that at Tufts, he could find a radical movement to join. It was not hard to do this in 1968. In an autobiographical essay he wrote for Tufts twenty years later, Blatt recalled that his "major was political science," but his "real major was the anti-war movement."[141]

In the fall of 1971, steeped in the language and strategies of protesting state violence, Blatt eagerly signed up for a course taught by Uri Davis, well known for his pacifism and his opposition to Israeli policies toward Palestinians.[142] Davis had traveled to the United States because he had been offered a fellowship in the sociology department at Brandeis University. But there he met with controversy. The dean of the college, Dr. Eugene Black, overruled the decision of the department to accept Davis, saying he was "concerned with action, with propaganda," which "flies in the face of the canons of scholarly research." Faculty members were quoted in the *Justice*, the Brandeis student newspaper, as saying that "pressure ha[d] been applied through some Israeli students and through some donors." Because of Davis's anti-Zionism, they added, the university grew "afraid Davis would use Brandeis as a center for a nationwide campaign against Israel." Fifteen faculty members signed a letter of protest arguing that the rejection of Davis's fellowship was "an infringement of academic freedom."[143] Student editors of the *Justice* questioned the idea that Davis's rejection was on "purely academic grounds." They argued that Dean Black did not live up to the university's commitment to "political neutrality" and to academic freedom. They wrote of how Brandeis, which was Jewish sponsored and nonsectarian, allowed antiwar opinions but censured dissent on Israel and Zionism:

"Why doesn't the University apply to its other candidates for admission the same standards it used in rejecting Davis? In other words, why not reject a committed opponent of the Vietnam War who is active in national politics and wants to study history or political science here? If there is a certain level of political activity that makes one ineligible to attend Brandeis, let's spell it out."[144] Richard Sennett, a professor of sociology and chair of the admission committee, spelled out the argument in a letter distributed at the faculty meeting on May 27, 1971, and then published in the *Justice*. In the letter, Sennett outlined the damage done to Brandeis's "reputation among scholars" by Davis's rejection and the university's vulnerability to what he described as "outside forces." "It has been picked up by Brandeis's enemies," Sennett wrote, "as a sign that Brandeis thinks of itself as a Zionist school and that its commitments are founded in the politics of the present Israeli regime as well as in being a University of academic excellence."[145]

Controversy followed Davis to nearby Tufts, a university with no modern religious affiliation, where Marty Blatt signed up for his course, titled Post-1967 Israel: A Non-Zionist Perspective. It was taught at Tufts Experimental College, founded in 1964 to offer innovative, credit-bearing courses to undergraduates, with students represented on its board. Davis's course, which focused on "non-armed social change and the Middle East," proved transformative for Marty Blatt. In the antiwar movement, Blatt was learning to fight for justice. "The Vietnam War was a horrible injustice," he said. Davis taught him that "Israel/Palestine was another injustice."[146] Blatt and his classmate, Paul Kleinbaum, became interested in the idea of draft resistance and conscientious objection, building on their own experiences with the American military draft for the war in Vietnam. With Davis's encouragement, Blatt and Kleinbaum began to pursue a research project, interviewing Israelis who refused to serve in the army.

In the summer of 1972, Blatt and Kleinbaum traveled with Davis to Israel to interview thirty men and women who refused to serve in the Israeli Defense Forces. Their transcribed interviews were later published in a work titled *Dissent and Ideology in Israel: Resistance to the Draft, 1948–1973*. The book included an introduction by linguistics scholar and activist Noam Chomsky, a frequently attacked critic of American and Israeli policies.[147]

Following pressure from Jewish communal leaders, student leaders at Tufts Hillel, the B'nai B'rith–sponsored Jewish organization with chapters on college and university campuses, moved to discredit Uri Davis. Indeed, the Hillel president had "appealed to various campus officials" to prevent Davis from teaching his course.[148] Responding to this and to the fact that all Hillel events mirrored larger communal Jewish events uncritical of Israeli policies, Blatt was moved to action. In late 1972, he joined students in forming the Tufts Hillel Non-Zionist Caucus, a group "committed to presenting the Middle East 'crisis' in a non- or anti-Zionist framework." They were also "trying to offer alternatives to the interpretations of recent events and history offered by the American Zionist community."[149] Blatt and others also organized a series of speakers on campus, including Fouzi el-Asmar, a Palestinian poet, and Noam Chomsky, among others.

Blatt had learned about dissent from his American antiwar activism and from the Israeli left. During that year, with Davis no longer at the Experimental College, Blatt decided to open up a space for dissent from American Zionism by offering a course there himself entitled Zionism Reconsidered. He took the course title from the Hannah Arendt essay of the same name, first published in Henry Hurwitz's *Menorah Journal* in 1944. In the Tufts catalog, Blatt described the course as taking "a critical look at Zionist theory and praxis." His assigned texts reflected his own politically left orientation: *The Other Israel: The Case against Zionism* by Arieh Bober, a member of the Israeli socialist and anti-Zionist party Matzpen; Arendt's *Eichmann in Jerusalem*; Maxime Rodinson's *Israel and the Arabs*; Gerard Chaliand's *The Palestine Resistance*; and Irene Gendzier's *Middle East Reader*.[150] Blatt also had the students read Theodor Herzl's *The Jewish State* and Arthur Hertzberg's *The Zionist Idea*.[151]

In his course, Blatt taught the history of Zionism, tracing it through to contemporary Zionism, which seeks "a priori privileged position for Jews" in Israel. Contemporary Zionism, he taught his students, meant that "Israeli-Jews live in a constant condition of tension and siege." Blatt dedicated class time to the idea that "anti-Zionism does not in any way equal antisemitism." "Those that [sic] make this assertion," he added, "are committed to the privileged position of Jews in Israel and recoil at any attempt to put forth a critical position."[152] Drawing from the anticolonialist movements, Blatt taught about Palestinian dispossession and resistance and about Israel's Cold War alliance with the United States.

On March 13, 1973, an in-class protest of Zionism Reconsidered brought Blatt and Tufts more publicity than his students, many of them Zionists, ever could have imagined. About fifteen members of the Jewish Defense League, five of them Tufts students, forcibly entered the classroom. They called the course an "anti-Jewish outrage" and passed out a flyer that read, "Not since Germany in the days of Hitler has any university dared to offer a course presenting a one-sided view of any national movement." The Jewish Defense League was a far-right, anti-Arab, Jewish nationalist group founded in 1968 by Rabbi Meir Kahane. Its members used intimidation tactics to threaten and silence anyone who supported Palestinian rights. In Blatt's Tufts classroom, however, there was not just intimidation but physical provocation. One member spat on Marty Blatt.[153] Blatt called the March 13 moment a "break-in."[154] The disrupters only left when one student called campus security.

At that point, Blatt says, the issue became one of free speech. Even the students who were strong supporters of Zionism agreed that Jewish Defense League members had no right to enter and disrupt the class. Despite the incident, the class finished well and Blatt's teaching evaluations were good. Not wanting to appear to be backing down from the protest, Blatt planned to run the Zionism Reconsidered course again the following semester, in the fall of 1973, teaching during the Yom Kippur or October War.[155]

Blatt's activism and course crossed the threshold of acceptable dissent on American Zionism and prompted an explosive response. Two separate sets of responses continued in the months that followed. First, the attack on Zionism Reconsidered, along with events in the Middle East, mobilized non- and anti-Zionist students in the Boston area to protest. In late 1972, they formed an "ad hoc, anti-Zionist coalition" of students aligned with the New Left.[156] In May 1973, as Blatt wrapped up his course, the group stood out at a "counter celebration of Israel's [twenty-fifth] anniversary." As Senator Edward Kennedy spoke at a pro-Israel gathering in Boston, the group had three hundred people at a teach-in about the Middle East at Boston University.[157]

Also that spring, Marty Blatt joined others on Brandeis's campus to protest Israel's prime minister Golda Meir's visit. Prior to the events, "fistfights" broke out in university cafeterias over these demonstrations of dissent from the forced Zionist consensus. Two hundred and fifty members of the anti-Zionist coalition reportedly stood outside with equal numbers of Jewish Defense League members.[158] Debates over Zionism, Jewish loyalty, and safety occurred in the student newspaper. Protestors drew attention to the "repressive and explotive [sic] nature of Zionism."[159] Some of the protesting students at Meir's speech held signs that read, "Not Arab against Jews, but Class against Class." Where some saw antisemitism in student dissent over Israel and Zionism, student Frances Hagopian wrote in her editorial that these protestors were issuing "a political call for unity to fight for socialism."[160]

In a letter to the editor in the student newspaper the *Justice*, student Greg Perkins compared Prime Minister Meir's visit with Brandeis's rejection of Uriel Davis two years earlier. "Brandeis turns out to be too small even for even a student whose views are anathema to Zionists," he wrote. "How much more open is Brandeis, may we ask, than a University which excludes opponents of the Vietnam war or of capitalism or whatever the sacred cow-golden calf [is] of middle America?" Perkins asked. "How free is a university if it is run by men—or dependent on money from men—whose attitude is Israel can do no wrong, or worse, that Israel's wrongs are to be justified, rationalized, excused?"[161]

The second set of responses to the attack on Blatt's Zionism Reconsidered course was composed of private and public condemnations of his criticism of Zionism and Israel. The course attracted the attention of the local chapter of the Anti-Defamation League and other Boston Jewish communal groups.[162] ADL leaders considered Blatt to be a disciple of Professor Uri Davis and saw Blatt's Zionism Reconsidered course as clear evidence of the "Israel propaganda" peddled by both men.[163] Blatt's course and the protest garnered attention from Jewish presses as far away as Michigan and Indiana.[164]

In the *Boston Phoenix*, Boston's alternative paper, journalist Sid Blumenthal wrote an article supporting Blatt. Blumenthal mocked the fact that the Jewish Defense League and "establishment Jewish groups" had the same goal: to end the class in the hopes of silencing criticism of Israel. Though Herman Brown, executive director of the Boston Jewish

Community Council, called the course "part of a propaganda war," Blumenthal instead likened Blatt to "a Talmudist in blue jeans" and "an itinerant shtetl scholar." Quoting position statements written by Blatt, Blumenthal wrote that "American Jews should free themselves from the dominant myths they receive in the press, the synagogues, and temples. They would then understand the dispossession of Palestinians that took place, cease to support the militarism and expansionism of the Israeli government, and lend support to the emerging, progressive forces inside Israel itself."[165]

Debate raged for weeks in the *Boston Phoenix* while Boston's Jewish communal leaders gathered to consider how to respond. These leaders expressed outrage that Blatt and Blumenthal had brought questions about Israel and Zionism into public conversations. They issued a statement: "Whereas the anti-Semitic implications of the Tufts University Experimental College course, 'Zionism Reconsidered' is a grievous affront to the Jewish community, the Jewish Community Council of Metropolitan Boston should take such steps as are appropriate to convey the seriousness of our concern to the President and Trustees of Tufts University."[166] A few months later, Hillel, the Anti-Defamation League, the American Jewish Committee, the Jewish War Veterans, and the Boston Jewish Community Relations Council each put in $100 "for the special courses developed at the last minute to counter the Martin Blatt course."[167] Boston's Jewish Community Relations Council resolved to "undertake a vigorous program of educating the Jewish and general community at large about our concern over this issue." It declared Blatt's course "an insult to the Jewish community" and said that it "basically was unfair to present an anti-Zionist course when the University had never presented a pro-Zionist course." Not acknowledging the fact that most mainstream media outlets and certainly most Jewish media outlets were dominated by voices supportive of Israeli policies, they saw the course, and Blatt, as part of an "anti-Israel propaganda effort" that could have a far-reaching, negative impact.[168]

Appointed by the Jewish community's Middle Eastern Affairs Committee, Dr. Gerald Wohlberg, a psychiatry professor, published an article about Blatt and his course in Boston's *Jewish Advocate* titled "Tufts Anti-Zionist Course Seen as Abuse of Academic Freedom." Wohlberg echoed the idea that Blatt's "politicization of learning" drew only from "propaganda"—civil and Palestinian rights organizations—that crossed the threshold of acceptable dissent in "linking Israel with Vietnam and with US Imperialism." Wohlberg said that he and other Jewish leaders supported academic freedom but found the course had a "lack of balance." Because Blatt was scheduled to teach his class again, they "supported a second course which would present a broader view on Zionism." He encouraged readers to take a "vigilant stand against any course which may even remotely promote anti-Zionism" by writing to the president of Tufts.[169]

In more exchanges in the *Advocate*, Blumenthal argued that Blatt's criticism of Israel was not grounded in "Arab propaganda nor lack of interest in Jewish affairs." Instead, Blumenthal asserted, it was because of the "Israeli government's own actions." "Israelis feel free to speak out on these matters," he concluded. "Why shouldn't American Jews?"[170] Phyllis Pomerantz, one of the Tufts students who formed the non-Zionist Hillel, also wrote a letter to the *Advocate* in which she challenged the idea of an "anti-Zionist conspiracy in the Boston area." Pomerantz called them a "concerned group of people growing every week, Americans, Jews and Arabs, interested in social change and convinced that Zionism can only be harmful to that goal."

Engaging in comparative victimology with anti-Black racism, Wohlberg had compared Blatt's course to one on the "genetic inferiority of Blacks." Pomerantz wrote that she and her peers were "trying to struggle against . . . the labelling of any people as inferior or targets of oppression." Echoing Blatt's own ideas, she wrote,

> The answer to two thousand years of persecution of the Jews cannot be a nation based on militarism and the upholding of a privileged position (i.e., full social, political, and civil rights) for one segment of the population only—the Jewish segment. What happened to the Jews cannot be used to justify what is happening to the Palestinians. The occurrence of all forms of prejudice, discrimination, and oppression must be fought against—that is the only assurance that the next two thousand years will not be like the last. Anti-Zionism is not a veil for antisemitism. It is its direct opposite.[171]

Pomerantz's assertion of anti-Zionism as the opposite of antisemitism built on generations of Jewish dissent on Zionism and Israel. Like other critics of Zionism, she disputed the idea that Israel made Jews safer. And she concluded with a reference to the skepticism toward state power engendered by the Vietnam War: "We have recognized the danger of the slogan 'America—right or wrong!' It is time for American Jews to stop giving blind support to Israel. 'Israel—right or wrong' is just as dangerous."[172]

This debate struck a chord in *Advocate* readers, and they wrote dozens of powerfully emotional letters to the Tufts University president and various deans condemning what they knew of Blatt's course. Nearly all were from the Boston area, were self-identified Jewish individuals, and were filled with fury and fear at Tufts for risking Jewish safety by teaching anti-Zionism. Most of the letters included equations of anti-Zionism with antisemitism and with the dangers of the Holocaust, with statements such as "An attack on Zionism is an attack on Judaism."[173] Many expressed urgency after the October 1973 war, with a heightened sense of Israel's vulnerability. A local rabbi called the course an "appalling situation," noting, "It is inconceivable to me, especially in light of the Yom Kippur War, that a university of the stature of Tufts would permit such a course to be offered in its hallowed halls." He feared the course would "undermine the Jewish state and in Jewish minds foster what could be a second holocaust [*sic*] in one generation."[174]

Some letters criticized Blatt. A Connecticut doctor wrote to the Tufts president that "there are two particular groups who are very anti-Israel: the self-hating Jews and the Arabists." Placing Blatt in the earlier category, he wrote, "I think that the first group is to be pitied more than censured."[175] These ideas stoked the fire of the controversy so wildly that Blatt himself received death threats. He picked up the telephone one day to hear someone say, "Your parents should not have been saved." The person on the other end of the line clearly knew that his mother's side of the family was German and had lost many to the Nazis.[176]

Many, though not all, of these letters invoked anti-Black racism in their response to Blatt's course. The struggle of Black Americans with white supremacy, they believed, was now far more visible, rendering Jewish struggles with antisemitism invisible. This development, which many saw emerging out of the liberation movements of the era, was perilous for Jews. To discredit Blatt's course and thus criticism of Israel, Jewish leaders and laypeople relied on racist constructions of Black people and Black activism. These narratives would soon be codified in Forster and Epstein's book, *The New Anti-Semitism*, published by the Anti-Defamation League in 1974.

The most striking example of this kind of response to Blatt's course appeared in a publication titled *Herut News* of the New England Region of United Zionists-Revisionists of America (UZRA). Herut was a far-right Zionist organization, marginal in its membership and impact. They called the course "a forum for anti-Israel propaganda," the product of "factually incorrect left-wing socialist attacks on Israel." The article ended by employing a familiar racist trope, analogizing Black liberation with Zionism in a fictional encounter between "a Jew and an important [white] member of the Tufts community":

> JEW: "I understand academic freedom but suppose the course was 'Civil rights Reconsidered' or 'Black Equality Reconsidered'?"
> TUFTS MAN: "That's simple. There would be a large hole in the Medford earth where Tufts used to be."
> JEW: "Can't you see that for us, this is the same kind of issue?"
> TUFTS MAN: "Look, we know you people are not going to make trouble. Why should we listen to you?"

Concluding the story was the statement "Tufts University at least has honest officials."

Comparative victimology forms the foundation of this article. UZRA members considered unqualified loyalty to Israel as essential to Jewish identity and to Jewish liberation. They compared the Jewish fight against antisemitism, here equated only with criticism of Israel, with the Black struggle against white supremacy. There is shame, then, that members of the Jewish community, "you people," failed to make the sort of demands that Black activists made and failed to back up those demands with violence. In Blatt's teaching, these members saw Jewishness and Jewish masculinity compromised, and thus in the competition for visibility, Black activists—"naturally" violent—were winning.[177] The course continued to run, and for UZRA members, this marked a loss for Jews.

Other community members invoked anti-Black racism in furious letters about Blatt's course. One person asked, "[Suppose] R. J. Herrnstein was to offer a course at Tufts in support of his own views?" Harvard University's reception of Herrnstein's ideas of the genetic inferiority of Black Americans spoke to this letter's author of "the changing definition of 'academic freedom.'"[178] Another letter identified Blatt as someone who "passed out handbills on the Tufts campus linking Israel with Vietnam and American imperialism." To make that comparison, the letter writer declared, was tantamount to "offer[ing] a Negro history course from the Ku Klux Klan point of view."[179] Another letter writer likened the course to one called the "Academic Basis for Black Inferiority" or the "Economic Imperatives of Returning Black Africa to Its Original European Ownership."[180]

In June 1973, President Hallowell announced that the Experimental College was to offer a course called the Rebirth of Jewish Nationalism in the fall, taught by Mr. Mitchell Knisbacher. This was very likely the course funded by Jewish communal leaders that was intended to "counter" Blatt's teachings in Zionism Reconsidered.[181] The controversy grew to encompass questions of academic freedom at Tufts and even at the Civil Liberties Union of Massachusetts.[182] And it continued to occupy the energy of Tufts leaders. Tufts President Burton C. Hallowell, Dean of the Faculty Bernard Harleston, and Chair of the Experimental College Harry Ritchie met with Jewish communal leaders, including Isidore Zack of the Anti-Defamation League. They arrived at a "fuller, mutual appreciation of the issues involved, including the identification in many minds of Anti-Zionism with Anti-Semitism."[183] Ultimately, though, Tufts administration "affirm[ed] support" for Blatt's class. Their findings separated criticism of Zionism and Israel from antisemitism. Thus Tufts administrators concluded, "Though not neutral in point of view, the course was not found to endorse, advocate, or teach anti-Semitism in any form whatsoever."[184]

There was historical continuity in the struggles of Morris Schappes, Marty Blatt, and all the (mainly) young people working to balance antiwar, civil rights, and Jewish commitments in these years. For decades, American Jewish leaders responded negatively to criticism of Israel and Zionism. But the scope and intensity of leaders' responses to those who crossed the threshold of dissent had increased. In part, this reflected the broader backlash of many white Americans, including Jews, against the era's left, anticolonialist movements and the sense that Black liberation and other movements had drowned out concerns over antisemitism. Many American Jews had gained access to public and private power through white privilege and social mobility, as the Zionist consensus aligned with some American Jews' rise to power in Cold War politics and society. Using the language of loyalty and patriotism, some Jewish leaders insisted that safety in and belonging to the United States depended on Jewish support of the war in Vietnam. For them, there was simply too much to lose. In this way, the threshold of dissent was tied to American Jews' power during the Cold War. And it played an important role in limiting access to dissent on Zionism, to Palestinian voices and perspectives, within the American Jewish world and beyond.

In the introduction to their book on conscientious objectors in Israel, *Dissent and Ideology in Israel*, Blatt and his colleagues, Uriel Davis and Paul Kleinbaum, wrote that liberal Jews in the 1970s United States act out of "ethical double standards" because they oppose US involvement in Vietnam but "give uncritical support to Israel."[185] They themselves "insist on applying our ethics and values universally."[186] Zionism, they believed, rested on the "domination of Palestinian-Arab people."[187] This means, they wrote, that "most young people in the Left are confused about Israel, much as we were, because they are unable to reconcile their anti-militarist insights and values in the United States to their feelings about Israel." Blatt, Davis, and Kleinbaum lamented the "collapse of Judaism into uncritical support of Israeli policies."[188] They saw the "structural complicity of interests" uniting Jews with Zionism and Israel.[189]

Blatt and his colleagues offered pointed observations on the stakes involved in debates over the Zionist consensus, belying the notion of a consensus among American Jews. The Tufts Experimental College website continues to spotlight the support Blatt received from the university in 1973, listing his course as an example of the "rights and responsibilities associated with academic freedom."[190]

Yet even in 2020, the Tufts administration continued to struggle with Jewish dissent over Israel. The campus group Students for Justice in Palestine allied with a campaign called "End the Deadly Exchange," sponsored by Jewish Voice for Peace, which seeks to end the militarization of campus and other police forces through training in Israel. The Office of Campus Life gave an award to Students for Justice in Palestine for collaborating with so many campus groups in voicing support and solidarity with Palestinian rights. Jewish community leaders, most visibly those of the Anti-Defamation League, accused Students for Justice in Palestine of fostering antisemitism. Notwithstanding the outpouring of letters from Jewish and non-Jewish allies, including Marty Blatt, Tufts president stated that the emotional responses of the Jewish community convinced him to revoke the award.[191] In 2020 as in 1973, the open space for Jewish criticism of Zionism at Tufts in Boston remained a narrow space indeed.

Conclusion: In Breira, Open Discussion of Vital Issues

In 1973, the organization Breira tried to fill the narrow space for dissent from the Zionist consensus. Breira is the Hebrew word for "alternative" and was a response to the common phrase "Ain breira" or "There is no alternative," an Israeli slogan that was used to justify military aggression. Breira was not an anti-Zionist organization. Rather, its members advocated mutual recognition between Israelis and Palestinians and had ties to the political left in Israel. Scholars and others who mention Breira trace its founding to the activist sentiments of the 1960s and 1970s, especially to the civil rights and the antiwar movements, and almost universally regard it as the start of American Jewish dissent on Israel.[192] In doing so, they render invisible organizations such as the American Council for Judaism, journals such as the *Jewish Newsletter* and *Jewish Currents*, classes such as Marty Blatt's Zionism Reconsidered, and indeed all the individuals studied in this book. American Jewish dissent on Israel began before Israel was a state, and Breira built on these legacies of dissent as it also drew from the era's social movements.

The near invisibility of this history of opposition fits neatly into Breira's platform, which focused, in part, on countering the silencing of dissent about Israel, the failure of Jewish communal leaders to account for, and reflect upon, diverse opinions. In December 1973, as the controversy over Blatt's course at Tufts continued in Massachusetts, Breira's national founders declared in their first public statement, "This is the reason we join together now—we deplore those pressures in American Jewish life which make open discussion of vital issues virtually synonymous with heresy." Drawing from the language of the antiwar movement, Breira criticized the low threshold for dissent on Israel and on communal priorities generally. The statement went on to say,

This attitude of "my country right or wrong" was reflected in all areas of American Jewish life because Israel is the 'glue' that holds the disparate elements of the community together, as well as the "cause" which unites separate and faltering fundraising efforts into an effective campaign. The lack of news and analysis in Jewish journalism, the one-dimensional level of Jewish education, the growth of the checkbook "mentality" as the basis of communal life, and the hierarchical and exclusive nature of Jewish organizational structures all mirrored an increasingly intolerable rigidity in Jewish affairs. Believing that Diaspora Jewry has more than a charitable stake in the future of the Jewish State, and more than an impersonal interest in the quality of Jewish life everywhere, this situation could not be ignored.[193]

Members of the press made clear that they regarded Breira as an outgrowth of the New Left, describing its members as a "loose coalition of Jewish intellectuals and of veterans of the civil rights and anti-Vietnam war movements of the sixties."[194] While some radicals did indeed join the organization, members positioned themselves as young Jewish insiders who sought to influence the community from within. Like Blatt's ally Phyllis Pomerantz, who declared that "Israel, right or wrong, is just as dangerous," Breira members tapped into the language of those who supported American war making in Vietnam. At their first conference, they used the phrase "My country right or wrong" without saying clearly whether they were referring to the United States or Israel as the country of American Jews, suggesting that they found American Jews far too quiet in voicing dissent on the policies of both nations.

Many Breira members were Zionists, and indeed they chose "Breira," the Hebrew word for "alternative," in part to "comment about the importance of Israel and the Hebrew language."[195] Rabbi Arnold Jacob Wolf, a Jewish chaplain and Hillel director at Yale University, was one of the group's founders, and he had been involved in both the civil rights and the antiwar movements. Jewish intellectuals, scholars, and more than one hundred Conservative and Reform rabbis supported Breira. Many of them were involved with the havurah movement in Judaism, which established layperson-led, alternative, spiritual communities that eschewed what they called the "establishment" Judaism of large, suburban congregations. Breira members included progressive Rabbi Al Axelrad of Brandeis University, Morris Schappes of *Jewish Currents*, and Rabbi Arthur Waskow, author of *The Bush Is Burning!* Breira members supported work toward greater equality for all people in Israel and toward greater freedom for opinions on Israel among American Jews. Breira drew in important ways from the feminist movement, too, in that its by-laws stipulated that one-third of its national board had to be women.[196] The story of Breira offers us a window into what scholar Michael Staub calls "the limits of dissent."[197]

Breira was founded in March 1973, when a group of American rabbis and graduate students met to talk about their deep concerns over Palestinian rights, Palestinian nationalism, and the growing Israeli settler movement. After the war in Israel a few months later, the group established itself as a formal organization, embracing the two-state solution for Israel/Palestine and encouraging other American Jews to do the same. They publicly criticized Israel's occupation and lamented the inability of the PLO and successive Israeli governments to make peace through mutual recognition. Breira members connected with members of the Israeli left, whom they considered potential forces for peace in Israel.[198]

In 1975, with the organization only a few years old, Breira leaders issued a statement that demonstrated attempts to carve out a space for a new definition of Zionism, one that respected Palestinian rights and self-determination. The United Nations had just passed a resolution condemning Zionism as racism, a resolution that in many ways represented a victory for the activists of the anticolonialist movements throughout the world. Breira's statement in response to the resolution contained some criticism, qualifying Israel's achievements to date. The statement pointed out that the "promise of Israeli sovereignty—security for the Jewish people and the flowering of Jewish culture in a land of justice and peace—is still to be fulfilled." For Breira members, the denial of Palestinian rights did not align with the original vision and realization of Zionism. In line with this, the following year, Breira members wrote letters to members of the Knesset, Israel's government, calling for an end to "rigorous suppression of Arab dissent." Fighting for human rights in Israel, Breira made a plea for Israel to stay true to what it described as the "Jewish commitment to human and national rights on which Israeli society was founded and is maintained."[199]

Yet Breira also joined the widespread American Jewish condemnation of the 1975 United Nations resolution equating Zionism with racism. They labeled it an "attempt to revive ideological arguments to undermine Israeli independence," which "obfuscates the real policy issues" and prevents a "just peace." Moreover, Breira members joined mainstream American Zionists in pointing fingers at anticolonialist leaders for the momentum behind the resolution. "As Jews," Breira members wrote, "many of whom consider [ourselves] Zionists . . . we have been disappointed with the response" to attempts to "present this message directly to those representatives of Third World nations which claim to oppose racism and to value a just resolution of the Middle East conflict." While the statement's conclusion reaffirmed Breira's commitment to what the organization described as "the fulfillment of Palestinian national aspirations" and the role of the United Nations in working toward justice and peace, it also reflected its members' careful balancing of criticism of Israel with loyalty to Israel.[200] According to Breira's statement, their members had hoped to work with anticolonialist movements toward those ends. But criticism of Zionism as racism, built into the expansive worldview of anticolonialist groups, stood in their way. Though the New Left and anticolonialist movements proved integral to the ideas and platforms of Breira, members of the group found it essential to Distance themselves from the left's fully developed critique of Israel.

At the Breira National Membership Conference in 1977, members adopted resolutions with titles that put the organization's priorities on display: "Freedom of Expression in Jewish Communal Life" and the "Independence of the Jewish Press." Members focused on gender equality, tzedakah (charitable giving), the "pursuit of social justice," and work for the "vitality" of Jewish communities outside of Israel. Breira members further affirmed what they described as the "interdependence of the Jewish people in both Israel and the Diaspora." They balanced support for Israel with a commitment to forces for peace and equality in Israel and to "safeguarding the rights of Arabs and other non-Jewish minorities within Israel."[201]

Clearly, Breira members, whose numbers reached a height of about fifteen hundred, were trying to redefine Zionism rather than reject it. They identified themselves as "American Jews who support a definition of Zionism which views the establishment of a secure Jewish State of

Israel as a necessary means to the goal of developing a society based upon the principles of justice, peace, and civil liberties as expressed in our tradition." They endorsed ideas that contributed to those goals, such as working for Palestinian rights, ending the "Orthodox monopoly" in Israeli civil affairs, and advancing the rights of Mizrahi Jews from North Africa and the Middle East. Breira also hoped to influence American foreign policy toward Israel, pressing for what it described as a "lasting settlement of the conflict between Israel and her Arab neighbors, including the Palestinians." In addition, they tried to diminish Israel's dependence on the United States for military aid.[202]

In seeking to carve out space for critical conversations about Israel and its role in American Jewish life, Breira members met with a storm of controversy. The second day of the 1977 conference was interrupted by Jewish Defense League youth carrying signs that read, "No Deals with Baby Killers" and "Death to Breira." According to the Jewish press, the youth eventually "disbanded at the request of the police."[203] In their own publication, the Jewish Defense League called out Breira members' "confusion and naivete," grouping Breira with the Black Panthers and other anticolonialist movements and indicating that none of these groups cared for Jewish interests, which they equated solely with an unquestioning commitment to Israel.[204]

It did not matter that Breira did not engage in debates over Israel and Zionism as anti- or non-Zionists, that they had joined American Jewish leaders in rejecting the United Nations resolution equating Zionism with racism. The threshold of dissent over Zionism and Israel had again decidedly shifted, and Jewish Defense League leaders counted Breira members as enemies of the Jewish people. Anti-Defamation League leaders followed suit. An article in the *Village Voice* noted that by 1977, the forces aligned against Breira were many and powerful and led by the ADL. These Jewish leaders launched campaigns indicating that Breira members, like the PLO, were "dedicated to the destruction of the Jewish state." At the ADL, which was affiliated with B'nai B'rith, leaders threatened to fire any employees, especially leaders of Hillel chapters on college campuses, who showed support for Breira, as they had to "refrain from promoting views contrary to those of B'nai B'rith."[205] Anti-Defamation League leadership described having "some concern" about Hillel staff's involvement in

Breira and about Breira's commitment to Israel's safety. B'nai B'rith set up a "panel" to investigate.[206]

Rabbi Isidor B. Hoffman, a former Hillel director at Cornell University, wrote to B'nai B'rith leaders to say he was "shocked and chagrined" to learn that Hillel staff members would face dismissal "if they participate in Breira or voice dissenting views about the Middle East peace and Israel." He called the threat "heresy hunting."[207] David Blumberg, president of B'nai B'rith, went on record to say that he found the Anti-Defamation League's message about involvement in Breira "unnecessary, unwarranted, and inappropriate." Blumberg said that "dissent is needed in Jewish life" and noted that some observers called the attacks on Breira "McCarthyism with a Jewish face."[208] The *Jewish Post* wrote that the campaign against Breira "bordered on hysterical," and its editors blasted the ADL for its "effort toward thought control."[209] Just below the article that contained this information ran another about Jewish Defense League students "invading" the office of a Hillel rabbi involved with Breira.[210]

In accusing Breira members of taking the side of "the Arabs" by faulting only Israel, Zionist leaders made clear that Breira's positions were beyond the threshold of acceptable dissent.[211] Attacks on Breira members were swift and often vicious. Many of these attacks were personal assaults on the "Jewish credentials" of individuals and distortions of their positions. Some were familiar and similar to accusations that had been leveled at critics of Zionism for generations. Breira members were accused of fomenting dangerous divisions in the American Jewish community. They were called "anti-Zionists" and told that supporting Palestinian rights, though simultaneously calling for the Palestine Liberation Organization to recognize Israel's right to exist, posed the greatest threat to Jews everywhere.

Joseph Shattan, a conservative journalist and speech writer, published some of these accusations in the magazine *Commentary*, founded and funded by the American Jewish Committee, and members of Breira responded with letters to the editor. Robert Loeb, who had been Breira's executive director, wrote that "by distorting the position and denying Jewish 'doves' a place within the consensus of support for Israel's basic rights and essential security needs, Mr. Shattan provides precisely that interpretation of 'dissent' within the Jewish community most likely to hearten Israel's enemies."[212] Rabbi Max Ticktin, a Hillel rabbi and one of Breira's early leaders, recalled that "the people who made the biggest donations and were behind the big Jewish organizations . . . could do what they did do, which was bring us to our knees."[213]

Despite the concerns voiced by Hoffman and Blumberg, among others, the cost of these campaigns for members of Breira was truly incalculable. Members were attacked, and some felt shunned for years, even decades. By January 1978, faced with mounting threats and debt, leaders issued an appeal explaining that the "organized Jewish community mounted a concerted attack on Breira." "The counter-response," they wrote, "drained us of our energy and funds." Only weakened and decentralized chapters remained.[214]

Breira members dedicated considerable thought as to why they were attacked, and interestingly, though not surprisingly, they spoke of themselves as representing the first real American Jewish dissent on American Zionism. "The irony is that extreme groups like Neturei Karta [an Orthodox anti-Zionist sect] on the one hand, and the Zionist Organization of America and the JDL on the other, openly challenge Israel without raising too much of a storm," they wrote. "Serious public criticism from within the mainstream of the American Jewish community was virtually unheard of before the creation of Breira. It is precisely because Breira is a child of the 'establishment' that it has caused a serious reevaluation of the future of Diaspora-Israel relations."[215] Here Breira leaders located the Anti-Defamation League and the Zionist Organization of America on the margins, no doubt the conservative margins, of American Jewish life. They located themselves in the center, legitimating their criticism. From the New Left, from Black liberation leaders and anticolonialist activists and, from the left in Israel, Breira members had learned lessons about colonialism and liberation. When they tried to locate the lineage of that brand of criticism in American Jewish life, they came up empty. They thought of themselves as the first serious Jewish critics of Zionism.

One critic of Breira, however, compared Breira to the American Council for Judaism with some regularity.[216] Working for the organization Americans for a Safe Israel, writer Rael Jean Isaac authored a well-funded and frequently circulated attack on Breira, a pamphlet titled *Breira: Counsel for Judaism*. This reference, even with the different spelling, surely was not lost on those who remembered Rabbi Elmer Berger and his organization. In her final sentences, Isaac drew a parallel between the two organizations by saying that at least the American Council for Judaism had been honest and straightforwardly anti-Zionist; Breira's danger lay in presenting itself as though it supported Israel but was actually working for Israel's destruction. As Isaac wrote, "The American Council for Judaism is a much less damaging organization than Breira. If there are Jews who draw back and assert what they feel to be their own interests against those of Israel, in the last analysis they may do so. But let them not take that flattering unction to their souls that they save Israel as they in fact facilitate her destruction. It is this that is the true corruption of Breira."[217]

According to Isaac's analysis, the American Council for Judaism was dangerous because its members felt that Zionism threatened American Jewish security just as Jewish integration and social mobility were largely underway. They rejected Israel because it was not in "their own interests" as American Jews. Breira members, on the other hand, located themselves within the "consensus of support" for Israel—and then contested what vision of Jewish and Palestinian coexistence was possible.

Isaac's analysis reflects the different historical contexts of Breira and the American Council for Judaism and the vastly higher stakes of the 1970s. By then, Israel was a major recipient of American military aid, and Israel was a site of Cold War political battles. Palestinian rights, long championed by Palestinians themselves, were now increasingly discussed in global human rights and activist communities. American Jews now held positions of power in the political, economic, and cultural life of the Cold War United States. To criticize Israel was to continue to play into fears of Jewish safety, and the criticism also played into a much wider set of perceived threats to America. To criticize Israel was to affirm anticolonialist activists' and intellectuals' visions of how Cold War imperialism in Vietnam, Israel, and the United States and across the world worked against marginalized populations and indeed against the interests of global safety and sustainability.

* * *

Attempts by Jewish leaders to sideline Jewish critics of Zionism began not with Breira's founding in 1973 but in the 1940s, and emotional responses to these critics began before the 1967 war in Israel.[218] This then is a counternarrative to the often told story of the Jewish 1960s, about American Jews who remained loyal to Israel and American Zionism, who made the "correct" selection when forced to choose between their anticolonialist, universalist activism in civil rights, antiwar, or Black liberation movements and their loyalty to Israel, American Zionism, and American Jewish life.[219] Many American Jews cared deeply for American Jewish life, criticized Israel, and remained in human rights campaigns or remained supportive of progressive currents in the US and Israel and worked to redefine American Zionism.[220] Many scholars and laypeople assert that Breira was the beginning of American Jewish controversy over Zionism. This work demonstrates that Breira's activism was but one chapter, and not the first, in a long history of American Jewish dissent over Israel and Zionism.

Breira began as an organization challenging the tenets of American Zionism, but not American Zionism itself. Those who had come before Breira, who created space for Jewish communal criticism of Zionism—the Council, Zukerman, Hurwitz, Blatt, and Schappes—were all anti- or non-Zionists, challenging American Jews to radically alter their relationships with Israel. Strong responses to Breira, which was neither anti- nor non-Zionist, spoke to just how far the threshold of acceptable dissent on Israel and American Zionism had moved. Any criticism of Israel's policies was outside of this threshold. This book's final chapter analyzes New Jewish Agenda (NJA), founded in the 1980s during an era of overwhelming political conservatism and the dismantling of social welfare and civil rights policies. Jewish activists who joined New Jewish Agenda dissented from multiple dissented from multiple aspects of American Jewish life but took great care in balancing criticism of American Zionism and Israel with professions of faith in Israel as a Jewish state.

4

The Threshold of Dissent in the 1980s

New Jewish Agenda and American Civil Rights

The story of the 1980s is, in part, the story of the sheer force of the Zionist consensus and in some ways its victory. The intense criticism and decline of Breira indicated how successful Jewish communal leaders' efforts were in building and reinforcing the consensus. While the Vietnam War and Watergate contributed to an immense loss of confidence in state power, Americans of all backgrounds now supported US aid to Israel as contributing to the image of America as what historian Shaul Mitelpunkt describes as a "benevolent actor in world affairs."[1]

The Camp David Accords between Israel and Egypt, which were signed in 1978, further convinced many Americans that Israel needed US support to flourish. The accords also meant an increase in US military aid to Israel. Both in the United States and in Israel, the late 1970s and early 1980s marked a rightward turn in political leadership, and the conservative alliances between the two nations only enhanced the chilling effect on dissent from unconditional American Zionism. American Jewish Zionist leaders' support was, then, deeply connected to domestic needs as well as to Cold War alliances between Israel and the United States.

Before the establishment of the State of Israel, American Jews had debated competing visions of American Judaism and the role of nationalism and Zionism in American Jewish life. Those who criticized or rejected American Zionism were at first tolerated, then marginalized, losing Jewish communal funding and support, and eventually often accused of threatening American Jewish safety and security even as American antisemitism largely diminished. Zionist leaders continued to see peril in American Jews' fractured unity on Israel because any criticism might be used to reduce US support for Israel. American Jews rarely gave voice to their anti- or non-Zionism within their communities. Even

American Jews who were Zionists and who criticized American Zionism and Israel paid a high price, as evidenced by those in Breira.

In the 1980s, the forced Zionist consensus had a strong hold on American Jewish life, as Jewish leaders grounded Jewish religious and community life, community belonging, and philanthropy in unquestioning loyalty to Israel and measured Jewish political behavior against this loyalty. As Israel's occupation and settlement building became normalized, those who wished to publicly oppose the conservative policies of elected leaders in Israel and the United States struggled to avoid the pitfalls and punishments meted out to those who had openly dissented from American Zionism in the previous decades.

Historian Shaul Magid notes that in the 1980s, many of the so-called New Jews who had embraced radical Zionism in the 1960s and 1970s were rabbis, journalists, scholars, and Jewish educators. "The political remnants of the New Jews," he observes, "had folded back into mainstream American liberal Zionism."[2] And some liberal Zionists continued to connect to the left in Israel. Wading into all debates about Israel and American Zionism, these American Jews necessarily identified as Zionists first. From 1979 to 1982, several former Breira members joined with other American Jews in forming the Shalom Network. Its members expressed public support for Peace Now, the pro-peace movement founded in Israel in March 1978; brought Israeli speakers from that movement to the United States; and worked for recognition of the Palestine Liberation movement and for a two-state solution in Israel/Palestine.[3]

The 1980s heirs to the dissent from unconditional American Zionism were the founders and leaders of New Jewish Agenda. NJA was a grassroots movement composed of individual chapters whose members often adopted their own local agendas. Members described themselves as progressive Jews and owed much of their initial organizational platform and structure to Breira; many of its founders had been Breira members. The Shalom Network merged with NJA's Middle East Task Force in 1982.

Active from 1980 until its dissolution in 1992, NJA learned essential lessons from Breira. They had no single group of prominent leaders, instead opting for a community-based model. They also moved away from Breira's "single-issue" focus on Israel/Palestine, a stance that allowed them to respond nimbly to local initiatives. This move also signaled recognition that there was a low threshold of tolerance for dissent on Israel.

Though New Jewish Agenda's positions belied any true consensus on American Zionism, its members consistently expressed their love for Israel and also emphasized their organization's broad Jewish dissent from conservative domestic policies. For over a decade, they embraced progressive positions and served as a counterforce to the conservative policies of President Ronald Reagan and of the American Jewish communal world, especially when American Jewish leaders built alliances with conservative organizations, citing their key support for Israel. NJA members' criticism of Israel and American Zionism was prudent and cautious. Still, their association with the left made them seem, at times, suspicious to mainstream Zionist Jewish leaders. One measure of that suspicion lies in the fact that the American Jewish Committee did not include them in their *American Jewish Yearbook* until 1986.

In the 1980s as before, American Jews' positions on Israel and Zionism were often intricately bound up in their positions on Black civil rights. Along with some Reform movement leaders, NJA members were among the most visible American Jews to commit themselves to the new challenges of the civil rights movement and its broader struggle against the war on the social welfare state, labor unions, and global militarism. Navigating and mediating conversations about Israel and Palestine, about antisemitism and white supremacy, about civil rights and Jewish continuity, NJA struggled to define American Jewishness outside of—or perhaps adjacent to—the Zionist consensus.

The equation of American Jewishness with unconditional support for Israel grew still harder to contest, and that fact had far-reaching implications for American Jews' positions on anti-Black racism. American Jews remained generally liberal on most social domestic issues, such as reproductive rights and social welfare. But Israel was the aberration from the liberal paradigm. Progressive Jews often felt stranded when trying to take stands *as Jews* against issues that were central to anticolonialist campaigns, such as antiapartheid and civil rights. For many, only organizations such as NJA offered a sense of Jewish belonging.

The Turn to the Right

In 1977, as the conservative Likud Party rose to power in Israel, American Jews who had long held on to the liberation narrative of Israel, who had seen it as a realization of dreams of collective living, grew still more uncomfortable.[4] Since 1967 many radical and liberal American Zionists had criticized the occupation of Palestinian land. Israel's Labor Party leaders had authorized the building of Jewish settlements on Palestinian territory, and this continued as Likud, under the leadership of Menachem Begin, came to power. As the 1970s drew to a close, mainstream American Jewish leaders "declared that the consensus among American Jews was that the West Bank settlements were legal." The Anti-Defamation League stood out among other American Jewish communal organizations in supporting the settlements unconditionally. Its leaders "reject[ed] the concept that Jews should not be free to settle and live in peace in Samaria and Judea" (the ancient biblical names for the occupied Palestinian territory of the West Bank).[5] No longer receiving funding from B'nai B'rith, the Anti-Defamation League by the 1980s had an enormous budget of $34.5 million, a staff of 350, and 30 regional offices. As scholar Jack Wertheimer notes, "Much of its [the ADL's] success derived from its shift to the right in the 1980s; it became far more aggressive in monitoring hate groups and more militant in its pursuit of foes, staking out a 'right of center' position on matters of Jewish defense."[6]

Liberal American Zionists, including members of Breira, allied with members of Israel's left, the Peace Now movement, in protesting these settlements. They voiced strong support for Israel but also insisted that American Jews were divided on the issue of new Jewish settlements on Palestinian land. A 1978 telegram, signed by writer and activist Leonard Fein, Nobel Prize–winning economist Kenneth Arrow, author Saul Bellow, and Rabbi Joachim Prinz, among others, declared its signers "lifelong friends of Israel" who "were distressed by the dangerous Middle East policies of the American government." They pointed out that "the fact that you criticize a government doesn't mean you don't support the country, its values, and its institutions."[7] Another 1979 protest letter to Prime Minister Begin, signed by Leonard Fein, Rabbi Balfour Brickner, and other liberal Zionists, read, "A policy which requires the expropriation of Arab lands unrelated to Israel's security needs and which presumes to occupy permanently a region populated by over 750,000 Palestinians we find morally unacceptable and perilous for the democratic character of the Jewish State."[8]

Even with their impressive Jewish and Zionist credentials, Leonard Fein and others were targets of American Jews and Israelis who saw the Zionist consensus as key to Jewish safety. One critic accused Fein of helping Israel's enemies, as "a divided Jewish community is just what the P.L.O. et al want." Another attacked Fein for taking his criticism of Israel to the mainstream press: no one should "mindlessly support every [Israeli] government policy," he wrote, but it threatens Jewish unity and safety to "take . . . disagreements to the American mass media."[9] Another critic of Fein and those who supported Peace Now wrote that when American Jews "try to influence Israeli foreign policy in the name of American Jewry, they render a disservice to Israel and to American Jewry."[10]

Lending his own power to reinforce the low threshold of American dissent on Israel, Prime Minister Begin wrote to Fein to assert that dissent created danger. While he affirmed that "Jews have the right to criticize the government of Israel," he urged Fein and others against "proffering advice, at least in public, within earshot of the enemies who conspire to do us evil." He declared that Fein's statement "lends—not, God forbid, intentionally—comfort to those who gleefully declare: 'Look, the Jews of America are turning their backs on Israel.'"[11] Jewish and other presses around the country covered these debates about American Jews, Israel, and American Zionism. Leonard Fein published an opinion piece in the *New York Times* titled "Criticism Is Not Fatal."[12]

Meir Merhav, economics editor for the *Jerusalem Post*, was born in Germany and left in 1933 for Palestine, where he became a Haganah fighter, defending the Jewish population during the British Mandate and then fighting for Israeli independence. Merhav wrote a column for the *Jerusalem Post* titled "Begin v. Fein." For Merhav, the press dispute between the two men represented historic divergences on many issues. He concluded his column, though, reflecting on what it meant for American and world Jewry that "every dissent is portrayed as comforting the enemy and bordering on high treason." He predicted that this would mean that "dissent and protest . . . will then be . . . stifled." This would be true for Jews around the world, Merhav asserted, and then reminded his readers that it "already started with Israeli Arabs."[13] He saw dissent and conversation as central to democracy and equality in Israel, and he feared what the loss of it meant for world Jewry.

Working for democracy and equality in the United States, some Black and Arab Americans had for decades felt solidarity with Palestinians, and they noted when Likud leaders' actions reflected links between Israel's settler colonialism and American racism. When visiting the United States, for example, Moshe Dayan, who joined the Likud-led government of Menachem Begin in 1977, said that the US Army was inferior because it relied on volunteers. He noted that "most of the soldiers are Blacks who have a lower education and intelligence." Congresswoman Shirley Chisholm was among those American leaders who rebuked Dayan for his remarks, saying that it "sounds like a warmed over Hitlerian statement on racial supremacy."[14] Using Holocaust language, Chisolm expressed the widely felt horror over the racism of leaders of a nation founded immediately after the Holocaust. For the public, statements like these laid bare the connections between American colonialism in the form of white supremacy, and the settler colonialism embedded in Israel's continued annexation of Palestinian land—just as they drew still more attention to the divide between Black Americans and white American Jews.

In the decades when American Jews were attacked for mentioning Palestinian rights, some prominent Black American leaders attempted Middle East peacemaking with visits to the Palestine Liberation Organization, linking the struggles against colonialism in both nations. In 1979, Washington, DC, delegate Walter Fauntroy and other Black leaders of the Southern Christian Leadership Conference, the organization founded in 1957 and led by Dr. Martin Luther King until his death in 1968, traveled to Lebanon to meet with Yasser Arafat, chairman of the Palestine Liberation Organization. Together Black American and Palestinian leaders sang songs from the civil rights movement. When Fauntroy and others requested to meet with state leaders in Israel on that same visit, they were refused. Israeli leaders explained their refusal by saying that the delegation had "prejudged Israeli policies."[15]

Israel proved to be a key issue in determining the voting patterns and alliances of American Jews in the 1970s and especially in the 1980s.

The election of Ronald Reagan as president in 1980 marked an anti-communist, American backlash against the social movements of the 1960s and 1970s and government commitments to fight racial inequality and poverty. Though American Jews were, for decades, reliable Democratic voters, they considered voting for the backlash politics of Ronald Reagan's Republican Party just as feminism, gay rights, and the AIDS crisis moved into public conversations. Some Jewish liberals argued that *both* political parties advanced Israel's interests. But the Republicans' strong military support for Israel made the choice still more comfortable for the small number of American Jews who voted for Reagan. Indeed, largely because President Jimmy Carter had sold weapons to Saudi Arabia and Egypt in 1978 and because Reagan was known to be an ally of Israel, Carter was the first Democratic candidate since the 1920s to receive less than 50 percent of the Jewish vote. American Protestants were also drawn into the "counterattack to liberalism" of this era, and many white evangelicals who saw Israel as central to end-times eschatology were fervent supporters of Zionism and Israel.[16]

By the 1980s, the split within Protestantism with regard to Israel was complete: white evangelicals offered strong support, while mainstream liberal Protestants often allied with global human rights campaigns, including that of Palestinians, and were more critical of Israel.[17] Historian Amy Weiss notes that Israel was central to the building of the alliance between Jews and evangelical Christians, an important segment of Reagan's base of support, even in the 1970s.[18] American Jewish Zionists found them a powerful partner in advocating for American foreign policy commitments to Israel in the 1980s, and these alliances shaped the visions of American Judaism that leaders worked toward in the broader American Jewish community.

Other elements of 1980s American conservatism appealed to American Jews. Many had already stopped supporting civil rights, and like many if not most white Americans, some had become troubled by affirmative action and other efforts to achieve racial equality.[19] The lives of many American Jews and African Americans diverged in the 1960s and 1970s. Many Jews had relied on low-interest, protected mortgages to exit cities for suburban communities built on state-funded infrastructure. Black communities, in contrast, were especially hard hit by the redirecting of social welfare resources to the military. Deindustrialization, job loss, and the murder of so many Black leaders during the civil rights movement added to social and economic distress.[20] As the *American Jewish Yearbook* pointed out in 1982, "Jewish opposition to programs for relieving the problems of [B]lacks, spearheaded chiefly by the Anti-Defamation League, continued, although specific court cases were not as heavily publicized as was the . . . Bakke case [challenging affirmative action]."[21] The *Regents of the University of California v. Bakke* was a 1978 Supreme Court case that challenged the use of racial "quotas" in a university's admissions process. The American Jewish Committee, the American Jewish Congress, and the Anti-Defamation League all supported Bakke and welcomed the Supreme Court's decision that quotas were unconstitutional. These groups feared that quotas designed to raise minority enrollment would shut out Jewish candidates, restoring the (anti-Jewish) quotas that had been abolished only a few decades before. The decision undermined attempts to open opportunities to Black students and students from other marginalized groups.

Some Black American leaders grew increasingly frustrated with both the Carter administration and the Democratic Party's inability to act on issues that were central to Black communities, including antipoverty programs, criminal justice reform, and labor rights. At a 1977 meeting of the Congressional Black Caucus Brain Trust, chaired by a delegate from Washington, DC, Walter Fauntroy, leaders noted that the Democratic Party's voter base itself was fractured partly because "there is a confrontation with the Jewish Community over the Bakke (affirmative action) case."[22]

Yet within this dynamic, too, Israel/Palestine emerged as an issue. Black Americans continued to support President Carter even though, as one Black newspaper reported, the "majority . . . feel that Israel should agree to a homeland for Palestinians."[23] As the 1983 civil rights March on Washington made clear, many Black Americans stood by the Democratic Party even as they drew attention to American support of what were seen as colonialist structures in both the United States and Israel, which was then, and remains, the largest cumulative recipient of American foreign aid since World War II.

When the energy of other liberation movements began to be felt in American Judaism and created conflict, Jewish leaders cited statements about a consensus of support for Israel as proof that American

Jewry remained united. When the Reform movement decided to ordain women as rabbis, for example, there was tension among members of the Jewish Welfare Board, and the Orthodox representative threatened to leave the organization. Sociologist Samuel Heilman echoed Jewish leaders who suggested that even amid the "current strife among Jews," American Jews ranked the issues that "united" them in this way: "support for Israel, rescuing Soviet Jewry, and fighting anti-Semitism."[24]

Surveys of American Jewish households only confirmed the centrality of Israel to American Jewish life. The 1981 National Survey of American Jews, sponsored by the American Jewish Committee, found "an overwhelming majority of the respondents (81 per cent) *disagree* with the statement" that "each American Jew should give serious thought to settling in Israel," but those polled rejected "the Zionist contention that Jewish life in the Diaspora is precarious or untenable." The report continued, "Reservations about classical Zionism do not inhibit deep, passionate, and widespread concern for Israel."[25]

Broadly speaking, unbiased measurements of American Jews' sentiments toward Israel were difficult given the mechanisms used to collect data. Participants were asked to respond to the statement "If Israel were destroyed, I would feel as if I had suffered one of the greatest personal tragedies in my life." The survey also asked participants to agree or disagree with the idea that "Jews should not vote for candidates who are unfriendly to Israel." Perhaps predictably, based on these data, this survey concluded that 94 percent of American Jews were "pro-Israel."[26]

In an essay titled "Liberalism and Pro-Israelism," sociologist Stephen Cohen, himself aligned with the Peace Now movement in Israel, recorded his interpretations of what the survey data revealed about American Jewish liberalism and support for Israel. "Some liberals have claimed," Cohen wrote, "that many Jews are leaving the liberal coalition because of their commitment to Israel." He concluded that while "American Jewish liberalism is not incompatible with pro-Israeli feelings," it does "restrain concurrence with certain hard-line policies of the Israeli government."[27]

Cohen's findings intended to reassure American Jews and others of Jews' continued faith in liberal paradigms, although adherence to unconditional Zionism and withdrawal from civil rights coalitions might have suggested otherwise.[28] Such studies emphasized American Jewish continuity, placing ritual observance, Jewish community birth rates, and fealty to Israel at its center. Cohen and others tried to show how Israel fit into the traditional understanding of Jews as Democratic voters, glossing over how a rigid "pro-Israel" approach to politics disrupted American Jewish patterns of supporting social welfare policies and Black rights.

Some liberal Zionists decried the rightward shift in American and American Jewish life. Rabbi David Polish of Chicago, for example, grew up in a secular, Yiddish-speaking, Zionist home. Ordained in the Reform rabbinate in 1934, Polish found his temple "in a cross fire between the Zionist ideology and the anti-Zionist ideology" of Reform Judaism. In the 1950s, he and his congregants broke away to form Temple Beth Emet, which as he recalled "did not only become a strong Zionist congregation but . . . was also deeply committed to some of the great social issues of our time. Like the issue of race, and later on the question of Viet Nam [sic]."[29]

Two years after his retirement from his pulpit, in a 1982 address to the national convention of the Labor Zionist Alliance at the Waldorf Astoria, Polish "pointed to a swing to the right not only in American politics, but in Israeli affairs as well as in the Jewish community." Citing the rights of workers, women, and minorities since the New Deal, he labeled the rightward trend a "growing retrogression . . . in the U.S. which takes the form of a frenzied effort to tear up the roots of a half century of social achievements." Polish encouraged Jews to reflect on these losses because he feared the rightward turn was also linked to attempts to silence conversations about what had been lost. He said that American Jews were "strongly dissenting in private" from Israel's actions, for example, and even suggested that Jews always had a right to this dissent. The case for the position that Jews needed to always agree with Israeli policies, he asserted, was "threadbare and discredited." Between Israel and the United States, he observed that "a relationship based on unquestioned support is not a healthy relationship." Polish called it a "contrived unity which collapses in times of stress."[30]

Yet this idea of "contrived unity" held sway throughout this decade. In the late 1980s, embattled by the controversy over his support for the Contra forces in Nicaragua, paramilitary operations to undermine Nicaragua's socialist regime, President Reagan argued that a "hostile Nicaragua" might endanger trade routes to Israel.[31] Liberal Jewish commentators

protested the veiled threat, including then liberal Zionist Henry Siegman, executive director of the American Jewish Congress and a fervent
critic of Israel's occupation. Siegman called out far-right Republicans for
using a "visceral appeal on the Israel issue," citing these efforts as "not so
subtle attempts at blackmailing the Jewish community." Siegman joined
the ranks of Jewish leaders who warned of the consequences of allying with evangelicals, those who supported "right wing fundamentalist
Christianized America" who opposed "equal rights amendments, affirmative action, humanism and social action programs."[32] Still, Reagan's
comment made clear that Israel was still seen as the single issue that
could be used to broker American Jewish support.

Some American Jews worried that the community's resources and
interests were also just too narrowly focused on Israel. By 1987, sociologist Nathan Glazer, a former member of Breira, noted, "The chief function of Jewish community organization in this country would appear to
be support of Israel. Indeed, this support almost fully defines the range
of interests of Jewish community organizations in politics. At the same
time, Israel occupies a major place in the content of Jewish life; it defines
much of the curriculum of the Jewish school and much of the subject
matter of the Jewish sermon."[33]

Zionist leaders such as Rabbi Polish, Henry Siegman, and Nathan
Glazer echoed concerns voiced by critics of American Zionism throughout the twentieth century. They worried about alliances formed over the
single issue of Israel. They also argued that a diversity of opinion and
interests within the American Jewish community was central to American diversity overall and respect for American Jews from other groups
in the United States. Leonard Fein stated his conclusions succinctly at
the American Jewish Committee's annual meeting in the spring of 1988.
"For every ounce of protection we thereby gain for Israel" by supporting "pro-Israel" right-wing ideologues such as Moral Majority leader
Jerry Falwell and Senator Jesse Helms, he said, "we will lose a pound
of protection for pluralism." Support for these figures, he declared, sub-
verts Jewish interests, Jewish values, and American Jews' "ability to help,
defend and protect the State of Israel."[34] Fein feared that as Jews allied
with right-wing leaders, they would remember Israel—and forget about
protecting American pluralism.

New Jewish Agenda: A "Mediating Discussion"

This snapshot of the 1980s captures the strength of the Zionist consensus in American Jewish communal life, its intricate connections to Israel, to Reagan conservatism, and to a turning away from pluralism and civil rights on the part of some American Jews. It captures, too, the predicament of liberal Zionists, whose critiques of Israeli policies often, though not always, stopped short of vocal support for Palestinian rights and who often expressed discontent with American Jewish priorities.

The 1980s witnessed a nadir of anti- and non-Zionist Jewish organizational work. When many former Breira members and other Jewish activists came together to create a new progressive Jewish organization after American voters elected Ronald Reagan in 1980, they self-consciously sought to avoid the attacks of Zionist leaders. They created a broad agenda encompassing many facets of American Jewish life and did not center Israel/Palestine in their organizational efforts. More than seven hundred people attended the founding convention of what two years later became New Jewish Agenda, whose "national platform upholds progressive Jewish values and affirms that the goals of peace and justice are attainable." The organization, which embraced and was built on antimilitarism, rights for the disabled, feminism, antiracism, economic justice, and lesbian, gay, bisexual, transgender, queer/questioning, intersex, and asexual (LGBTQIA+) rights, had at its height five thousand members with about forty-five active chapters.[35]

Ezra Berkley Nepon, author of a history of New Jewish Agenda, wrote of their interview with former NJA national director and Middle East Task Force member Reena Bernards and NJA cofounder Rabbi Gerry Serotta about how the group's members thought of their place in the debates over Israel and Palestine among American Jews. "There were other places to do social justice work [as Jews]," Bernards said, "but really no other place to express your desire for Israel/Palestine peace. Friends of Peace Now was getting organized right around the same time, but they were much more cautious, because their Israeli partners kept them cautious." And Rabbi Serotta added, "They were single-issue, and directed by the Israeli peace movement. Agenda was the only place since Breira had died for criticism from the Diaspora."[36]

New Jewish Agenda was not an anti-Zionist organization. Its original "Statement of Purpose" included not one word on Israel or Palestine, and its members intentionally did not use the word "Zionism" anywhere in the broader platform of which the statement was one small part. Instead, in their platform, members declared a commitment to inclusion for all, notwithstanding those "whose visions differ from ours," and a commitment to peace and justice. While local chapters had the freedom to choose campaigns and commitments, NJA held to five primary campaigns through their national task forces: Middle East Peace, Worldwide Nuclear Disarmament, Economic and Social Justice, Central American Solidarity, and Jewish Feminism. Their campaigns served as critiques of—and alternatives to—the campaigns and arrangements of traditional American Jewish life. To cite just two examples, NJA members wanted to ally American Jews with global peace work instead of Cold War militarism and worked to challenge the traditional, patriarchal definitions of family with feminism as well as gay and lesbian inclusion.

In the final sentences of the statement's section on antisemitism, NJA first mentioned Israel when they wrote that manifestations of antisemitism included judging Israel "by standards other than those used for other countries, or when all Jews are held responsible for Israeli government actions." The platform section ended with an endorsement of coalition building, stating, "As key to ending Jewish oppression, we in NJA will make alliances with other oppressed groups on the basis of mutual respect and struggle." In a section on racism, too, NJA members pledged to "build alliances" across racial, ethnic, and other boundaries, observing that the alliances would "seek to end Jewish isolation and foster mutual respect for the goals of all peoples." Recognizing how the Zionist consensus had contributed to this isolation, NJA voiced support for affirmative action, civil liberties, environmental protection, and the labor movement.

Committed to Israel yet open to criticism of Israeli policies, NJA members created a place for themselves as progressive Jews who could join forces with people of color in coalitions for change. In so doing, they were among the first Jewish organizational leaders to openly build alliances based on an explicit acknowledgment of the interrelatedness of antisemitism and white supremacy. Members wrote that the schism between Black and (white) Jewish Americans "weakens the fight against antisemitism and racism." They also included in their platform an antiracist plank that linked the rise in all forms of racism to the nation's "economic deterioration" and also linked the "Arab-Israel conflict" to Jews' "negative view of Arabs and Islam."[37]

The final pages of NJA's platform, separate from its "Statement of Purpose," focused specifically on Israel and Palestine, noting that the struggles for Middle East peace were part of the "mutual responsibility" of all members of the "Jewish people." The organization's members allied themselves with those working for "peace and justice" in Israel and affirmed the right of Jews and Palestinians to self-determination. NJA declared that "a comprehensive peace settlement is a necessary first step to returning Israel to a position of non-alignment in the superpower conflict." They called for an end to Israel's occupation, to terrorist violence on all sides, and to Jewish settlement building on Palestinian land. They supported negotiations with the PLO, a highly controversial stand, even when aligned with firm commitments to Israel's safety. They wrote that Israel's alliances with "repressive dictatorships" such as the one in South Africa, among others, violate their "sense of Jewish ethics."[38]

NJA's Middle East Task Force also worked to provide an alternative, in this case to the American Jewish forced consensus on Israel and Zionism. In an interview with Ezra Berkley Nepon, sociologist Gordon Fellman, who served as cochair of the Middle East Task Force for five years (1982–87), noted that NJA struggled as an organization with tensions that resulted from both the anti-Muslim sentiment among Jews and the anti-Israel sentiment among activists on the left. Fellman expressed his hope that American Jews would not have to choose between the activism of the left and belonging to the Jewish community. The organization's task, he said, "was to persuade Jews not to be anti-Arab racists and to persuade Leftists not to be anti-Israel rejectionists. I found that kind of exciting," he added, "a challenge because nobody else was doing that at the time. Within Agenda were people who wanted to give up on the Jewish community and stand firmly with the Left. I, and a number of others thought that was a mistake and we should really be working in the Jewish community to change consciousness as well as on the Left. We went through this over and over again."[39]

Walking a fine line with regard to Israel, NJA members acknowledged that Israel and Zionism were often the key issues that isolated American Jews from peace and justice activism and also kept activist coalitions in a state of tension with American Jewish communal life. In maintaining this balance, NJA served as a magnet for those disaffected from Jewish life. As Aliza Becker of the American Jewish Peace Archive put it, "NJA's Middle East grassroots organizing engaged large numbers of American Jews who had not been raised as Zionists, and others who had abandoned Zionism as adults. For them, Zionism had come to mean uncritical support for the settlement enterprise supported by most American Jewish organizations." Becker identified the low threshold for dissent from American Zionism as the reason so many American Jews had departed the American Jewish community in the 1960s and 1970s: "This [uncritical] support [for Israel] was among the reasons that many of these Jews were unaffiliated," she explained, "but they still longed for Jewish community. NJA filled that need."[40]

Indeed, NJA's public statements drew on that idea directly, indicating how the "stifling of dissent" in the American Jewish community had led to widespread disaffection and how NJA's inclusiveness countered that current and encouraged Jewish affiliation, even unity, among those previously "unconnected": "To those Jews whose images of Jewish life and Jewish goals differ from our own we say let us join in dialogue. In the spirit of ahavat Yisrael, love and acceptance of all Jews, let us try to develop an authentic Jewish unity, one that grows out of respect and understanding for diversity, and not from enforced unanimity, intolerance, or the stifling of dissent."[41] NJA statements were carefully crafted not to oppose any one idea, organization, or individual. Instead, its members hoped to supplement—perhaps supplant—old agendas and initiate new conversations about Israel and other topics in American Jewish life.

In distancing itself from mainstream Jewish perspectives on issues including American Zionism and Israel, NJA members created room for resistance to the conservative politics of the Reagan administration, including battles over civil rights and American military interventions in Central America. American Jewish communal leaders had for decades marginalized dissent, limiting access to Jewish voices that criticized or rejected American Zionism. NJA's positions, therefore, demonstrate the degree to which American Jews' unconditional allegiance to Israel diminished their capacity to ally with liberal and left activists.

In the 1950s, Zukerman and the American Council for Judaism were sources for journalists from Black newspapers reporting on anticolonialism. In the 1980s, NJA leaders served as sources for journalists from Black newspapers exploring American Jewish support for conservative leadership in Israel and the United States and how that support, in part, led to tension between Black and Jewish Americans. In 1984, for example, mainstream Jewish Zionist leaders decried the anti-Jewish comments of the Reverend Jesse Jackson, a minister, civil rights activist, and presidential candidate. They called out the positions taken by Jackson and others who allied with civil rights and anticolonialist movements, criticized Israel as a "theocracy," called Prime Minister Begin a "terrorist," and urged Israeli talks with the PLO to advance peacemaking.[42]

American Jewish leaders linked Jackson's comments to his pro-PLO and therefore anti-Israel and anti-Jewish worldview. The Jewish Defense League disrupted Jackson's campaign events, calling him a "Jew hater."[43] In the mainstream *Detroit Free Press*, Hyman Bookbinder, Washington representative of the American Jewish Committee, called Jackson a "scoundrel" and an "opponent of Israel and Jewish American interests." To counter that, the *Michigan Chronicle*, a Black newspaper, printed a statement of NJA members who asserted that Bookbinder did not speak for "the general Jewish community." They noted that Presidents Truman and Nixon had made remarks similar to those of Jackson but had not apologized as Jackson had. They praised Reverend Jackson's work to channel money from the military budget to social welfare policies. And they concluded by noting that Bookbinder and other Jewish leaders would do well to move beyond "name-calling" to "engage in dialogue," in that way following the model Jackson provided with regard to the "Israeli-Palestinian impasse."[44]

Some Reform movement and other Jewish leaders offered even more poignant explanations for Jewish attacks on Rev. Jackson. Political scientist Adolph Reed Jr. quoted Albert Vorspan, president of the Union of American Hebrew Congregations (the Reform movement in American Judaism), who noted the heated response to Jackson's comments. "For many Jews," Vorspan said, "this is an excuse to bolt concern for [B]lacks, cities, and the rest of it. For others, it will be an excuse to go for Ronald Reagan." Reed also quoted Arthur Hertzberg, former president of the American Jewish Congress, as saying that the "revolt against liberalism among middle-class Jews" was "motivated by a desire to protect their class interests as 'haves.'"[45]

NJA leaders also challenged reports that cited antisemitism as a justification for military involvement in Nicaragua. The Reagan administration joined the Anti-Defamation League in using these reports to gain Jewish support for funding the Contras, paramilitary operations to undermine Nicaragua's socialist regime, the Sandinistas. The Sandinistas' ties to the PLO were commonly known, as they formed partly in the spirit of revolutionary and national liberationist movements and partly because of Israel's long-standing ties to the Somoza dictatorship, which was overthrown by the Sandinistas in 1978–79. Divisions among American Jews about Nicaragua fell along political lines. Mainstream newspapers had reported that Elliot Abrams, Reagan's assistant secretary of state for human rights and humanitarian affairs, stated that "communism poses a very real threat to their very survival as Jews [in Nicaragua]." To counter this reporting, the *Atlanta World*, a Black newspaper, published an article noting that NJA members took a "fact-finding mission to Nicaragua" in August 1984. "We intend to investigate," NJA members stated, "whether anti-Semitism exists in Nicaragua or whether these charges are part of a plan to manipulate Jewish concern about anti-Semitism."[46] The delegation found "no anti-Semitism" and indeed almost no people who identified as Jewish in Nicaragua. As Marjorie Hyer of the *Washington Post* reported, NJA members "charged the Reagan administration with using allegations of anti-Semitism in Nicaragua to fuel 'an all-out, full court press effort' directed at the American Jewish community 'to bolster support for its policies' against the Sandinista regime."[47]

Finally, in contests over Israel and Palestine at the United Nations Conferences for Women, held beginning in 1975 to commemorate the International Women's Year, NJA members sought to maintain Black/Jewish alliances and keep open the possibility of peacemaking between Jews and Palestinians. In 1975 in Mexico City, in 1980 in Copenhagen, and then in 1985 in Nairobi, these conferences drew from more than one hundred governments and nongovernmental organizations. They focused on women's employment, health, and education and their rights regarding property, child custody, and inheritance. These events also sought to promote peace and gender equality.

Some Jewish feminist activists reported feeling attacked at these conferences, as anticolonialist activists criticized Israel; allegiance to Israel prevented the Jewish activists from joining coalitions opposing apartheid, for example.[48] Journalists at the *Philadelphia Tribune*, a Black newspaper, turned to NJA members to learn that these sentiments were not shared by all members of the American Jewish community. NJA executive director Reena Bernards noted that at the 1975 and 1980 United Nations conferences, "divisions over the Middle East overshadowed the programs." But NJA leadership stepped in to challenge these divisions, the *Philadelphia Tribune* reported.[49] Christie Balka, then cochair of the Middle East Task Force, who traveled with NJA for the 1985 UN Decade for Women conference in Nairobi, Kenya, said the group sought to have a "mediating influence on the [Middle East] discussion."[50] Their mediating influence, however, was only made possible by their walking a fine line with regard to Israel. In Nairobi, NJA leaders organized the first public United Nations forum in which Israeli and Palestinian representatives acknowledged one another's right to national self-determination. Importantly, the dialogue guidelines agreed to by both parties in this historic workshop labeled the equation of Zionism and racism "divisive and inaccurate" and described Zionism as a "movement for Jewish national liberation."[51] Five hundred women from many countries attended. In preparation for the meeting, the *Philadelphia Tribune* reported, "Jewish, Arab, and Black women" held forums "to prepare for the potential polarization that could occur."[52]

Upon their return from Nairobi, NJA members continued to run feminist gatherings to talk about the Nairobi conference and the divides among Black women, Arab/Muslim women, and (white) Jewish women.[53] They committed to these gatherings despite being attacked by some Jewish leaders as those who *promoted* "Zionism as racism" (though NJA had protested this UN resolution) and who spoke of Israelis only as Nazis.[54] NJA's attempts to bridge the divides among American Jews and Arab/Muslim and Black Americans involved in anticolonialist movements, however, did not have significant staying power. Self-identified Jewish women remained largely, but not entirely, absent from coalitions with women of color in anticolonialist causes such as the fight against South African apartheid. Jewish activists often cited Israel/Palestine as the central reason for this absence.[55]

Still, New Jewish Agenda created rare Jewish forums for American Jews—rabbis as well as laypeople—to give voice to dissent from unconditional Jewish support for Zionism and Israel and American Jewish communal ties to conservative American foreign and domestic policies. In 1982, Philip Klutznick, former president of the World Jewish Congress and secretary of commerce in the Carter administration, spoke to two hundred people at a meeting sponsored by New Jewish Agenda, insisting he had a "'moral obligation' to speak out rather than be silent as some have advised him." "We are doing great damage to Israel by our acts that give rise to serious questions of credibility of our own American Jewish institutions, our own Jewish American leaders who are perceived in too many places as acting as rubber stamps," Klutznick told his audience at Temple Sinai in Washington, DC. He reaffirmed his commitment to Israel's security but ended with a wistful lament: "I wish our Jewish community was as open and respected differences and the right to differ as much as the State of Israel," he said.[56] For his stand, Klutznick was often cited as both a "prominent American Jew" and an "advocate for dissent" who had criticized Prime Minister Begin and Israeli policies.[57]

From the start, critics of New Jewish Agenda's "right to differ" noted its membership overlap with Breira. With echoes of anti-communist crusades, journalists accused NJA of using Breira's membership "list."[58] Certainly NJA counted members who had been in Breira, and among its award recipients was Breira supporter Morris Schappes.[59] Yet its path differed from Breira's because its members acted on their "right to differ" in diverse campaigns. According to one report in the Jewish press, "The New Jewish Agenda which had leaned over backwards soft-pedaling criticism of Israel in order to avoid the fate of Breira finally spoke out" during the war in Lebanon.[60] The organization's response to the war marked a high tide of American Jewish dissent on Israeli policies and actions, challenging the threshold of acceptable dissent and offering further proof that no consensus existed among American Jews. It also placed NJA at the forefront of political controversy.

American Jews and the War in Lebanon: "We've Come to a Watershed Now"

On June 6, 1982, Israeli troops, led by Defense Minister Ariel Sharon, invaded Lebanon in an initiative called Operation Peace for Galilee with the goal of preventing the Palestine Liberation Organization from launching military attacks on Israel. Israel was aided by American military operations.[61] Israeli troops traveled far beyond Israel's initial territorial limits and left behind massive civilian casualties and destruction, in part because of their use of American cluster bombs. American politicians largely supported the invasion, as it aided American interests in targeting Soviet-supported Syrians.

American interests in the Cold War and American Jews' interests in unconditional Zionism were thus closely aligned. American and Israeli leaders felt that Israel's war in Lebanon clearly advanced American Cold War interests in the region, while others, such as attorney and activist Colin A. Moore, asked in the *Amsterdam News*, a Black newspaper, "Lebanon, a New Vietnam?" Moore's analysis noted what the two wars had in common, including a lack of American "honesty and prudence," support for the "losing side," and opposition against democracy and truly representative government.[62] On the whole, he wrote, the war "further tarnished" world opinion of Israel "outside of the political right."[63]

At the same time, mainstream journalists like Carl Rowan writing in Black publications questioned American funding of Israel in the wake of the invasion. Rowan had headed the US Information Agency in the mid-1960s. In the wake of the Lebanese invasion, he suggested that both the PLO and Israel were acting like terrorists.[64] Given the fact that the leaders of American Jewish Zionist organizations supported the war, these journalists saw mainstream Jewry as largely allied with the political right.

New Jewish Agenda was the only Jewish organization to publicly oppose the war from its beginning, which was soon after the organization's founding in 1982. NJA leaders published a full-page advertisement in the *New York Times* on June 30 "denouncing the Israeli invasion of Lebanon politically and spiritually, and signed by the entire membership of NJA, including more than 40 American rabbis." At the top of the advertisement was a quote from an Israeli popular song from 1973, "I promise you my little girl that this will be the last war," and was followed by the organization's first public statement, balancing its commitments to Jewish life in Israel and outside of Israel: "We are American Jews deeply concerned about the physical and moral survival of our people and the Jewish State of Israel." Quoting coverage of the Israeli left, the Peace Now movement, in the Israeli newspaper *Haaretz*, the signers of the ad declared, "There has never been a war like this in Israel's past." Laying equal blame at the hands of Israelis, Palestinians, Syrians, and Lebanese soldiers and leaders, NJA members urged a withdrawal of Israeli and Syrian troops from Lebanon, mutual recognition, and work toward a "just and viable peace."[65]

In this new age, characterized by a new, rising conservatism among American Jews and a low threshold of acceptable dissent from Israeli policies, the Israeli invasion of Lebanon tested the American Jewish consensus on Israel as perhaps no war had before.[66] While NJA members stopped short of rejecting Zionism or questioning Israel's right to exist, they and others voiced their opposition to Israeli actions. *Village Voice* columnist Nat Hentoff, who wrote a series critical of Israel's invasion, said that he had received letters from American Jews who were also deeply upset but had "no contacts anymore in the Jewish community . . . and felt they had no place to go." "These people would be lost to any organized Jewish identity without the New Jewish Agenda," he observed.[67]

Yet some organized Jewish religious leaders would not tolerate such dissent, rejecting NJA's dissent on Israel and their support of domestic issues such as LGBTQIA+ rights. In 1982 three rabbis formed a *beit din*, a religious Jewish court, and excommunicated several NJA members along with others, including Noam Chomsky. The rabbis criticized NJA's support of "Palestinian and homosexual rights." Reena Bernards, one of those who had been excommunicated, noted that rabbis who had composed the *beit din* had been "harassing our [NJA] chapter in Boston." Rabbi David Werb, president of the Massachusetts Board of Rabbis, which represented Orthodox, Conservative, and Reform rabbis, challenged the "excommunication." "I think it's a political means to express chagrin at the criticism of Israel," he said. "Personally, I share that chagrin, but not the method they used to express it."[68]

Despite this backlash, other American Jews followed suit in publicly criticizing the war. Sixty-seven American Jewish scholars, writers, and rabbis signed an advertisement published in the *New York Times* in July 1982 in support of Israel's Peace Now movement. The ad expressed "grave misgivings" over the fighting in Lebanon and advocated "national self-determination" for the Palestinians while positioning its signers as aligned with what they saw as the authentic vision of Zionism, dedicated to the liberation of Jews and democracy in the Middle East. The ad also posed a question to American Jews: "Is it not time for us as supporters of Israel to speak out critically about those Israeli policies we know to be mistaken, self-defeating, and contrary to the original Zionist vision?" The signers, a group that included Saul Bellow, E. L. Doctorow, Alfred Kazin, Irving Howe, Meyer Schapiro, Daniel Bell, Nathan Glazer, and Seymour Martin Lipset, also noted the silence of American Jews on the invasion: "The views we express here are widespread in Israel, as they are among American Jews. Unfortunately, although Israelis have spoken up in opposition to their Government's policies, American Jews have been largely silent, thereby possibly contributing to the Israeli Government's misperception that American Jews support it in this war."[69]

While liberal American Jews, many of them Zionists, wrestled with the ethics of the war, and while hundreds of thousands of Israelis marched in the streets to protest the massacre, some American Jewish leaders began to respond harshly to media coverage that was critical of Israel. Writing in the Omaha *Jewish Press*, for example, Rabbi Irving Greenberg identified the Jewish critics of the war as a few "professors from Cambridge." Echoing the urgency of equations of criticism of Israel with antisemitism, he concluded that "some of the media vis-a-vis Israel represents a feckless internalization of the messages of the delegitimation of Israel campaign being pursued by would-be genocidal enemies."[70]

* * *

Over the course of that summer, Zionist American Jewish leaders began coaching members of the community on how to respond to the negative press Israel was receiving. A memo sent in August from the American Israel Public Affairs Committee (AIPAC) to the group's members spoke too of "a coordinated and well-oiled campaign" that was "producing a volume of anti-Israel letters, phone calls, and ads aimed at the Congress and the White House in unprecedented numbers." AIPAC advised Jewish leaders to present Israel as the "victim" of PLO raids and to promise a victory over terrorism, over Syria, and over the Soviets. They encouraged their members to issue reassurance that "Israel's action in Lebanon serves the strategic interests of the United States and will help promote a lasting peace in the region."[71] The Israeli embassy in Washington distributed memos accusing the media and "some governments" of a "disinformation and propaganda campaign," and they sought to dispel "baseless rumors" of "fabricated" casualty numbers.[72]

To respond to criticism of Israel, some Jews were advised to repeat standard narratives, reminding readers of the anticolonial Jewish heroes who defeated the colonizing British to establish the State of Israel. In August, Thomas A. Mann, former chairman of the Conference of Presidents of Major Jewish Organizations, distributed to leaders of mainstream Jewish organizations a memo titled "'Morality' and the War in Lebanon." The memo challenged what he described as the "severely critical media attention" focused on Israel's war in Lebanon. Mann assured his readers that this was the "right war at the right time" and that Israel was fighting with "uncommon restraint." Above all, Mann pushed back against the idea that the PLO were "anti-colonial insurgents, deserving of sympathy." And he offered a corrective: "The anti-colonial battle was fought by the Jews in Palestine against the British," he wrote. He went on to say that "Palestinian nationalism has been fatally flawed from the outset because it was based not on a desire to send colonialists home, but on a desire to expel Jews who are already home and have no other."[73]

Some of the coaching on how to respond to the negative press that Israel was receiving also relied on traditional fundraising tropes equating the safety of American Jews with the urgent need for an American Jewish consensus on Israel. Beginning in mid-July, presidents of New England Jewish organizations, for example, received a mailing titled "The Propaganda War: We Cannot Remain Silent." The goal was to counter any feelings of "complacency" as Israel sank still further in global world opinion and to put American Jews to work repairing Israel's reputation.

The document indicated that it was "critical" that Congress maintain its support for Israel. Israel's attacks supported American interests in the area, the authors asserted, and would lead to greater safety for the region. American Jews had the responsibility to respond to what the document described as a "well-financed and concerted Arab campaign" against Israel and to restore the "traditional support" Israel had "within the American public and in Washington." Recipients were urged to write letters and to "increase your contribution to the UJA [United Jewish Appeal, the umbrella philanthropic organization for mainstream Jewish groups]."[74]

In September 1982, the Anti-Defamation League released a study prepared by public opinion analyst David Garth, who had worked on multiple New York City mayoral campaigns. The study examined the nightly newscasts of the three major television networks from June through August. Garth alleged that distortions and biases had crept into reporting about the number of civilian casualties inflicted by the Israeli military.

CBS and ABC rejected the Anti-Defamation League's charge that their coverage had turned public opinion in the United States against Israel. They did concede, however, that for various technical reasons, the reporting of Palestinian casualty figures had been exaggerated. News stories about the ADL report cited especially its focus on visual coverage of "the wounded or dead," on an image of "Yasir [sic] Arafat holding a baby." The *New York Times* quoted the report directly: "Lingering and graphic daily coverage of the wounded and suffering," the report said, "overwhelmed or overlooked the political, historical and military context of the situation."[75] Coverage of the war in Lebanon drew attention to the Cold War alignment of American and Israeli political strategies, an alignment supported by many American Jews.[76] They saw Israel's safety as under siege and also felt that their own safety was under siege.

The division among American Jews over the war in Lebanon was the newest chapter in the long history of Jewish disagreements over Zionism and Israel and the threshold of American Jewish dissent with regard to both. It was also a strong example of the role played by American Jewish mainstream organizational leaders in supporting American foreign policy. All major mainstream Jewish organizations supported the invasion. An NBC poll showed that a majority of Americans of all religions did not support it, while an American Jewish Committee poll showed American Jews evenly split.[77] Just a few days later, the *New York Times* ran an article under the headline "Discord among U.S. Jews over Israel Seems to Grow." After first stating that "virtually all American Jews support Israel's invasion of Lebanon," reporter Paul Montgomery noted that supporters of Israel interviewed for the story suggested that "critics of Israel in the United States had become more vociferous, but not more numerous." Yet writer and activist Leonard Fein pointed out, "There was practically no debate in 1967 or 1973. This is Israel's first optional war, and the first with large numbers of civilian casualties. This creates an emotional distance that permits—even encourages—debate."[78]

Investigative journalist and author I. F. Stone, another independent Jewish voice on Zionism, also reported that dissent was "much more widespread than ever before," commenting that "people who used to call him and Noam Chomsky 'stooges of the P.L.O.' were now joining him in petitions for peace." Calling the group who had signed the July letter "dissidents," Norman Podhoretz, whom Montgomery identified as "the editor of *Commentary* Magazine and perhaps the most unbending supporter of Israel among secular intellectuals," dismissed them as people "who had shown little concern for Israel in the past." Podhoretz noted that "groups that raise money for Israel are exceeding projections since the invasion of Lebanon."[79]

The *New York Times* article largely sidestepped the history of American Jewish critics of Zionism who, like NJA members, also cared about Israel and American Jewish life. One rabbi interviewed for the article suggested "a psychological component of the dissent," which he labeled that of a "self-hating Jew."[80] The words of Rabbi Balfour Brickner, a longtime social justice activist and liberal Zionist, closed the story. He said the invasion of Lebanon had "touched a nerve of pain in an ambivalent Jewish community." He rejected the idea that "dissent" on Israel's invasion "gave comfort to Israel's enemies." That, he claimed, was the "kind of argument that's trying to make everybody march in lockstep." Rabbi Brickner used an antiwar trope utilized by others who dissented from Zionism. "It's 'My country right or wrong,'" said Brickner, "but I've never adopted that for America and I'll be damned if I'll adopt it for Israel."[81]

Perhaps the most urgent response to criticism of Israel's war in Lebanon was the eleven-page article titled "J'Accuse," written by Norman Podhoretz and published in *Commentary* in September. The title "J'Accuse" was taken from a document written by novelist Emile Zola in support of Alfred Dreyfus in 1898 France, when Dreyfus faced false accusations of treason because of antisemitism.

Podhoretz argued that the "explosion of invectives" in attacks on Israel was "unprecedented in the public discourse of this country." He denied that the attacks, now increasingly from "respectable" media outlets who historically supported Israel, signaled Israel's loss of "moral stature." He rejected comparisons between Israel and Vietnam. Instead, Podhoretz posed a counternarrative that he analogized with allied troops landing in Normandy. "The purpose of the Israelis in 1982 was to liberate Lebanon from the PLO," he wrote, asserting that the "Lebanese people greeted the Israelis as liberators." Israel remained, for him, a "light unto the nations." Most vociferous were his harsh words for those who had compared Israel's treatment of Palestinians to the Nazis' treatment of Jews. Those who betrayed Israel were antisemites, he asserted, and also guilty "of the broader sin of faithlessness to the interests of the United States and indeed to the values of Western civilization as a whole."[82]

Editors of the *New York Jewish Week* cited Podhoretz's arguments, asserting, "We must therefore sadly agree with the editor of *Commentary*, who said recently that he sees the worldwide media campaign against Israel as a sophisticated case of anti-Semitism that had been bottled up for a number of decades . . . and was now testing the waters and coming out into the open."[83]

Although the PLO withdrew from Lebanon in August, the following month brought additional tragic news that created still more division and disillusionment among American Jews. Toward the end of September, Israeli military officials controlled an area in which the Phalange, the Lebanese Christian right-wing militia, slaughtered thousands of Palestinian families in the refugee camps of Sabra and Shatila, near West Beirut. Estimates of those murdered ran from several hundred to several thousand. Israeli troops not only looked on but abetted the militia.

The tragic losses resulting from the Sabra and Shatila massacre weighed heavily on many American Jews. A *Newsweek* poll found that 65 percent of American Jews "considered Israel at least partially responsible for the killings."[84] Many people reckoned with the idea that their support of Israel was implicated in the tragedies. A group of Jewish Bostonians wrote to Israeli diplomats and local, state, and communal leaders declaring, "As American Jews, it is incumbent upon us to urge the Israeli government to come to its senses. For too long we have lobbied for Israel blindly."[85]

For their part, New Jewish Agenda members continued to write letters to Jewish and mainstream newspapers arguing against the war.[86] They sent cables to Israeli political leaders.[87] Defense Minister Sharon resigned in February 1983 after an Israeli commission recommended his dismissal or resignation when it discovered that Israeli military leaders were "indirectly responsible" for the massacre of Palestinians. A few months later, leaders of the State of Israel Bonds Organization invited former defense minister Sharon to speak at a fundraising dinner in Philadelphia. NJA members protested during the event. Rabbi Devorah Bartnoff spoke on behalf of NJA, calling Sharon "not an appropriate representative of Israel" because his "own people have held him responsible for the Shatila and Sabra massacre."[88]

"Across a Threshold"

By the 1980s, most American Jews had largely been told a single story about Israel. They believed Israel ensured Jewish life, safety, and survival and that Israel's survival depended on unconditional American Jewish support. Yet the Sabra and Shatila massacre awoke some American Jews to the need for more information. In an interview in *New York Magazine* in October 1982, for example, Rabbi Alexander Schindler, who led the Reform movement from 1973 to 1996, said that the relationship of American Jews to Israel had changed dramatically as a result of the war in Lebanon. "Maybe," he said, "our past silence in some way contributed to the present nightmare. But even if it didn't, we are across a threshold."

The article reported that Schindler, close to Israel's prime minister Menachem Begin, had told Begin to fire Ariel Sharon on Israeli television. Schindler elaborated,

> We haven't been *completely* silent in the past . . . but we've certainly been reticent. I fear that our past *public* support of the government of Israel, no matter its policy and no matter our private reservations, was used by the Israelis to project a world Jewish community completely in accord with its goals and methods. We were used like cows. We were milked for both financial and moral support—and for the influence we could bring to bear on Washington—and when we were used up we were put out to pasture. . . . But we've come to a watershed now, and our open criticism will continue and increase.[89]

An aide to Prime Minister Begin later reported that Begin called Schindler a "traitor."[90]

Rabbi Schindler spoke publicly about how the war in Lebanon had led to "widespread soul-searching" among American Jews. "We have slipped into the sloppy equation which says that Judaism equals Zionism equals Israel," he told Reform rabbis at their annual conference. And he added, "We do ourselves irreparable harm when we make Israel our surrogate synagogue."[91] President Reagan's support for Israel may have been good for Jews, Rabbi Schindler suggested, but Reagan also chose to "multiply missiles rather than mitigate human misery." He urged American Jews to form closer ties with the poor, who were "cry[ing] for relief." "Will we heed them or block our ears so long as we see President Reagan's benign smile when he speaks of Israel?" Rabbi Schindler wanted Jews to cease being a "one-issue community."[92]

For his part, as head of the Reform movement and an ardent Zionist, Rabbi Schindler proved largely untouchable and escaped harsh criticism from other Jewish leaders. In the late 1990s, the *New York Times* consulted Rabbi Schindler for an article that ran under the headline "Feeling Abandoned by Israel, Many American Jews Grow Angry." Rabbi Schindler called the moment "an internal convulsion" in a long line of historical contests among Jews. "I'm less nervous than other people are," he said, "because from the perspective of Jewish history there was never a time in Jewish life of ideological consensus."[93]

The war in Lebanon challenged the low threshold of acceptable dissent on Israel and American Zionism. According to one scholar, after the war in Lebanon, "The public positions that only a few years before had made pariahs of Breira advocates were now being expressed by members of the establishment."[94] Yet some critics believed that the dissent of NJA members did not suffice because Zionism—even liberal Zionism—had no place on the left as a settler colonialist ideology. They believed that it stopped short of challenging the true history of Israel's founding, its violence against Arabs and Palestinians, and the discrimination against Mizrahi Jews. According to these critics, the war in Lebanon and the Sabra and Shatila massacre led only to the "safe" criticism of "Begin and Sharon," a "close-to-condemnation of Israel's atrocities," which meant that "Zionism need not be reexamined."[95]

Ultimately, US foreign aid to Israel did not decrease, and mainstream American Jewish organizations did not lessen their focus on unconditional Zionism. Accordingly, the distance between American Jews and civil rights and other social justice coalitions remained, perhaps even widened. The very narrow and fragile bridge connecting organized American Jewry to these coalitions was maintained by New Jewish Agenda members and a few Reform Jewish leaders. Ultimately, their bridge proved almost too narrow and fragile to constitute any real connection.

American Jews, Zionism, and the 1983 March on Washington: "Israel Exempt"

Civil rights leaders planned the 1983 March on Washington, in part, to commemorate the two decades since the 1963 March on Washington for Jobs and Freedom at which the Reverend Dr. Martin Luther King Jr. had made his famous "I Have a Dream" speech. The idea was originally proposed by the Reverend Walter E. Fauntroy, a civil rights leader and congressman who had served as the District of Columbia coordinator for the 1963 march. Dr. King's widow, Coretta Scott King, borrowed her husband's phrase when she said that the march's goal was to create a new "'coalition of conscience' committed to the thesis that 'our problems cannot be considered apart from one another, that the problems of unemployment, the arms race and retrenchments of civil rights enforcement . . . are inter-related.'"[96]

Leaders of the march insisted that this was not to be a trip down memory lane because they were marching with the urgency of the moment, as the movement struggled against the era's conservatism. As one journalist wrote, it was a "strong indictment lodged against Reagan Administration policies that was a primary catalyst in bringing this broad base of people together."[97] The multi-issue nature of the march gave many civil rights organizations pause, and in fact the National Association for the Advancement of Colored People and the Urban League did not support the event, citing their fear that its broad focus would lack appeal and thus not draw significant numbers. They also cited a lack of funding.[98]

Scholar Manning Marable, however, wrote that the organizers, many with firm ties to the political left, saw the expansive call for jobs, peace, and freedom and the coalition of civil, women's, LGBTQIA+, labor, disability, and environmental rights activists as keys to rejecting what he described as "Reaganism, racism, and economic reaction through the creation of the broadest possible front of liberal, moderate, and progressive constituencies."[99] Marable observed that some Black leaders bowed to "corporate and administration interests" in avoiding the march, as "the left was an open and unambiguous current within the rally."[100]

Many Jewish groups cited the criticism of Israel among some liberal and left-wing groups in refusing to participate in the march. Leaders of the Anti-Defamation League cited the criticism among civil rights leaders specifically. In the *New York Jewish Week*, Walter K. Lewis reported that "major Jewish organizations which supported the civil rights movement in the 1960s are faced with the problem of how to abstain discreetly from a 20th anniversary observance of the 1963 march on Washington that is tainted by anti-Israel, pro-PLO and Soviet propaganda overtones."[101]

Jewish communal and religious leaders mainly echoed these ideas. In an article titled "Why AJCommittee Won't 'March on Washington,'" Donald Feldstein, the AJC's executive vice president, wrote that in the early 1960s, civil rights had "clear-cut goals" for equal access to public services, mortgages, and jobs. "Jews gave selflessly of their energy and substance in support of equal rights," he wrote. But now, he noted, Jewish and Black Americans are not "of one mind on how best to end racism's legacy in America."

Feldstein then patronizingly scolded the march's conveners for linking domestic civil rights to foreign policy questions, which he dismissed as irrelevant to civil rights goals. While most of the march leaders were "admirable and respected Americans," he wrote, "they have repeatedly shown themselves to be no friends of the Jews or of Israel."[102] Equating dissent on Israel and Zionism with antisemitism, Zionist leaders accused civil rights leaders of betraying Jewish safety.

* * *

Tolerance for American Jewish criticism of Zionism and Israel had diminished as many Black leaders broadened their worldviews and altered their positions on Palestine. Rev. Fauntroy, one of the leaders of the march, was typical in this regard. In August 1975, he and other members of the Congressional Black Caucus supported a resolution opposing the expulsion of Israel from the United Nations. The resolution compared the "people of Israel" to "the oppressed peoples of Southern Africa," citing Israel as the product of the Jewish people's struggle for "self-determination and nationhood."[103]

In the years that followed, Fauntroy adopted the anticolonialist lessons of other global movements. In 1979, he met with Chairman Yasser Arafat of the Palestine Liberation Organization on a peacemaking mission, sparking feelings of "anger and betrayal" among Washington's Jewish community.[104] In 1982, he refused to support a congressional resolution opposing efforts to expel Israel from the UN General Assembly because of Israel's invasion of Lebanon. In response to his demonstration of support for Palestinian rights and in defense of Jewish withdrawal from the 1983 march, the *New York Jewish Week* accused Fauntroy of being a follower of "leading Arab propagandists."[105]

Supporting the 1983 march were the Jewish organizations whose leaders recently had most visibly criticized both Israel *and* the singular focus on Israel and Zionism among American Jews. New Jewish Agenda and the Reform movement's organization, the Union of American Hebrew Congregations, led by Rabbi Schindler, "unhesitatingly endorsed and took part in the march," the Jewish press reported.[106] Reform Jewish leader Albert Vorspan defended the group's decision to march. "Can one exert more influence in defense of Israel and Jewish concerns from within," he asked, "or by abandoning the field to those who wish to exploit civil rights for Third World gains?"[107]

Vorspan had worked with Dr. Martin Luther King Jr. and been active in civil rights work. He had also, like Dr. King, spoken out against the Vietnam War. His question accused those who supported the march's agenda of unthinkingly linking Israel to colonialism. But, Vorspan concluded, "to have a friend, one must be a friend. An American Jewish community which expects allies to defend and support Israel and Soviet Jewry, must learn—once again—to understand and empathize with the concerns of others as well. Coalitions, like friendships, are two way things, and the future of the American Jewish community may be adversely affected by judgments being made in the summer of 1983."[108]

The absence of mainstream Jewish groups and the controversy over Israel surrounding the 1983 march did not go unnoticed. In the Baltimore *Afro-American*, reporter George W. Collins commented on America's "drastically different . . . military posture" in 1983 as compared to 1963 and focused on that and other "sharp contrasts" between the two. The political and economic climate was surely different, as was the presidential response. While Kennedy had greeted the march's organizers, Reagan exited Washington and was on vacation at his ranch. "In fact," Collins wrote, "the demand by some sponsors of the march that America end its involvement in the Middle East is causing concern in the American Jewish community. Tension created by disagreement over that issue between sponsors of the march and some leaders of the Jewish community is expected to be reflected in the participation—or lack of the same—by that community."[109]

One of the planners of the march, Donna Brazile, told an interviewer that part of her work was to dispel myths about Black leadership's ability to raise both enthusiasm for the march and broader support for the march. She also worked to dispel the myth that "Black people could not raise enough money without Jewish support," which had been central to the 1963 march.[110]

New Jewish Agenda leaders tried to build support for the march within the Jewish community. To that end, Moe Rodenstein, an NJA spokesperson, and Betsy Cohen, chair of the National Steering Committee, wrote to a group of "national Jewish leaders" explaining how they themselves had come to support the march. Noting the ties between positions on Israel/Palestine and Black civil rights, Rodenstein and Cohen freely admitted that their organization's "Middle East position may differ from a few coalition members." They spoke of the role of American Jews in civil rights actions of the 1960s, adding that "New Jewish Agenda is determined not to allow a handful of people to isolate the Jewish community from people who in the past have been some of our strongest allies."

Rodenstein and Cohen, however, sounded similar notes about separating domestic and foreign policy issues and insisted that their presence was important precisely because there was disagreement on Israel: "We feel our concerns about continued support for Israel best can be expressed from within the coalition's broad umbrella," they said. If they "abandon[ed] the coalition," they feared that "the Middle East may arise as an issue and none of Israel's defenders would be around to speak out."[111]

Rodenstein advocated for the removal of "any reference to a reduction of aid to Israel" in the march's agenda and press materials. But James Zogby, executive director of the American-Arab Anti-Discrimination Committee, resisted this effort, saying that the "people who want the language to go away really want the problem to go away—and that's not going to happen."[112]

Jewish groups testified to their own intransigence on Israel and American Zionism in refusing to join the march. Bernice S. Tannenbaum, chairman of the World Zionist Organization–American Section, declared that "American Zionists and most Jews will be conspicuously absent from the ranks of the March on Washington on Aug. 27, despite the presence of the New Jewish Agenda and the Union of American Hebrew Congregations." With these words, Tannenbaum ignored the fact that both organizations counted many American Zionists as members. Here she demonstrated that the threshold of tolerance for any dissent on Zionism and Israel had shifted among American Jewish leaders. Zionists who joined coalitions with those who criticized Israel earned strong and negative responses. "This is not a bona fide commemoration," she said of the march, "because the anti-Semitic, anti-Zionist and anti-Israel views and actions of so many of its leaders and participants betray the spirit of the historic 1963 event when Martin Luther King, Jr. and Rabbi Joachim Prinz marched hand-in-hand as allies in the struggle for civil rights, social justice and [B]lack-Jewish brotherhood."[113]

Ultimately, the pressure brought by Zionist Jewish groups won the day, and leaders of the march agreed to tone down criticism of Israel in the official literature and coverage of the event. Just a few days after Tannenbaum released her statements on the march's "strange company," the *Washington Post* reported that "several Jewish groups had been at odds with March leaders in recent weeks over expansion of the March's focus to include foreign policy questions, specifically criticisms of U.S. arms shipments and involvement in the Middle East," and that "march leaders promised Jewish groups last week they would avoid any specific statements about U.S. foreign policy." Only after this concession did the American Jewish Committee grant its support to the march. The American Jewish Congress, under the leadership of Henry Siegman, ultimately decided to support the march as well.[114]

Beginning with the growing US protests over the war in Vietnam, American Jewish Zionists had carefully extricated criticism of Israel and American Zionism from broader global criticisms of colonialism and the abuses of Western militarism. The success of Jewish groups in distancing the march's agenda from these criticisms put on display the power of the forced Zionist consensus.

The march was on a Saturday, the Jewish Sabbath, and so on the night before, at the start of the Sabbath, two religious Jewish services were held, both with prominent speakers. The Reform movement's service was held at Temple Sinai, and about six hundred people attended.

Dr. Benjamin Hooks, executive director of the National Association for the Advancement of Colored People, told those who gathered, "We appreciate the support of Jews who were in the very forefront of the battle for civil rights for Blacks." Citing the controversy around Israel, Hooks said, "We must submerge our differences and remember the things that join us together and strengthen us, not the things that keep us apart." Coretta Scott King spoke too: "Jews have supported Black Americans in their quest for equality because it is morally right," she said. "It is for this same reason that responsible Black Americans will continue to vigorously oppose anti-Semitism in America." Also participating in the service were representatives of the American Jewish Congress, B'nai B'rith, and the Greater Washington Jewish Council, most of whom had agreed to support the march after references to Israel and Palestine were removed from its agenda. Rabbi Alexander Schindler delivered the benediction. "We differ from one another in color and creed," he said, "But our destinies are intertwined."[115]

As religiously observant Jews would not travel in cars, New Jewish Agenda provided guest homes and its own, second, Friday night Shabbat service so that observant Jews would not have to miss the march. This service was held at American University, with about five hundred people in attendance. Here, Martin Luther King III, age twenty-five, spoke. He was joined by Susannah Heschel, age twenty-seven, daughter of the late theologian Rabbi Abraham Joshua Heschel, in blessing the Sabbath candles.[116] Rabbi Heschel, who was active in civil rights, had been present at the 1963 march. The younger King and Heschel lit candles and recited a prayer that they dedicated to Dr. King and Rabbi Heschel. Martin Luther King III said that he "was sad about the distance now" between "all the old allies of the civil rights movement," but he predicted that "sooner or later . . . [they] would march together again."[117]

Between two hundred thousand and four hundred thousand people attended the March on Washington for Jobs, Peace, and Freedom at the Lincoln Memorial, where Dr. King's image adorned buttons and signs. Andrew Young, mayor of Atlanta, told the crowd that all "came as individuals" in 1963 but came today "as organizations." Mayor Young spoke of a "steering committee" that would "steer Americans away from death and destruction, and toward life and development." John Lewis, a member of Atlanta City Council and later the US House, said that those in attendance had a "mandate from martyrs who gave their lives for this struggle for human rights." Speakers protested against nuclear weapons, advocated for women and LGBTQIA+ rights, and linked freedom in El Salvador and throughout Latin America to Dr. King's dream.[118] Marchers, organizers, and speakers demonstrated the interconnectedness of these human rights campaigns.

Even with concessions with regard to the agenda, Siegman and others faced attacks from right-wing, Zionist Jewish leaders for their decision to participate in the march. Rael J. Isaac, author of *Breira: Counsel for Judaism*, accused Siegman in the *Jerusalem Post* of pursuing the "tired 'progressive' agenda, much of it—like so-called affirmative action (i.e. quotas)—directly contrary to Jewish interests in the U.S." Above all, Isaac accused him of having a compromised loyalty to Israel.[119] Various editorials likened Jewish participation in the march to destruction and martyrdom. "Jews decide to march on Washington for the sake of human rights," wrote Rabbi Emanuel Rackman, "even though the march includes enemies of the Jewish people and explicitly affirms that one of its goals spells the end of Israel."[120] In the *New York Jewish Week*, Walter Lewis dismissed the march as "tainted by anti-Israel, pro-PLO and Soviet propaganda overtones."[121]

The Anti-Defamation League strongly supported the idea that there was no safe place for Jews in civil rights coalitions and that Jews who marched were not loyal to the Jewish community. One month after the 1983 March on Washington, members of the Anti-Defamation League's National Executive Committee received the organization's official report prepared by Mira Lansky, described as their "Washington Fact-Finding Director." Lansky stated that the Anti-Defamation League "chose not to participate in this demonstration because of a wide range of complex and controversial issues unrelated to civil rights," noting that "chief among these was criticism of U.S. support for Israel and other democratic allies."

Lansky drew attention to communist and "Arab propagandist" connections, pointing to signs held at the march that were related to Irish independence, indigenous rights in North America, and liberation for people across Africa and the Middle East, including Palestinians. Lansky focused mainly—and inaccurately—on how each group linked its cause back to Palestinian liberation, especially in endorsing the work of the PLO. Because the American-Arab Anti-Discrimination Committee was one of the "conveners" of the march, she wrote, they were "advancing the perception of ADC as a 'civil rights' organization" and thus of Palestinian rights as a civil rights issue. Activists at the march focused on American aid to Israel, contending that the millions of dollars going to Israeli military aid annually were "needed for domestic programs." Lansky noted the contents of a cable of solidarity from Chairman Yasser Arafat of the PLO—and the presence of a few Jewish organizations, including New Jewish Agenda.[122]

Lansky expressed frustration with what she gauged as the failure of the march organizers, Representative Fauntroy and Coretta Scott King, to live up to assurances they had offered to NJA members. They had pledged that they would "publicly disavow" any "divisive" acts, such as those that were "anti-Israel or anti-Semitic or defamatory of any group in the coalition," as "inconsistent with the spirit of the march." Lansky drew attention to ADC leader and former US senator James Abourezk, in particular, for a press release from before the march in which he said that his group's members were "disappointed," particularly in Jewish groups that wanted to "exempt Israel" from calls for peace, antimilitarism, and the "self-determination of all people." Though Lansky noted that ADC leaders made no overt statements about Israel from the podium, she found one part of his speech, where he called out the "massacre of thousands of innocents in Indochina, Latin America, and Lebanon," sufficiently damning. Here again the analogies of Israel with Vietnam raised the hackles of those who balked at any criticism of Israel.[123]

* * *

When Susannah Heschel and Martin Luther King III lit Sabbath candles at the New Jewish Agenda Shabbat service the night before the 1983 March on Washington, one newspaper reported that they were trying to "rekindle" the coalition of Black and Jewish groups fighting together for civil rights. Many forces had contributed to the snuffing out of that coalition: social mobility, white privilege, suburbanization. But another powerful influence driving the withdrawal of Jewish groups from participating in the 1983 march was the forced Zionist consensus within American Jewish life.

In defending the decision of the Reform movement to join the hundreds of thousands of people who marched on Washington, Albert Vorspan wondered about the cost of other Jewish organizations' absences from coalitions for change: "Will Jewish groups ever again be able to be part of broad-based coalitions if we require a 100 percent certified kosher rating for every organization in the coalition?" he asked, referring to "pro-Israel" sentiments as "kosher." To American Jews, he asked two pointed questions: "Are we painting ourselves into a corner of irrelevance in American life? And what interest does our splendid isolation serve?"[124]

Conclusion: The End of New Jewish Agenda, outside the Consensus

In 1984, journalist Arthur Magida wrote an article published in the *Baltimore Jewish Times* about New Jewish Agenda that appeared under the headline "Radical Gadflies: Always on the Outside, the New Jewish Agenda Wants to Heal the Rift between Jews and Progressive Politics." "Jews began to leave the Left after it had excoriated Israel in the wake of the Six-Day War," Magida explained. New Jewish Agenda intended to heal that rift, insisting that its "new" agenda was really the "old agenda of American Jews." "Jews used to be concerned with social issues and justice," noted Rabbi Gerry Serotta, a leader in Breira and a cofounder of NJA. "In the last 20 years, the Jewish community has become extremely self-oriented."[125]

The diminishment of visible Jewish commitments to Black civil rights and global human rights was an important component of that transformation. Although Magida quoted Mike Tabor, a Baltimore NJA leader, on the organization's goal to "decrease tensions" between Jewish and Black Americans, Magida himself steered clear of mentioning the civil rights march of the previous year.[126]

But for some, the 1983 March on Washington had demonstrated the extreme "self-orientation" cited by Rabbi Serotta. The absence of anti- and non-Zionism in American Jewish life was notable. Leaders of some mainstream American Jewish organizations felt that American Zionism and therefore American Jewishness could not be aligned with political commitments to broader struggles for justice. To march and work alongside those who criticized Israel was too great a threat, and in this way, the march proves an instructive example of the threshold of dissent on Zionism in the 1980s.

The end of New Jewish Agenda is also instructive. In a 1995 examination of NJA, historian Jack Wertheimer noted that the organization had achieved some major successes, gaining "communal legitimation" with "its chapters gaining admission to the local Jewish council or Jewish federations" in Kansas City, New Haven, Ann Arbor, and Los Angeles.[127] Wertheimer contrasted NJA favorably with Breira. While Breira presented itself as the "alternative" to the "established" American Jewish community, he observed, NJA embraced "a deliberate program of seeking inclusion in that very establishment."[128]

So if NJA members managed to walk this fine line, what led to its end in 1992–93? Leaders suggested that the organization folded for myriad reasons. Among them were its grassroots nature, which led to a lack of funding; infighting among progressive Jews about issues and strategies to bring about change; and the displacement of multi-issue organizations with single-issue organizations. Some believed that the organization had focused too little on the Middle East, while others said that attacks on Israel/Palestine led ultimately to the tensions that brought about its decline.

Ezra Berkely Nepon, who wrote the only dedicated history of NJA, observed that the marriage of domestic human rights campaigns with advocacy for Palestinian rights led to the organization's end. "NJA was isolated," Nepon wrote, "because the mainstream Jewish community was not prepared to embrace NJA's progressive visions of a two-state solution in Israel/Palestine and a sanctified place in the community for Lesbian and Gay Jews."[129] Ethan Bloch, the last chair of NJA's Middle East Task Force, noted its internal divisions were "partly along Zionist vs. non-Zionist lines," though he pointed out that "'non-Zionist' did not mean 'anti-Zionist' [because] the NJA platform always supported the right of Israel to exist." "If we were naive about the mainstream Jewish community," he continued,

> we were completely unprepared for the unbelievable intolerance for dissent found in that world. Our real crime, as it were, was ultimately neither image, nor naivete, nor even leftist views, but our explicit belief in the

need to break the hegemony that the mainstream Jewish organizations had, and particularly to challenge the one-sided views they promoted in the 1980s about the Israeli/Palestinian conflict. NJA's bold stance opposing the 1982 war in Lebanon, at a time when public Jewish criticism of Israeli government policies was even more rare than today, was both a catalyst for NJA's early growth and a source of much enmity.[130]

Some of the most virulent attacks on NJA emerged from Americans for a Safe Israel, the same organization to which Rael Isaac belonged when she wrote the attack on Breira a decade earlier. In 1987 Isaac wrote a pamphlet titled *The New Anti-Jewish Agenda* that attacked NJA leaders' work as undermining American support for Israel. In 1990, the World Zionist Organization journal *Midstream* published another piece by Isaac attacking NJA: in this, she wrote that the organization's members were "a step ahead of the PLO in its zeal to advance that organization's interest." Locating the origins of their dissent only outside of the Jewish community, Isaac noted that NJA members "worked with the most radical Arab groups." "The American Jewish community's consensus," she wrote, was that "the safety of Israel must be the overriding *national* concern of modern Jewry." Her article was titled "New Jewish Agenda: Outside the Consensus."[131]

Other American Jewish organizations took hold of this message. In 1989, a member of the Philadelphia chapter of the American Jewish Committee wrote *Dissent or Disloyalty?* The committee issued a report after some controversy over a request by the local NJA chapter to participate in community events such as the Israel Day parade and to "have its views aired in the local Jewish newspaper, the Philadelphia *Jewish Exponent.*" The report questioned NJA's "commitment to the State of Israel."[132] Americans for a Safe Israel then circulated this report, amplifying its message and its attacks on NJA.

To defend themselves against the idea that their critical positions on Zionism and Israel demonstrated their disloyalty, NJA members released an official response to the unpublished report. They stood by their dissenting views by citing the American Jewish Committee's 1989 survey data, which relied on an instrument designed to capture the American Jewish Zionist consensus. "Even when they disagree with the actions of the Israeli government," NJA members noted, "82% of American Jews surveyed" said that "it does not change how close they feel to Israel." "Critique of and commitment to Israel are not mutually exclusive," they concluded. NJA members sought to reassure the Jewish community that they did not cross beyond the threshold of dissent on Israel and Zionism. "Disagreement," they asserted, "is a richly supported tradition in Judaism."[133]

In his 1984 article, Magida quoted local leaders in Baltimore who relied on familiar tropes to attack the organization, accusing New Jewish Agenda members of presenting "a kind of pathology." "Thirty or forty years ago," one leader noted, "the same kind of people who are in New Jewish Agenda would have been anti-Zionists."[134] His point was well taken. NJA built on the legacies of other critics of Zionism across the twentieth century. But in the 1980s, to gain any traction in the Jewish community, NJA's critiques of Israel *required* first a commitment to Israel, a position that earlier dissenters might have resisted. The sum total of a century of Jewish communal attempts to discredit and marginalize anti- and non-Zionism among American Jews contributed to that state of affairs. Only with that commitment could organizations like NJA create a Jewish space to connect to civil and human rights issues, domestic and global—and still be loudly criticized.

Indeed, in his praise of NJA's quest for Jewish communal legitimation, Jack Wertheimer specifically noted evidence of this "balance" in the fact that its members "had worked behind the scenes to keep the issue of the Middle East off the agenda of a major civil-rights march on Washington in 1983."[135] To keep the new agenda acceptable within the American Jewish world, this clearly had been the correct choice.

By the 1980s, then, the threshold of acceptable dissent had decidedly shifted. The lesson was clear: make plain support for Zionism and Israel to gain attention, acceptance, and funds in the American Jewish world. For more than a decade, New Jewish Agenda members pushed against parts of the Zionist consensus without questioning its very foundation. They drew from past critics of Israel and Zionism and also from the social movements of the 1960s and 1970s, and their work created a new space for Jewish progressives to ally with civil rights and antimilitarism and with environmentalism, feminism, LGBTQIA+, and disability rights. Theirs were, in some ways, new, more inclusive models of American Jewish life.

In those years, young Jews drifting from Jewish affiliation became an urgent topic of the Jewish communal world, and there was a tremendous focus on interfaith marriages and declining ritual observance (as reflected in American Jewish Committee surveys). Jewish communal leaders might have looked, instead, at how young Jews put off by the carefully wrought and intensely policed American Jewish consensus on Zionism had found a place for Jewish affiliation in New Jewish Agenda.

Conclusion

American Jewish Critics of Zionism and the Cost
of a Forced Consensus

An examination of statements made by Jewish critics of American Zionism and Israel over nearly a century makes clear that the threshold of dissent has long been a central and defining feature of American Jewish life.

1937: "Even the intolerance of criticism, the most distressing feature of middle-class Zionism, seems to be passing. It is now almost possible to criticise Zionism and not be called an anti-Semite."[1]

1946: "All Americans have a stake in Palestine because it is a key to the peace of the world. Let them study the proposals for a Jewish State in light of democratic principles for which they stand as a people. They believe in equal rights for all citizens without regard to race or creed. They believe in the separation of church and government. They believe that one group shall not dominate the others. They believe in the right of self-determination. The Jewish State cannot be reconciled with these principles."[2]

1953: "Have we lost our capacity for indignation at wrong? . . . What Jewish organization has lifted its voice on behalf of the Arab refugees numbering some 800,000 people? . . . Does Jewish nationalism crowd out every feeling of sympathy for any other group than Jews?"[3]

1955: "Any American Jew who doubts the sincerity of the Israeli politicians' protestations of peace is denounced as a pro-Arab, a partner of feudal barons, or an anti-Semite."[4]

1973: "A call for unity of 'the oppressed classes' of Jews and Arabs [sic] against a government, in this case, the Israeli government, cannot be construed as anti-Semitic. The reaction against the demonstration was one instance of reading anti-Semitism into a situation where none existed."[5]

1977: "We deplore those pressures in American Jewish life which make open discussion of vital issues virtually synonymous with heresy."[6]

2003: "It is not anti-Semitic to be angry at those Jews who support Israeli policies that are oppressive. It is anti-Semitic when the anger gets directed at all Jews or gets articulated in anti-Jewish language."[7]

2019: "The organized American Jewish community has become one of the greatest threats to free speech in the United States."[8]

* * *

This history began in the late nineteenth century, listening to American Jews debate how best to find belonging in white America while maintaining their safety and their Jewish distinctiveness. They asked what ideas and practices were most compatible with American belonging. The main narrative of American Jewish communal history tells of the gradual acceptance of Zionism as compatible with Americanism, and it largely presents American Jews as of one mind about the role of Israel and Zionism in American Jewish life. Yet there was always a small but important minority of American Jews who criticized or rejected that idea, who defied the claim that there was any consensus on Zionism's role in American Jewish life. They had other visions of both Israel and the relationship of American Jews to Israel. This group was large and vocal enough to be considered a threat, and they were treated as such. This was especially true after the Holocaust, when leaders felt that Jewish unity was central to Jewish safety.

Beginning in the 1960s, mainstream Jewish communal leaders insisted that anti-Zionism emerged as a force from outside of American Jewish life, blaming "Black antisemitism" and "Arab propaganda" for impinging on Jewish unity and puncturing the consensus. Though Jews encountered antisemitism in debates over Israel, American Jewish leaders dissembled in locating the origins of criticism of Zionism exclusively outside of their community. In truth, anti-Zionism first emerged within mainstream American Jewish life, and debates over Zionism took place there as well.

American Jewish Zionists, anti-Zionists, and non-Zionists wrestled with the same questions about how best to balance a deep concern for Jewish communal life with Americanism and a commitment to universalist ideas of human rights and equality. However diverse the meanings they assigned to those values, they were an integral part of the contests over what it meant to be Jewish and American, to be Jewish and a citizen of the modern world.

In 1959, William Zukerman wondered in his *Jewish Newsletter* how American Jews could be "integrationists" at home, allying with African Americans for civil rights, and yet "segregationists" in their support of Israel. American Jews knew they had much to gain by integrating into the United States, he said. Fighting racism would make them, as Jews, safer. Zukerman predicted that unqualified support for Zionism would ultimately stand in the way of American Jewish liberalism, broadly defined, and that this stance would exact a cost.

I will end, then, with a prophetic meditation by the cultural critic, activist, and writer James Baldwin on American Jews, whiteness, and the cost of this forced consensus on Zionism. In 1984, an essay by Baldwin that was titled "On Being 'White' . . . and Other Lies" was published in *Essence* magazine. In this work, Baldwin saw whiteness as a "moral choice," made possible only by "justifying the Black subjugation" and by denying the "genocidal history" of Black and indigenous people on the North American continent. He discussed diverse groups of American ethnics who had become "white" and "paid the price of the ticket." But Baldwin devoted the most space to American Jews, connecting clearly their whiteness to Zionism and to Israel:

> It is probable that it is the Jewish community—or more accurately, perhaps, its remnants—that in America has paid the highest and most extraordinary price for becoming white. For the Jews came here from countries where they were not white, and they came here, in part, because they were not white; and incontestably in the eyes of the Black American (and not only in those eyes) American Jews have opted to become white, and this is how they operate. It was ironical to hear, for example, former Israeli prime minister Menachem Begin declare some time ago that "the Jewish people bow only to God" while knowing that the state of Israel is sustained by a blank check from Washington. Without further pursuing the implication of this mutual act of faith, one is nevertheless aware that the Jewish translation into a white American can sustain the state of Israel in a way that the Black presence, here, can scarcely hope—at least, not yet—to halt the slaughter in South Africa.[9]

Baldwin drew attention to Israel's alliance with apartheid South Africa. He acknowledged the global anticolonialist work ("the Black presence, here") of Black Americans in fighting apartheid. He also saw that this work placed into stark relief the role that Israel and colonialism played in the divisions between Black Americans and American Jewish Zionists. To Baldwin, support for Israel did not mean support for American Jews but support for dispossession and colonialism. Choosing to support Israel was, then, choosing *not* to support anticolonialism and Black freedom.

In this work, Baldwin touches on many of the themes addressed in these chapters. His allusion to the "remnants" of the Jewish community, for example, recalls William Zukerman's romantic view of Jewishness as intricately connected to a liberal worldview. In 1937, Zukerman wrote about what it would mean for the elite ruling classes to be victorious in Israel, to rule over a state based on the oppression of the Palestinians. It was almost fifty years later that Baldwin sat down to write.

American Jews, who had long equated all critiques of Israel with antisemitism, even after serious, political antisemitism largely waned in the 1950s, felt forced to choose between antiapartheid, civil rights, and other progressive causes and their loyalty, as Jews, to Israel. American Jews who pushed back against an unconditional loyalty to Israel, who first dared to tie America's growing intimacy with Israel to American imperialism in Vietnam, were marginalized and accused of self-hatred, antisemitism, or communism.

From their first moment in North America, most Jews who were descended from Europeans traveled within United States borders with state protection of their bodies. Though they faced social exclusion and certainly prejudice, they negotiated their way to whiteness and white privilege. What, then, do we make of Baldwin's observations? To be white, he asserted, meant more than just essential state protection of Jewish bodies. It was about withdrawing from the struggle against white supremacy and supporting colonialism; it meant allying one's self with the white majority in erasing the past and present of indigenous life on the continent and participating in—and profiting from—Black oppression.

In 2006, American Jewish historian Eric Goldstein published *The Price of Whiteness: Jews, Race, and American Identity*. Goldstein begins his exploration of this topic by citing another of Baldwin's writings, his

1967 essay "Negroes Are Anti-Semitic Because They're Anti-White." Baldwin wrote this essay during the civil rights movement, between the tragic murders of Malcolm X and Dr. King and before he had largely lost hope in redeeming America from white supremacy. While Baldwin argued that their whiteness "had created a wholly welcoming, unproblematic environment for Jews in American society," Goldstein writes, Baldwin then ignored the "heavy price" of whiteness for American Jews. American Jews' "entry into that world," he writes, brought privilege but also "alienation, communal breakdown, and psychic pain." Goldstein chronicles Jewish negotiations with American whiteness through the 1950s, and so his analysis necessarily stops short of identifying how Baldwin linked American Jewish whiteness to the threshold for dissent from the Zionist consensus.[10]

Baldwin's analysis of "the highest and most extraordinary price" begs a fuller accounting of the 1980s and beyond, taking this consensus into account. By 1980, many white American Jews, like other white Americans who benefited from federal policies (mortgage insurance, low-interest loans, and investment in infrastructure creation such as schools and highways), had exited cities and moved to the suburbs. Young people raised with ties to Jewish life departed when Jewish leaders didn't mirror their social and political commitments and when they found that suburban communal life left them wanting. There was the loss of communal unity—and perhaps strength.

Goldstein ends his 2006 book with an analysis of a question: Are American Jews positioning themselves for the "End of Whiteness"? "Many Jews at the turn of the twenty-first century seem particularly conscious of the way that being seen as white delegitimizes their claim to difference as Jews," he wrote. Far from predicting a "tribalist" or religious revival that enhances Jewish difference or a wholesale renunciation of whiteness, Goldstein leaves open the question of how American Jews will wrestle with their "impatience with the constraints of whiteness."[11]

Though his language might recall the rejection of Zionism on the part of Reform rabbis—the careful balancing of distinctiveness and integration—the historical currents of the last two decades instead lead us back to the insights of Zukerman, Blatt, and Pomerantz; to Breira and New Jewish Agenda; to predictions about what would happen to a community that does not allow for meaningful dissent. They felt that the stifling of dissent would chill the Jewish community's capacity for participation in struggles for justice. This new century has seen the increased visibility of white supremacist, colonialist ideologies embraced by far-right leaders, which reveal the deep interconnections among antisemitism, xenophobia, and racism. Many Jews, especially young Jews, felt alienated by the conservatism of communal leaders who asked only where candidates stood with regard to Israel. They turned to the courageous activists in the Black Lives Matter movement, who stood with Black activists throughout American history in linking Black and Palestinian oppression. And many American Jews of all ages turned to Jewish Voice for Peace, the heir to Breira and New Jewish Agenda, and showed a newfound willingness to cross the threshold of tolerance for dissent.

Jewish Voice for Peace was founded in 1996 when a group of Jewish women in the San Francisco Bay area felt they had to speak out as Jews against Israel's brutal occupation. Though the organization endorsed the idea that criticizing Israel was not antisemitic at its founding, its members decided at first to "abstain from taking a position on Zionism" and to "raise our voices as Jews supporting Palestinian rights." Historically, mainstream American Jewish leaders spoke of Israel and Zionism as the issues that pushed them away from the Black Lives Matter coalition of supporters. Jewish Voice for Peace was among the very few Jewish groups to unreservedly voice support for Black Lives Matter in 2016 when its members released a platform describing Israel's treatment of Palestinians as a genocide.[12]

In 2018, learning lessons from activists involved in the Black Lives Matter and the Boycott, Divestment, and Sanctions movements, Jewish Voice for Peace members declared that they now saw Zionism "as damaging to Jewish identity and spiritual life," and the organization issued its first-ever statement on Zionism, stating that their members "unequivocally oppose Zionism because it is counter" to a "vision of justice, freedom, and equality for all people."[13] Other groups such as IfNotNow began to publish statements about how the forced consensus had actually made Jews less safe and how twenty-first-century racism was a pressing concern for them as Jews.[14]

Some mainstream Jewish organizations continue to see criticism of Israel and support for Palestine as obstacles to joining progressive coalitions, especially for the Movement for Black Lives.[15] As activists unmasked anti-Black racism in the summer of the deaths of George Floyd and Breonna Taylor at the hands of police officers and raised awareness about the savage racial inequalities in criminal justice, food security, and health care, especially during the COVID-19 pandemic, American Jews struggled to align themselves and keep pace with growing public sympathy for Black Lives Matter. By 2020 leaders of some Jewish groups had backtracked with regard to this issue, removing the online evidence of their 2016 rejection of Black Lives Matter in order to find their way back to supporting it.[16]

Indeed, in the summer of 2020, a full-page advertisement appeared in the *New York Times* announcing the following: "On this 57th anniversary of the 1963 March on Washington for Jobs and Freedom, institutions representing over half of American Jews publish the following letter." The letter offered unequivocal support to Black Lives Matter, explaining, "We know that freedom and safety for any of us depends on the freedom and safety of all of us."[17]

The letter included not one word about Israel or Zionism, the issues that had prevented most Jewish groups from participating in the 1983 anniversary march. Instead, it focused on the connection between antisemitism and other forms of hate. One statement made clear that the collaborative work toward justice had been interrupted: "When Jewish people join together with our neighbors across racial and religious differences, as we have in the past, we can protect each other and build the future of freedom and safety we all deserve."[18]

Claiming that this letter reflected the sentiments of more than half of American Jews, the signers clearly positioned themselves as the majority, those who would not let the Zionist consensus stand in the way of their support of Black freedom and civil rights. In so doing, they placed a spotlight on mainstream Jewish leaders who refused to support this movement and were thus increasingly out of step with most American Jews. Jewish communal life and American Jewish relations with Israel are showing signs of large-scale change. Jewish Voice for Peace now has seventy chapters all over the United States, and its membership has soared since 2016. Its members seek to build support across rights movements (including LGBTQIA+, disability, Black, and indigenous people of color) and ultimately to build what the organization describes as a "Jewish community that supports Palestinian rights."[19]

In the realm of foreign policy, the *New York Times* reported in 2021 that Israel's dependence on US aid is diminishing and that the country has largely achieved "military autonomy." The *New York Times* also reported that Israel's right-wing leadership now no longer needs to pay heed to "Washington's bipartisan consensus" in support of Israel.[20] Jewish communal organizations might see this moment of escalating dissent as an opportunity to refocus their energy and resources. With less attention on the threshold of dissent, Jewish leaders might rekindle their relationships with other groups working toward justice. But before true, large-scale coalition building can even begin, American Jews will have to reckon with a long and troubled history of enforcing a community consensus on Israel.

Any analysis of the cost of Jewish silences on Zionism's abuses must begin and end with the fact that the highest price for Jews' forced consensus was paid by those whose oppression went largely unheeded in the American Jewish community, including Palestinians, Black Americans, Black South Africans, Arab and Muslim Americans, and others. Through their silence, American Jews, including myself, were long complicit and contributed to violence against members of these groups.

To be sure, since the 1950s, the intense pressure within American Jewish political life was to speak *less* about Palestinian rights for fear of crossing the threshold, getting on the wrong side of political divides, or losing funding or allies. Zionist Jewish leaders convinced their communities that only this consensus kept Jews safe. The price of that pressure within the Jewish community was diminished relevance to struggles for justice, the deterioration of American Jewish life, and the alienation of those who sought communal connections to these broad struggles for justice playing out in their own lifetimes. Ultimately—and tragically, too—the forced consensus on Zionism has made the world safer for antisemitism and racism and, consequently, less safe for us all.

Coda

A New Chapter in American Jewish Dissent?

Forty-three years ago, during the first war in Lebanon, the author and activist Leonard Fein (1934–2014) drew attention to the threshold of dissent when he declared that American Jewish criticism of Israel was decidedly not "fatal."[1] Fein, a lifelong and dedicated Zionist, saw connection to Israel as vital to American Jewish communal life. He also believed that a healthy American Jewish community included debates over what that connection might look like and what Israel as a state should be. With his declaration, Fein gently pushed back against those Jewish leaders who insisted that only an unquestioned consensus on Israel would ensure a safe Jewish future and that any dissent on Zionism and Israel would prove dangerous, even fatal, for American Jews.

In November 2022, as this book was nearing completion, there was lively dissent within the American Jewish community over what some saw as a shocking turn of events in Israel. Israelis elected into office a coalition headed by former prime minister Benjamin Netanyahu that is the most right-wing ruling coalition in the nation's history. As hundreds of thousands of Israelis protested in the streets, American Jews reassessed their own relationships with Israel. An article published in March 2023 in the *New Republic* asked a question framed not only by the election but also by the threshold of American Jewish dissent and by the activism of the historical figures who are discussed in this book, including Leonard Fein: "Can American Jewish Support for Israel Survive This New Government?"[2]

This governing coalition in Israel includes many far-right nationalists within the Religious Zionist Party. Bezalel Smotrich, the party's chair, has denied the existence of the Palestinian people and described himself as a "proud homophobe."[3] Itamar Ben Gvir, leader of the right-wing Otzma Yehudit Party, which joined a coalition with the Religious Zionist

Party, is a disciple of Meir Kahane, known in the United States for his leadership of the Jewish Defense League and in Israel for his leadership of the racist Kach Party that was banned in 1994.

In addition to increasing violence against Palestinians, these leaders positioned themselves as seeking to diminish the power of more liberal denominations of Judaism in Israel and to restrict the rights of women and all LGBTQIA+ people. Meanwhile, Netanyahu is facing charges of fraud and corruption; some members of his coalition have pledged to overhaul the judiciary, and critics alleged that one motivation was to undo the charges against him. Protesting Israelis cited their fear that the future of Israeli democracy was at stake.

For nearly a century, many American Jews have described their dedication to Israel as bound up with the ideals of democracy, articulating how Israel's political values mirror those of the United States and describing Israel as a thriving democracy in the Middle East. The values espoused by the new ruling coalition challenged these ideas. And so American Jews protested as well, writing a new chapter in the history of American Jewish criticism of Zionism.

Was this election indicative of something dramatically new? Did it reflect a seismic shift to the right and a departure from Israeli democracy? Or was it, as scholar Shaul Magid declared in the *New Republic* in March 2023, "the logical outcome of what's been going on for the last 50 years"? To the question "How could this be happening?" Magid answered, "It was always happening."[4] And the election begged still broader questions: If more American Jews, including Zionists, grew fearful of or even rejected what was happening in Israel in 2023, would that stance create more room for open conversations about American Zionism? This coda looks briefly at the American Jewish community after the Israeli election and the start of the Israel-Hamas war and asks, Where does the threshold of dissent on Zionism now lie for American Jews, and what will that mean for American Jewish life?

* * *

In the years since the 1983 March on Washington, debates over Israel and Zionism have continued: through the First (1987–93) and Second (2000–2005) Palestinian Intifadas (translated as "shaking off"); the continued aggressive building of Jewish settlements in Palestine; the Oslo

Accords (1993); Jewish and non-Jewish criticism of Israel; the rise in power of the American Israel Public Affairs Committee (AIPAC); the 2006 Israeli war in Lebanon; the passage of the new Nation-State Law (2018); the continued growth of the Boycott, Divestment, and Sanctions movement; and other resistance from Palestinian activists and their allies. Across these decades, the low threshold of tolerance for dissenting viewpoints on Israel meant that American Jews who wanted to protest Israeli policies *as Jews* had few places to go.

Even with the growth of organizations such as Jewish Voice for Peace and IfNotNow, AIPAC's strong influence in the 2022 midterm elections in the United States might be a measure of just how low the threshold for dissenting views on Israel had sunk in advance of Israel's election. AIPAC launched its own super PAC, an independent political action committee that raised millions of dollars to support the campaigns of what it termed "pro-Israel candidates," a stand that has long meant that at times, American Jews appear to support antidemocratic candidates, positions, and parties.

Howard Kohr, chief executive of AIPAC, responded to a question about the super PAC and its role in AIPAC's strategy by indicating that it was in response to "the rise of a very vocal minority on the far left of the Democratic Party that is anti-Israel and seeks to weaken and diminish the relationship."[5] Yet among those who benefited from AIPAC's funds were thirty-seven Republicans who refused to certify the 2020 election of President Joe Biden and two who refused to testify to the congressional panel investigating the insurrection of January 6, 2020, when supporters of Donald Trump stormed the US Capitol in a vigilante attempt to overturn the election results. AIPAC defended its support of these candidates by noting it is a "single-issue organization."[6]

Some "pro-Israel" organizations voiced concern over AIPAC's funding of these candidates, among them the Jewish Democratic Council of America and J Street, the "pro-Israel, pro-peace" organization founded in 2007 as an alternative to AIPAC. The Anti-Defamation League and other mainstream Zionist Jewish organizations held two seemingly contradictory positions. They condemned the vicious antisemitism embraced by these figures who allied with the political far right, including the white nationalist extremism of the insurrectionists, even while they maintained that their unconditional support of Israel aligned with

AIPAC.[7] Since the 1980s, American Jewish Zionist leaders' enforcement of a consensus position on Israel and their marginalization of those who breached the threshold of tolerable dissent have meant that their organizations have often openly allied themselves with right-wing conservatives, overlooking their positions on other essential issues such as civil, women's, and LGBTQIA+ rights, because they offer unflagging US support for Israel. In this way, the funding and alliances of the 2022 American midterm elections continued this stance.

With far-right figures leading Israel, more American Jews questioned that support. Members of dissenting organizations echoed Magid: they saw nothing new in the Israeli elections, only the continuing tragedy of injustice in Israel and Palestine to which they have drawn public attention for decades.

Members of IfNotNow described their November 2022 protest as the first against the new Israeli government. They rallied outside of the Boston offices of the Jewish National Fund, an organization founded in 1901 to promote Jewish settlement in what was then Palestine. Critics have identified the Jewish National Fund's contemporary work as contributing to Palestinian dispossession and displacement.[8] Wearing shirts emblazoned with the words "Jews against Apartheid," IfNotNow members drew from Amnesty International's February 2022 report categorizing Israel's treatment of Palestinians as apartheid.[9] At their protest over the election, IfNotNow members chose to showcase the Jewish National Fund tzedakah (charity) boxes, nearly ubiquitous in Jewish life as a place to drop coins as donations to the organization. Members created two "human-sized Tzedakah boxes": one with the traditional Jewish National Fund logo, the other labeled "Justice and Equality."[10]

Jewish Voice for Peace leaders also continued their dissent from any Zionist consensus after the Israeli election. Beth Miller, the group's political director, reported that the election signaled only a "moment of exposure" for Israel's historic "Jewish supremacist" policies, and she predicted a "moment of reckoning here in the U.S."[11] As historian Hasia Diner noted, American Jewish Zionists have continued to live in a "fantasy" of Israel as a defendable project in liberalism and democracy.[12] As for IfNotNow and Jewish Voice for Peace and others who pushed past the threshold of dissent, they hoped that the Israeli election might dispel that fantasy.

* * *

Examining the fragmented responses of mainstream Zionist Jewish organizations to the fall 2022 Israeli election provided an opportunity to gauge whether the threshold had indeed moved and whether American Jews were growing more tolerant of dissent over Israel and Zionism. The American Jewish Committee and other groups issued statements supporting Israel's democratic election but warned of the threat posed to the priorities of "pluralism, inclusion, and increased opportunities for peace and normalization."[13] The Anti-Defamation League congratulated Israel's new leadership, affirming that its members were "eternally committed to Israel." They also voiced concern, saying they "would not shirk from calling out expressions, policies, and actions by the Israeli government and particularly Israeli leaders that are hateful, racist, anti-Arab or homophobic, anti-democratic or harmful to the non-Orthodox streams within the Jewish people."[14] Anti-Defamation League leaders pledged to continue their "advocacy for Israeli-Arab normalization," working for a "two-state solution" even as they maintained their efforts "to counter anti-Zionism" because they feared that some people would be emboldened by the election to "engage in the relentless demonizing of Zionism."[15]

Some liberal American Zionists, often staunch defenders of Israel, publicly criticized Israel's new government in print. In February 2023, Martin Peretz and scholar Michael Walzer, authors of the 1967 article "Israel Is Not Vietnam," joined critic Leon Wieseltier and writer Paul Berman in writing an article titled "We Are Liberal American Zionists. We Stand with Israel's Protestors," which appeared in the *Washington Post*. The four authors began by reaffirming the fact that they have "always regarded American support for Israel as a point of patriotic pride," as they hold fast to a vision of Israel as an "essential refuge for oppressed and persecuted Jews." They added that they see the aggressive building of Jewish settlements and "extremist Jewish vigilantism" as threats to "Israel's standing in world affairs."[16]

The authors stopped short, however, of considering any lessening of American support for Israel. Though they described these protestors as "the hope for the decent and liberal state that the world needs," they rejected the idea that the United States should reduce the amount of foreign aid it sent to Israel. "Israel still needs and deserves the maximum in US military aid," they wrote, "because Israel has real enemies, and its enemies are no less strong than before," and because it has "served the Jewish people so well in the past."[17]

Other American Jewish Zionists coalesced around a brand of dissent that rejected individual Israeli politicians and their political positions. They supported the results of the election but publicly declared that these newly elected officials would not be permitted entry into their Jewish institutions. One hundred and forty American Jews signed a document titled "Statement from American Jewish Leaders: Smotrich Should Not Be Given a Platform in Our Community." They declared that those who meet with Finance Minister Bezalel Smotrich need to see that it will "harm, rather than help, support for Israel." Drawing from the idea that Israel's democratic values mirror those of the United States, some American liberal Zionists, then, saw protesting the positions of this far-right leader as within the boundaries of acceptable dissent. Smotrich has "long expressed views that are abhorrent to the vast majority of American Jews," they wrote, "from anti-Arab racism, to virulent homophobia, to a full-throated embrace of Jewish supremacy."[18] Three hundred and thirty Jewish clergy also signed a letter opposing invitations for any members of the Religious Zionist Party to speak at their congregations and organizations, citing their "commitment to our Jewish and democratic values."[19] The Anti-Defamation League, the Conference of Presidents of Major Jewish Organizations, and even the American State Department condemned Smotrich's violent, hateful speech.

Halie Soifer, chief executive officer of the Jewish Democratic Council of America, called her organization "an unabashedly pro-Israel organization" and wrote that Smotrich's visit to Israel Bonds in March 2023 found her protesting an Israeli government official "for the first time in her life." Soifer identified herself as one who was "publicly declaring support for Israel and hope for peace" during the Second Intifada. After the elections, however, Israel was diverging from the "shared values on which the U.S.-Israel relationship is based, including pluralism and democracy." She identified herself not as heir to past critics of Israel and Zionism but in line with the many American Jews who have been fighting "right-wing extremism" in the United States since 2016.[20]

Strikingly, one American Jewish Zionist, Rabbi Jeremy Kalamofsky of Ansche Chesed, a Conservative synagogue on Manhattan's Upper West Side, made clear that the 2022 Israeli election forced him to rethink the role of Zionism in Jewish communal worship. He had already signed the letter denying members of the Religious Zionist Party entrance to his synagogue, but he then took his dissent still further: he decided to stop leading the Prayer for the State of Israel, which has been a part of Shabbat liturgy for many synagogues since 1948.

Rabbi Kalamofsky, a "staunch, lifelong Zionist," was not a "rabble-rouser," noted Jodi Rodoren, editor of the *Forward*; instead, he is a "sober thinker" who "felt the situation demanded a more sustained response."[21] The standard prayer expresses hope for the success of Israel's leaders, ministers, and advisers. Rabbi Kalamofsky considered the government "a Jewish Klan," undeserving of these words. On his synagogue blog, he acknowledged "friends who take a dimmer view of Zionism," those who "believe that this grim turn was all but inevitable, baked into the cake of an ethnic nationalism that would inevitably devolve into supremacist aggression." He disagreed, and the bookends of his blog post are instructive in demonstrating his own position. He began by describing how his son used to ask him, "'When does Israel do something so outrageous that you stop supporting it?' I would invariably reply: nothing. Nothing could shake my support of the state of Israel, the national home of the Jewish people." He concluded by noting that he remains an "unshakably loyal lover of the Jewish national project" who supports Israel but opposes the current government.[22] This was a dissent that allowed for criticism of Israel and perhaps even for associations with those who have come to reject Zionism. The public pronouncements of this dissent, however, still supported the Zionist project and still centered Israel and Zionism in American Judaism.

* * *

To find thoughtful deliberations on the election that directly questioned the Zionist project and the threshold of dissent, one perhaps had to look outside of US borders. Hillel Halkin's essay in the *Jewish Review of Books*, published in the winter of 2023, immediately after the election, began with the words "This time it's different." An American-born critic, novelist, and translator, Halkin has long been a fervent, devoted

Zionist, author of the famed *Letters to an American Jewish Friend: A Zionist's Polemic*, a 1977 book that urged all American Jews to move to Israel. He devoted much of his article to charting the demographic and political shifts in Israel that led to the election's outcome.

"Zionism wanted to make us a normal people," he wrote, but it grew "warped in the process." He confessed to not heeding "the warnings" of aggressive Jewish settlements and then mused on how he used to think that a "point of no return" for Jews and Palestinians in Israel would occur long in the future, a distant day. Perhaps, he concluded, "it was, all along, the starting point." In 1945, I. F. Stone described a Jewish state with no Palestinian rights as a "blind alley."[23] In the winter of 2023, Halkin saw Zionism and the forces that built Israel, with "Benjamin Netanyahu in tow," leading Jews into an "abyss."[24] Halkin had moved from the United States to Israel in 1970. Taking note of Halkin's piece, one prominent anti-Zionist outlet published an article headlined "Another Prominent Zionist Admits the Project Failed."[25]

* * *

Was this moment of the election different? American critics of Zionism have, for decades, cautioned against the perils of ethnonationalism, about the global implications of settler colonialism in Israel. They have linked Israel's oppressive policies to the rise of global antisemitism and rejected equating all criticism of Zionism with antisemitism. They drew attention to the dangers of centering Israel in American Jewish life, of denying meaningful debate over Israel and Zionism. These critics drew from the lessons of the Holocaust and the goal of Jewish safety. They drew, too, from the currents of their moments in American and world history—the Reform movement, the Yiddish left, anticolonialism, the Black freedom movement, feminism, and LGBTQIA+ rights—and crafted visions of what American Jewish life might look like. Indeed, American Jews drew from these currents to express outrage over Israel's current government—its racism, its sexism, and its homophobia.

Because most of the mainstream Jewish leaders who fervently and publicly disagreed with Israel's new governing coalition always reaffirmed their commitment to Zionism, the inclusion of anti-Zionism within the threshold of dissent remained elusive. But debates over whether criticism of Zionism is antisemitic continued.

Jewish Currents, the publication Morris Schappes edited that young Jewish leftists have revitalized, reported on the response of American Jews to *The U.S. National Strategy to Combat Antisemitism*, a document released by President Biden's administration in May 2023. In the June 1, 2023, weekly newsletter of *Jewish Currents*, Mari Cohen, associate editor, observed how the fragmented American Jewish responses to the report reflected vociferous disagreements over what it meant to criticize Israel in that moment's political climate. Both liberals and conservatives praised the report, she observed, claiming victory in these heated debates.

Liberals had feared that the report would mark the formal adoption of the International Holocaust Remembrance Alliance's "working definition of antisemitism," which defines certain kinds of anti-Zionist speech as antisemitism. But that did not happen. Though the report acknowledged the Alliance's definition, it also acknowledged that antisemitism "frequently occurs alongside other manifestations of hatred—including racism, Islamophobia, and anti-LGBTQ sentiment—and is best fought in coalition."[26] As *The Threshold of Dissent* makes clear, critics of Zionism, especially progressive activists, have long argued this point.

Even with this interpretation of *The U.S. National Strategy to Combat Antisemitism*, and even if AIPAC's formation of a super PAC might have indicated that the Israel lobby feels vulnerable, there are still millions of dollars flowing to "pro-Israel" candidates and from the United States to Israel. In the summer of 2023, the policing of criticism of Israel on American college campuses continued, creating a climate of fear among teachers when tasked with illuminating the complex realities of historical and contemporary Zionism. In that moment, many educational institutions created obstacles to students' open engagement with the history of settler colonialism in Israel, and thus meaningful movement of the threshold of acceptable dissent appeared unlikely.

* * *

As this book heads to press in November 2023, yet another chapter in this history is unfolding in American Jewish responses to tragic events in Israel/Palestine. Last month, Hamas brazenly attacked Israel, killing twelve hundred people, and Israel responded by launching missile attacks and then invading Gaza. The space to criticize Israel, which appeared immediately after the fall 2022 Israeli elections, collapsed rapidly.

American Jewish Zionists insist that reaffirming unqualified commitment to Israel is an essential first step to engaging in any conversation about the events that dominate each day's news. There is little room for discussions of the history of centuries of violence against Palestinians, the tens of thousands of Palestinians dying in Gaza, and the Palestinian perspectives that remain unwelcome and marginalized in mainstream media and on college campuses. Since the fall, progressive Jews had protested the policies of Prime Minister Netanyahu. Rabbi Rachel Timoner, a "well-known voice for Progressive Jews" in Park Slope, Brooklyn, wrote to her Congregation Beth Elohim members after the Hamas attacks that now was "a time to stand in unequivocal solidarity with Israel and Israelis."[27]

The threshold of dissent from the manufactured consensus on Zionism appears to be at a low mark, perhaps an unprecedented low, and many who step beyond the threshold are accused of antisemitism and self-hatred, purged from mainstream Jewish life. In October 2023, the Jewish Community Relations Council (JCRC), an umbrella Jewish organization, moved to expel the Boston Jewish Workers Circle after its members participated in a rally outside of Senator Elizabeth Warren's office. The rally, organized by IfNotNow and supported by members of Jewish Voice for Peace, called for a cease-fire and de-escalation of the violence in Israel/Palestine. The Workers Circle is a secular, progressive Jewish community founded in the early twentieth century by immigrant Jews from Eastern Europe. Drawing from Yiddish culture and the Jewish left, the organization focuses on education and social action; it was one of the JCRC's founding organizations in 1944, when local Jewish groups united to fight antisemitism. After the rally, JCRC leaders pointed to a 2019 resolution that said no JCRC member can partner with a "self-described Jewish organization that declares itself to be anti-Zionist." The CEO also noted that since its founding, JCRC leaders "have embraced a 'big tent' approach to our network—which is comprised of 40 organizations—striving to welcome all voices advancing the interests of the organized Jewish community and we have been committed to representing a diversity of viewpoints."[28] In fall 2023, at the onset of the Israel-Hamas war, the big tent did not extend to those with critical analyses of Israel's long history of violence against Palestinians.

Soon after the rally, Workers Circle members wrote about how the group decided to resign rather than go through the lengthy, time-consuming process of being expelled from JCRC. They responded with frustration that "JCRC has refused to draw any moral lines for its far-Right extremist members, including the Zionist Organization of America (ZOA)." The ZOA, Workers Circle members noted, had recently hosted Israeli minister Bezalel Smotrich; Circle members had asked JCRC "for the expulsion of ZOA several years ago because of the way its ideology endangers our multiracial, multiethnic Jewish community as well as communities of color in Boston." Their requests were denied. Workers Circle members wrote of the "choice" put before them: for "retribution and endless occupation . . . and mutually assured destruction" or for "a future of equality, freedom, and safety for all Palestinians and Israelis." Echoing the rhetoric of Jewish critics of Zionism across the last century, they concluded by taking note of the "growing moral cry" coming from American Jews and asserted that JCRC was moving further away from serving as a "representative body of our community."[29]

Media outlets now speak of a "fracture" in American Jewish support for Israel over the war. Scholars and others wonder if the intolerance for dissent is growing.[30] Equations of anti-Zionism with antisemitism abound. *The Threshold of Dissent* examines past American Jewish critics of Zionism, and they too were accused of divisiveness by mainstream Jewish leaders. These critics instead asserted that Zionist leaders' shrill insistence on a consensus on Israel was the fracturing force. They often took a hard look at the white, patriarchal, heteronormative American Jewish model of American Judaism, with an imposed consensus on Israel and the routing out of "antisemitic" criticism of Zionism and Israel at its center, and found it wanting. Like the Workers Circle members, they forged their own paths, often building alternatives—organizations, publications, college courses—to illuminate new ways of thinking and new models of American Jewish life, often tied to progressive coalitions. Many American Jewish critics of Zionism paid a very high price for doing so.

This book has argued that supporting unquestioning loyalty to Israel, in part by marginalizing dissent, has, for a century, made it more difficult for American Jews to reconcile their Jewishness with political commitments to social justice, democracy, pluralism, and liberation and that this ultimately weakened Jewish communal life and the prospects for Jewish belonging, particularly among younger Jews. This book has also argued that enforcing this manufactured consensus was deeply intertwined with the fraught process of Euro-American Jews' century-long effort to claim whiteness. In this era of ascendant white nationalism, perhaps we can see the growth of IfNotNow and Jewish Voice for Peace as aligned with historian Eric Goldstein's prediction that more American Jews would come to wrestle with the "constraints of acceptance in white America."[31] Young American Jews are still and again building exciting and laudable community institutions, alternatives that connect them in coalitions that center on LGBTQIA+ rights, Palestinian self-determination, and antiracism. As this book goes to press, these expansive coalition politics are on display across the US: JVP protests and demonstrations draw from Holocaust consciousness and anticolonialism, civil and gay rights.

American Jewish Zionists often continue to ally with conservative forces in supporting American and Israeli militarism, citing their fear for Israel's and Jews' vulnerabilities and their motivation to keep Jews safe. On October 27, 2023, Arielle Angel, editor in chief of *Jewish Currents*, wrote in the journal's Shabbat reading list first an acknowledgment that these fears are real and then the observation that a "liberal myopia" was at work in looking *only* at this fear. "To perversely posit young American Jews as the central victims of the earth-shattering violence in Palestine—and, for that matter, in Israel—seems in its own way a form of denial."[32] She cited an essay by American literary critic Saree Makdisi in which Makdisi described the everyday violence of the occupation, the deaths of women and newborns and others that "never constituted news in the Western world." Makdisi placed the "appalling violence" of Hamas within the "wider historical context of colonialism and anticolonial resistance . . . of absolute violence, domination, suffocation, and control" that produce "appalling violence in turn." "What we are not allowed to say," he wrote, "is that if you want the violence to stop, you must stop the violence that produced it." Even the "most progressive of Democrats," he wrote, care about "gender and racial equality" and "climate change" yet "*seem* not to see Palestinian suffering because they literally do *not* see or recognize it."[33]

Across the last century, American Jewish Zionist leaders enforced a threshold of dissent by marginalizing progressive American Jews who were able to see Palestinian suffering. Theirs is a fraught and difficult history and one entangled with immense destruction in the name of

Jewish safety. If mainstream Jewish communal organizations continue to hold fast to unqualified support for Israel, insisting that American Jews and American politicians subscribe to a forced Zionist consensus, will young American Jews continue to look at American Jewish life and find it wanting? And, finally, how might future historians assess the impact of this forced consensus on the safety of Jews and all others?

ACKNOWLEDGMENTS

I offer my thanks to all the individuals and institutions that helped make this book possible. A fellowship at the Goldstein-Goren Center for American Jewish History at New York University allowed time to research and write at a key phase of the book's development. The Babson Faculty Research Fund also helped support my work on this book with time and resources.

I am grateful for the assistance of staff members at the archives and libraries where I completed my research: the Center for Jewish History, the YIVO Institute for Jewish Research, the American Jewish Archives, the New York Public Library, Yeshiva University Archives and Special Collections, Tamiment Library and the Robert F. Wagner Labor Archives at New York University, the Wyner Family Heritage Center of the New England Historic Genealogical Society, and Tufts University Archives. I am especially thankful to the heroic archivists who sent me material when the pandemic prevented travel: David Gartrell at the University of California Santa Barbara Library, Lindsay Murphy at the Wyner Family Jewish Heritage Center of the New England Historic Genealogical Society, Chloe Gerson at the Brandeis University Archives and Special Collections, and Rachel Greenblatt at the Brandeis University Judaica Collection.

Lawrence Bush spoke to me about Morris Schappes and *Jewish Currents* and sent me helpful materials. Professor Martin Blatt welcomed me to his home and shared with me his personal archives about his teaching and activism at Tufts University and beyond. I am grateful to both of them.

I thank the colleagues who offered me feedback on pieces of this work over the course of my writing: Matt Berkman, Peter Eisenstadt, Emmaia Gelman, Josh Leifer, Geoff Levin, Pamela Pennock, and Adolph Reed. Ri Turner offered feedback and also aided me throughout with Yiddish and Hebrew translations, for which I am deeply grateful. I owe a special thanks to Geoff Levin for guiding me to sources and talking over ideas. Constance Rosenblum offered editorial support that improved the book greatly.

I could not ask for better colleagues than Kevin Bruyneel and Stephen Deets, who have always offered support, solidarity, wise and calm counsel, and humor. I also thank my chair, Kandice Hauf, for her feminist leadership and boundless optimism. Meenakshi Khanna has cheered me on for the last three decades, even across oceans, and I feel so happy that she is a part of my life. Thanks to Anita and Meredith for their friendship and laughter, especially while working our jobs and parenting during the pandemic.

Hasia Diner offered helpful feedback on this work, especially in its earliest stages, and essential encouragement during the pandemic. I have great respect for her integrity, courage, and intellect, and I am grateful for her friendship, humor, and support. At New York University Press, I thank Eric Zinner for supporting this book and for shepherding it through to publication. I am also grateful for Furqan Sayeed's support at NYU Press.

My deepest thanks go to my family for their patience and enthusiasm. Izzy and Nathan teach me about hope and resilience and the need for a better world. I admire and love them more than I can say. Michael read every single page of this book multiple times, and his partnership and love made it possible. I dedicate this book to Michael, Izzy, and Nathan with all my love, always.

NOTES

INTRODUCTION

1 "Millennials are the only generational cohort in which fewer than half (43%) sympathize more with Israel. And about a quarter of Millennials (27%) sympathize more with the Palestinians, the highest share of any generation." Samantha Smith and Carroll Doherty, "Five Facts about How Americans View the Israeli-Palestinian Conflict," Pew Research Center, May 23, 2016, www.pewresearch.org.

2 "Older Jews are more likely than younger Jews to see caring about Israel as an essential part of what being Jewish means to them. More than half of Jews 65 and older say caring about Israel is essential for their Jewish identity (53%), as do 47% of Jews ages 50–64. By comparison, 38% of Jews in their 30s and 40s and 32% of Jewish adults under age 30 say caring about Israel is central to what being Jewish means to them." "A Portrait of Jewish Americans," Pew Research Center, October 1, 2013, www.pewforum.org.

3 Eric Alterman, "The Fraying Ties between Liberal American Jews and Israel," *Nation*, May 23, 2018, www.thenation.com.

4 Eric Alterman, "Does Anyone Take the B.D.S. Movement Seriously?," *New York Times*, July 29, 2019, www.nytimes.com.

5 Eric Alterman, "Altercation: Israel and Palestine and the Absence of a Solution," *American Prospect*, June 3, 2022, https://prospect.org.

6 Eric Alterman, *We Are Not One: A History of America's Fight over Israel* (New York: Basic Books, 2022). In over four hundred pages of political analysis, Alterman covers some material that is also studied in this work.

7 Melvin I. Urofsky, *American Zionism from Herzl to the Holocaust* (Garden City, NY: Anchor Press, 1975).

8 In the 2nd edition of his *American Judaism*, Jonathan Sarna included a revised conclusion in which he took note of historical controversies over Israel. "Glimmers of dissent" from the idea of Israel as "the great unifier among America's variegated Jews" appeared "as early as 1973," he writes. Here he mentions Breira, an organization studied in chapter 3. Jonathan Sarna, *American Judaism: A History*, 2nd ed. (New Haven, CT: Yale University Press, 2019), 377–78.

9 Shaul Magid, "On Antisemitism and Its Uses," in *On Antisemitism: Solidarity and the Struggle for Justice*, by Jewish Voice for Peace (Chicago: Haymarket Books, 2017), 68.

10 Noam Pianko, *Zionism and the Roads Not Taken: Rawidowicz, Kaplan, Kohn* (Bloomington: Indiana University Press, 2010); Adam Rovner, *In the Shadow of Zion: Promised Lands before Israel* (New York: New York University Press, 2014).

11 This study builds on the work of those who have asked essential questions about American Jews and Israel: Dov Waxman, *Trouble in the Tribe: The American Jewish Conflict over Israel* (Princeton: Princeton University Press, 2016); Peter Beinart, *The Crisis of Zionism* (New York: Times Books, 2012). Outside of Jewish studies are these important works: Keith Feldman's *A Shadow over Palestine: The Imperial Life of Race in America* (*Minneapolis: University of Minnesota Press*, 2015); Amy Kaplan's superb *Our American Israel: The Story of an Entangled Alliance* (Cambridge: Harvard University Press, 2018); Shaul Mitelpunkt's *Israel in the American Mind: The Cultural Politics of US-Israeli Relations, 1958–1988* (Cambridge: Cambridge University Press, 2018).

12 Tallie Ben-Daniel, "Zionism's Frontier Legacies: Colonial Masculinity and the American Council for Judaism in San Francisco," *American Studies* 54, no. 4 (2016): 49.

13 Waxman notes that "the connection between religious faith and attachment to Israel is understandable given the fact that the Land of Israel (*Eretz Yisrael*) is a core element in Jewish theology, and the notion of an eventual return to the 'Promised Land' is deeply embedded in Jewish ritual and belief." Waxman, *Trouble in the Tribe*, 27.

14 Gideon Shimoni, "From Anti-Zionism to Non-Zionism in Anglo Jewry, 1917–1937," *Jewish Journal of Sociology* 28, no. 1 (June 1986): 19.

15 Shimoni writes that "emancipation implied a moral-social contract whereby the Jews were accepted as equal participants in the environing nation on the clear understanding that they undertook to integrate into that nation in all respects." Only "religious doctrines and practices" were to separate them out as Jews. Shimoni, "From Anti-Zionism to Non-Zionism," 21.

16 Shimoni, 26.

17 Jason Lustig, "Resigning to Change: The Foundation and Transformation of the American Council for Judaism" (master's thesis, Brandeis University, 2009), 69.

18 Hillel Halkin, "What Ahad Ha'am Saw and Herzl Missed—and Vice Versa," *Mosaic Magazine*, October 5, 2016, https://tikvahfund.org.

19 Shimoni writes, "For the Zionist Organization, to permit the formation of a legislative council reflecting the clear Arab majority which prevailed (as it was likely to, unless ingenious alternative devices could be found) would spell disaster for the development of the National Home; but to oppose its formation would place the Zionists in the invidious position of being anti-democratic." Shimoni, "From Anti-Zionism to Non-Zionism," 38. "Arab majority" is the term used for the Palestinian people.

20 Shimoni, 42. Shimoni's second article in the *Jewish Journal of Sociology* followed the story forward, analyzing the divide between non-Zionists and Zionists during World War II. He explains the "acrimony" between the two groups as emerging

out of the "heightened assertiveness" of the Zionists during the war, the growth of Zionism's popularity, and the "capturing" of leadership positions by Zionist Jews (91, 95). British and American non-Zionists leaders joined forces and spoke of the "Zionization" of organizational boards and referred to "Zionist manipulators." Quoted in Gideon Shimoni, "The Non-Zionists in Anglo Jewry, 1937–1948," *Jewish Journal of Sociology* 28, no. 2 (December 1986): 100.

21 Shimoni, "Non-Zionists in Anglo Jewry," 109, 110.

22 In 2000, Rory Miller, a scholar of Mediterranean studies, published *Divided against Zion: Anti-Zionist Opposition to the Creation of a Jewish State in Palestine 1945–1948* (New York: Routledge, 2000). Miller focuses on Jewish and non-Jewish anti-Zionism in London and argues that studying the common themes and arguments of anti-Zionism is of "vital importance" in understanding the history of Britain and the Middle East in that era (2).

23 Here, Berger referred to the American Jewish Committee, whose members referred to themselves as non-Zionist through to 1967. Rabbi Elmer Berger to Mr. Clarence Coleman Jr., April 10, 1959, Papers of the American Council for Judaism, box 1, folder 5, American Jewish Archives, Cincinnati, OH.

24 Yakov M. Rabkin, *A Threat from Within: A Century of Jewish Opposition to Zionism*, trans. Fred A. Reed with Y. M. Rabkin (London: Zed, 2006).

1. JEWISH ANTI- AND NON-ZIONISM

1 Shari Rabin, *Jews on the Frontier: Religion and Mobility in Nineteenth-Century America* (New York: New York University Press, 2017).

2 Joseph Kip Kosek and Jon Butler, eds., *American Religion, American Politics: An Anthology* (New Haven, CT: Yale University Press, 2017), 62.

3 Michael A. Meyer, *Response to Modernity: A History of the Reform Movement in Judaism* (New York: Oxford University Press, 1988), 265.

4 The Pittsburgh Platform's inclusion in *American Religion, American Politics* by Kosek and Butler, preeminent scholars of American religion, offers a gauge of its historical significance.

5 Meyer, *Response to Modernity*, 269.

6 The full text of the Pittsburgh Platform can be found at the Jewish Virtual Library, "Reform Judaism: The Pittsburgh Platform (November 1885)," www .jewishvirtuallibrary.org.

7 Earl Raab, "Attitudes toward Israel and Jews: The Relationship," in *Antisemitism in the Contemporary World*, ed. Michael Curtis (Boulder, CO: Westview, 1986), 288.

8 Discussing the American Council for Judaism, Matthew Berkman writes, "Central to the Council's view of antisemitism . . . was an understanding of Zionism as a racializing force." Matthew Berkman, "Antisemitism, Anti-Zionism, and the American Racial Order: Revisiting the American Council for Judaism in the Twenty-First Century," *American Jewish History* 105, nos. 1–2 (January–April 2021): 128.

9 Meyer, *Response to Modernity*, 210.

10 Yaakov Ariel, *Evangelizing the Chosen People: Missions to the Jews in America, 1880–2000* (Chapel Hill: University of North Carolina Press, 2000), 18.

11 Ariel, 13. On the historical alliance between Evangelical Christians and Jews over Zionism, see Yaakov Ariel, *An Unusual Relationship: Evangelical Christians and Jews* (New York: New York University Press, 2013). Donald M. Lewis also studies the role of restorationism in Christian support of Zionism. See Lewis, *A Short History of Christian Zionism from the Reformation to the Twenty-First Century* (Downers Grove, IL: InterVarsity, 2021).

12 Hasia Diner, *Julius Rosenwald: Repairing the World* (New Haven, CT: Yale University Press, 2017), 72–73.

13 Diner, 72–73.

14 Eric Goldstein, *The Price of Whiteness: Jews, Race, and American Identity* (Princeton, NJ: Princeton University Press, 2006), 90. Goldstein charts the arguments over the idea of a Jewish "race," with both Zionist and anti-Zionists using the term for "Jewish self-description" while debating the idea of a Jewish nation (93).

15 Meyer, *Response to Modernity*, 294.

16 Quoted in Waxman, *Trouble in the Tribe*, 32.

17 Meyer, *Response to Modernity*, 330. Reform leaders described the Columbus Platform as a "guide for the progressive elements of Judaism." The statement on "Israel" read as follows: "We affirm the obligation of all Jewry to aid in its upbuilding as a Jewish homeland by endeavoring to make it not only a haven of refuge for the oppressed but also a center of Jewish culture and spiritual life." The full text of the Columbus Platform is available at the Central Conference of American Rabbis, "The Guiding Principles of Reform Judaism," www.ccarnet.org.

18 Lustig, "Resigning to Change," 35. Importantly, the text reads "a" center, leaving room for other (diasporic) centers, marking this perhaps as a transitional document between the 1885 Pittsburgh Platform and full support for American Zionism. On this, see Shaul Magid, "From the 1885 Pittsburgh Platform to Judith Butler: Living in the Diaspora as Home," the 2018 Robert P. Kogod Annual Lecture at the Shalom Hartman Institute on June 5, 2018, www.hartman.org.il.

19 Leaders of American Zionist organizations such as the Federation of American Zionists were in fact members of the German Jewish community, some even from the Reform rabbinate. But importantly, as Thomas Kolsky writes, German Jewish Zionist advocates before 1914 were "a distinct minority," and "many of these leaders were attracted to Zionism as a result of their encounters with East European Jews." Thomas Kolsky, *Jews against Zionism: The American Council for Judaism, 1942–1948* (Philadelphia: Temple University Press, 1990), 25.

20 Naomi Cohen, *Not Free to Desist: A History of the American Jewish Committee, 1906–1966* (Philadelphia: Jewish Publication Society of America, 1972), 104.

21 Moses Rischin, "The Early Attitudes of the American Jewish Committee to Zionism (1906–1922)," *Publications of the American Jewish Historical Society* 49, no. 3 (March 1960): 188–201.

22 Cohen, *Not Free to Desist*, 109–10.

23 "Protest to Wilson against Zionist State: Representative Jews Ask Him to Present It to the Peace Conference. Reject 'National Home' Idea. Against 'Political Segregation,' Contrary to Democratic Ideals," *New York Times*, March 5, 1919, 7, quoted in Rischin, "Early Attitudes," 199–200. Committee members supported minority rights for Jews in the nations where they resided, including autonomy over communal institutions, language, and religion. Joining in a coalition with some Zionists at the Paris conference, these leaders made it clear to President Wilson that they did not see these rights as a pretext for Jewish nationalism, much to the chagrin and anger of some of the Zionist leaders in their coalition. See James Loeffler, *Rooted Cosmopolitans: Jews and Human Rights in the Twentieth Century* (New Haven, CT: Yale University Press, 2018), 13–14.

24 "Protest to Wilson," quoted in Rischin, "Early Attitudes," 200. These statements also of course reveal the nativist attitudes of AJC members and their hostility to new immigrants, Jewish and non-Jewish.

25 "Protest to Wilson," quoted in Rischin, 200.

26 Rafael Medoff, *Zionism and the Arabs: An American Jewish Dilemma* (Westport, CT: Praeger, 1997), 58.

27 Rischin, "Early Attitudes," 198.

28 Rabbi Wise was one of the cofounders of the American Jewish Congress. See, for example, "Zangwill Calls Political Zionism a Vanished Hope," *New York Times*, October 15, 1923, 1. A critic of Zionism, Israel Zangwill spoke here to AJCongress.

29 Cohen, *Not Free to Desist*, 255. On Magnes, see David Barak-Gorodetsky, *Judah Magnes: The Prophetic Politics of a Religious Binationalist*, trans. Merav Datan (Lincoln: University of Nebraska Press, 2021), 181–84.

30 Geoffrey Levin, "Liberal Whispers and Propaganda Fears: The American Jewish Committee and Israel's Palestinian Minority, 1948–1966," *Israel Studies Review* 33, no. 1 (Spring 2018): 84.

31 Raab defined "political anti-Semitism" as an "attempt to establish the corporate Jew as a generalized public menace, the implication being that some official public remedy is called for." Earl Raab, "The Black Revolution and the Jewish Question," *Commentary*, January 1969, 23.

32 See Maddalena Marinari, Unwanted: Italian and Jewish Mobilization against Restrictive Immigration Laws, 1882–1965 (Chapel Hill: University of North Carolina Press, 2020), esp. chap. 3.

33 Zvi Ganin, *An Uneasy Relationship: American Jewish Leadership and Israel, 1948–1957* (Syracuse: Syracuse University Press, 2005), 16, 86.

34 Diner, *Julius Rosenwald*, 207.

35 Diner, 129.

36 See Michael Beizer, "American Jewish Joint Distribution Committee," YIVO Encyclopedia of Jews in Eastern Europe, 2017, www.yivoencyclopedia.org.

37 Quoted in Diner, *Julius Rosenwald*, 142.

38 Yehuda Bauer writes of Julius Rosenwald's "anti-Zionism" and of the fact that he was "the most important financial supporter of JDC." See Bauer, *My Brother's*

Keeper: A History of the American Jewish Joint Distribution Committee, 1929–1939 (Philadelphia: Jewish Publication Society of America, 1974), 22.

39 Bauer, 135–37, 158–68. Bauer records that JDC's early leaders' non- or anti-Zionism did not stop the organization from funding projects in Palestine in the 1920s.

40 Kolsky, *Jews against Zionism*, 51. On Rabbi Elmer Berger, see Jack Ross, *Rabbi Outcast: Elmer Berger and American Jewish Anti-Zionism* (Washington, DC: Potomac Books, 2011).

41 Ganin, *Uneasy Relationship*, 12.

42 Kolsky, *Jews against Zionism*, 4.

43 Kolsky, 9. In 1942, Isaac M. Wise, son of Isaac Mayer Wise, founder of American Reform Judaism, asked to join the American Council for Judaism. Rabbi Berger wrote an enthusiastic reply, commenting, "We hope that we in the Council have the means of restoring American Judaism to the character your father planned for it." Rabbi Elmer Berger to Isaac M. Wise, September 10, 1943, Papers of the American Council for Judaism, box 1, folder 1, American Jewish Archives, Cincinnati, OH.

44 The full text of the Biltmore Conference Declaration can be found at Zionist Congresses: The Biltmore Conference, Jewish Virtual Library, May 6–11, 1942, www.jewishvirtuallibrary.org. The American Jewish Conference, founded in 1943 as a "democratically based parliament of American Jewry" had an "agenda . . . confined to advancing the Zionist cause." As historian Doug Rossinow notes, when the Conference delegates voted on endorsing the Biltmore Program, "those representing the AJC left the meeting, which in turn provoked anger among those who blamed the AJC for disrupting the Jewish united front." Doug Rossinow, "'The Edge of the Abyss': The Origins of the Israel Lobby, 1949–1954," *Modern American History* 1 (2018): 27.

45 Urofsky, *American Zionism*, 426, 429.

46 Rabbi Morris Lazaron, "In the Shadow of Catastrophe," speech delivered at the Annual Meeting, Baltimore Chapter, American Council for Judaism, October 23, 1956, Papers of the American Council for Judaism, box 1, folder 4, Center for Jewish History, New York.

47 "Jewish Postwar Problems: Paper Read by Rabbi Morris Lazaron at the Meeting of Non-Zionist Rabbis," June 1, 1942, Papers of the American Council for Judaism, box 1, folder 1, American Jewish Archives, Cincinnati, OH.

48 Edith Rosenwald, "The Council's Ten Years—as I Remember Them," American Council for Judaism, 10th anniversary conference, San Francisco, May 10, 1953, Papers of the American Council for Judaism, box 6, folder 5, American Jewish Archives, Cincinnati, OH.

49 Lessing Rosenwald, "Why Americans of Jewish Faith Are Opposed to the Establishment of a Jewish State," *Life* Magazine, June 28, 1943, 11. Rosenwald uses the term "Palestinian" to refer to residents of then Palestine.

50 Shlomo Shafir, *Ambiguous Relations: The American Jewish Community and Germany since 1945* (Detroit: Wayne State University Press, 1999), 103; Kolsky,

Jews against Zionism, 5. Wayne Cole writes that the America First Committee "tried to avoid the stigma of anti-Semitism." In 1940, Lessing Rosenwald became a member along with Henry Ford, whose antisemitic campaign in the early 1920s was well remembered. Rosenwald resigned from the America First Committee after a few months due to its association with antisemitism, and the committee subsequently asked Ford to leave. Though "prominent Jews were invited to serve on the committee" after Rosenwald's departure, none of the invitations were accepted. Wayne S. Cole, *America First: The Battle against Intervention, 1940–1941* (Madison: University of Wisconsin Press, 1953), 132–33.

51 Marinari, *Unwanted*, 100.

52 Raab, "Black Revolution," 24.

53 Amy Weiss, "'Making the Desert Blossom as the Rose': The American Christian Palestine Committee's 'Children's Memorial Forest' and Postwar Land Acquisition in Palestine," *Holocaust and Genocide Studies* 33, no. 2 (Fall 2019): 247.

54 Medoff writes that the meetings of the American Jewish Conference and the Zionist Organization of America in 1943 both addressed Arab civil rights, interest that was "likely to have been stimulated by recent attention drawn to the Arab issue by Judah Magnes's Ihud organization and the anti-Zionist American Council for Judaism." Medoff, *Zionism and the Arabs*, 122.

55 "Listening in on Lessing J. Rosenwald: A Radio Interview by Tex McCrary on WEAF, September 19, 1946," Papers of the American Council for Judaism, box 1, folder 4, Center for Jewish History, New York.

56 On the Anglo-American Committee, see Medoff, *Zionism and the Arabs*, 142–45. See also "The Case against a Jewish State in Palestine: Albert Hourani's Statement to the Anglo-American Committee of Inquiry of 1946," *Journal of Palestine Studies* 35, no. 1 (Autumn 2005): 80–90; and Walid Khalidi's "On Albert Hourani, the Arab Office, and the Anglo-American Committee of 1946," *Journal of Palestine Studies* 35, no. 1 (Autumn 2005): 60–79.

57 Anglo-American Committee of Inquiry, *Report to the United States Government and His Majesty's Government in the United Kingdom*, Lausanne, Switzerland, Harry S. Truman Library, April 20, 1946, www.trumanlibrary.gov.

58 "Listening in on Lessing J. Rosenwald."

59 Professor Elizabeth V. L. Stern, December 13, 1943, meeting of the ACJ executive committee, quoted in Kolsky, *Jews against Zionism*, 89.

60 Kolsky makes this point in *Jews against Zionism*, 99.

61 On behalf of members of the Council who wished "to contribute to the relief, resettlement, and other humanitarian needs of Jews and others abroad" but "did not wish to go through the UJA [the Zionist-learning United Jewish Appeal]," Rabbi Berger sought out non-Zionist agencies working for Jewish refugees. Rabbi Elmer Berger to Jacob Karlinsky, January 26, 1949, Vaad Hatzala Collection, box 46, folder 10, Yeshiva University, New York. The Vaad Hatzala (translated as "rescue committee") was a group of Orthodox rabbis who engaged in relief and rescue efforts for Jews in Europe during the Holocaust. In 1953, Rabbi Berger wrote "The Last of the

DP Camps" for *Council News*, which is a collection of his thoughts on Foehrenwald, one of the largest displaced persons camps, in Germany. Berger strongly criticized the Joint Distribution Committee for what he saw as its near-exclusive focus on Israel and its neglect of the displaced persons camps. Berger, "The Last of the Jewish DP Camps," *Council News*, January 1953, Papers of the American Council for Judaism, box 1, folder 18, Center for Jewish History, New York.

62 I. F. Stone, "Jewry in a Blind Alley," *Nation*, November 24, 1945, 543–44.

63 Kolsky, *Jews against Zionism*, 91–94.

64 Rabbi Irving F. Reichert, "The Jewish State and the Status of the Jew," speech given at the Third Annual Conference of the American Council for Judaism, Philadelphia, Pennsylvania, February 12, 1947, then published and distributed by the Council, Papers of the American Council for Judaism, box 2, folder 4, Center for Jewish History, New York. Reichert resigned from the Council in 1956, asserting that the organization had become as focused on public policy as had the Zionists.

65 Mondoweiss, a journalist outlet critical of American Zionism and Israel, published Reichert's 1943 Yom Kippur sermon about Zionism in 2013: Jack Ross, "'Where Do You Stand?' A 1943 Yom Kippur Sermon Challenged the American Jewish Community on Zionism," Mondoweiss, September 13, 2013, https://mondoweiss.net.

66 "CHOOSE NOW" membership mailing, n.d. [ca. 1950], Papers of the American Council for Judaism, box 2, folder 4, Center for Jewish History, New York.

67 Elmer Berger (on behalf of twenty-one Reform Rabbis of the COUNCIL) to Dr. James Heller, president, Central Conference of American Rabbis, May 7, 1942, Papers of the American Council for Judaism, box 1, folder 1, American Jewish Archives, New York.

68 Elmer Berger to Henry Hurwitz, June 11, 1945, Papers of the American Council for Judaism, box 1, folder 1, American Jewish Archives, Cincinnati, OH.

69 Copy of "Resolution," sent by Fred Herzberg, Community Relations Committee of Los Angeles Jewish Community Council, to Isaiah M. Minkoff, National Community Relations Advisory Council, September 10, 1947, Papers of the American Council for Judaism, box 1, folder 17, Center for Jewish History, New York.

70 Richard Gutstadt, Anti-Defamation League, to Isaiah Minkoff, April 17, 1946, Papers of the American Council for Judaism, box 1, folder 17, Center for Jewish History, New York.

71 David Petegorsky to Fred Herzberg, September 22, 1947, Papers of the American Council for Judaism, box 1, folder 17, Center for Jewish History, New York.

72 Historian Derek Penslar writes of how American Jews' emotions were mobilized in support of Zionism and especially Zionist fundraising; Jews had a right to a state in Israel because the need was "urgent and apparent" after the Holocaust, and any "failure to acknowledge that right was a source of unequivocal moral condemnation by American Jewish activists." Derek Penslar, "Solidarity as an Emotion: American Jews in Israel in 1948," *Modern American History* 4, no. 44 (2022): 38.

73 Kolsky, *Jews against Zionism*, 141.

74 Cohen, *Not Free to Desist*, 309.

75 "Rosenwald Explains ACJ to AJC," n.d. [ca. October 1949], Papers of the American Council for Judaism, box 1, folder 17, Center for Jewish History, New York. Geoffrey Levin finds that in the 1950s and early 1960s, Lessing Rosenwald became "friendlier" with Israeli officials, including Theodore "Teddy" Kollek, director of the prime minister's office and future mayor of Jerusalem from 1965 to 1993. These relationships emerged after Rosenwald accepted an invitation from Ben-Gurion to visit Israel in 1957, part of a concerted Israeli "effort to win over the Sears-Roebuck heir." See Geoffrey Phillip Levin, *Our Palestine Question: Israel and American Jewish Dissent, 1948–1978* (New Haven, CT: Yale University Press, 2023), 169.

76 Ganin, *Uneasy Relationship*, 85.

77 Indeed, Dov Waxman uses the word "disinterest" to describe "the American Jewish relationship with Israel" for the period 1948–67. Waxman, *Trouble in the Tribe*, 33.

78 Blaustein was likely the richest Jewish person in the United States in this era. He was the owner of the American Trading and Production Corporation and was also a diplomat and philanthropist.

79 See Ganin, "The Blaustein–Ben-Gurion Understanding of 1950," in *Uneasy Relationship*, esp. 81–86.

80 American Jewish Committee press release, "Israeli Premier's First Official Declaration Clarifying Relationships between Israel and Jews in United States and Other Free Democracies Hailed by Blaustein as 'Document of Historic Significance,'" American Jewish Archives, September 10, 1950, https://ajcarchives.org.

81 "American Jews in Relation to Israel: Summary of Press Reaction on Ben-Gurion-Blaustein Statements," American Jewish Archives, October 6, 1950, https://ajcarchives.org.

82 Waxman, *Trouble in the Tribe*, 30, 31.

83 On Lazaron's early career and relationship to Zionism and the Reform movement, see Monty Noam Penkower, "The Genesis of the American Council for Judaism: A Quest for Identity in World War II," *American Jewish History* 86, no. 2 (June 1998): 167–94.

84 Derek Penslar analyzes how in late 1948, "American Jewish public opinion turned against the [Palestinian] refugees," part of an "emotional regime" that inspired pride in Israel and "disregard for Palestinian suffering" among American Jews. Penslar, "Solidarity as an Emotion," 45.

85 Rabbi Morris Lazaron, "Israel and Jewish Nationalism: Approaching a Solution," American Council for Judaism, 10th anniversary conference, San Francisco, May 8, 1953, Papers of the American Council for Judaism, box 6, folder 5, American Jewish Archives, Cincinnati, OH.

86 Lazaron.

87 Lazaron.

88 Lazaron.

89 Lazaron.

90 "Massacre at Kibya," *Time*, October 26, 1953, 34.

91 Letter from American Council for Judaism, Henry C. Moyer, vice president, to the Honorable John Foster Dulles, secretary of state, October 20, 1953, American Council for Judaism Papers, Center for Jewish History.

92 Berger felt that Secretary of State Dulles identified "Zionism in a kind of adversary relationship to American interest" and that the "United States would have to take steps to remove Arab fears of what the Secretary courageously identified as 'expansionist Zionism.'" From Israel and American Zionists, he wrote, "came the predictable fire storm." Elmer Berger, "Memoirs of an Anti-Zionist Jew," *Journal of Palestine Studies* 5, nos. 1–2 (Autumn 1976–Winter 1976): 28, 29.

93 "Zionists Voice Shock That U.S. Joins Reprimand," *Jewish Advocate*, November 19, 1953, 1; and "Eisendrath Announces Tripling of Reform Temple Membership," *Jewish Exponent*, November 6, 1953, 38.

94 Rabbi Elmer Berger, "In Moral Indignation," *Council News*, December 1953, 3–20, quoted in Mark Glickman, "One Voice against Many: A Biographical Study of Elmer Berger, 1948–1968" (rabbinical diss., Hebrew Union College, 1990), 86.

95 Henry Hurwitz, "Israel, What Now?," *Menorah Journal* 42, nos. 1–2 (Spring–Summer 1954): 2. Hurwitz is discussed further in chapter 2.

96 "Pulpit Freedom," *B'nai B'rith Messenger*, January 8, 1954, 3.

97 Doug Rossinow asserts that in the wake of the Kibya killings and after the UN Security Council's censure of Israel over the killings, the "censure became the pivotal interval for the restructuring of pro-Israel advocacy in American power centers." Rossinow, "Edge of the Abyss," 35.

98 Mitelpunkt, *Israel in the American Mind*, 32.

99 Isaac Alteras writes of the close relationship between Secretary of State Dulles and the members of the American Council for Judaism as a means to explain the gap in uncritical American support for Israel under President Eisenhower. See Isaac Alteras, "Eisenhower, American Jewry, and Israel," *American Jewish Archives* 37, no. 2 (November 1985): 258–74.

100 At first, Israel received an invitation to the 1955 conference of independent Asian and African states in Bandung, Indonesia. But "no sooner had the invitation been issued than Indian premier Jawaharlal Nehru withdrew it" under pressure from Egypt, other Arab states, and Pakistan. Sasha Polakow-Suransky, *The Unspoken Alliance: Israel's Secret Relationship with Apartheid South Africa* (New York: Pantheon Books, 2010), 2. This exclusion was a "serious diplomatic defeat" for Israel, as it meant that "Asia viewed Israel neither as an Asian state nor as one rightly belonging to the nonaligned group of new nations then in the process of developing." The conference proved a platform for Egypt's president Nasser and other Arab Middle East delegates' "verbal onslaughts" against Israel and Zionism. Ran Kochan, "Israel in Third World Forums," in *Israel in the Third World*, ed. Michael Curtis and Susan Aurelia Gitelson (New Brunswick, NJ: Transaction Books, 1976), 253, 201, 252. On the broader historical importance of the Bandung Conference

for anticolonialism, see Penny M. Von Eschen, *Race against Empire: Black Americans and Anticolonialism, 1937–1957* (Ithaca, NY: Cornell University Press, 1997), 168–73.

101 "Leonard R. Sussman, Executive Director, American Council for Judaism," September 1958, Papers of the American Council for Judaism, box 7, folder 2, American Jewish Archives, Cincinnati, OH.

102 Leonard R. Sussman, "The Meaning of Bandung," *American Council for Judaism Newsletter*, June 1955, 6, Papers of the American Council for Judaism, box 1, folder 18, Center for Jewish History, New York.

103 Sussman.

104 On the tenure of Leonard Sussman at the Council, see Ross, *Rabbi Outcast*, 102, 160.

105 Leonard R. Sussman, *A Passion for Freedom: My Encounters with Extraordinary People* (Amherst, NY: Prometheus Books, 2004), 58. Sussman died in 2015.

106 Jack Ross tells this story in *Rabbi Outcast*, 96.

107 Ross, 62.

108 Sussman began serving as executive director of Freedom House in 1967. Beginning in the late 1980s, scholars and others criticized Freedom House for "its particular neo-Conservative political affiliation and alignment with government interests." Emily A. Zerndt reveals Freedom House's "increasing endorsement of U.S. foreign policy actions, even when those actions were detrimental to democratization in other countries." Emily A. Zerndt, "The House That Propaganda Built: Historicizing the Democracy Promotion Efforts and Measurement Tools of Freedom House" (PhD diss., Western Michigan University, 2016), 205, 222. Scholar Emmaia Gelman led me to this source.

109 Memo to Bill Gottlieb, from "ABB" [Albert Benton], "Inquiries from Smithtown Chapter of Hadassah," January 5, 1959, American Council for Judaism Records, box 3, folder 4, American Jewish Archives, Cincinnati, OH. The answer listed is that "there is no categorical yes or no to the question" but that "certain parts of the land did belong to the Arabs and their (forcible or voluntary) self-evacuation created the acute Refugee problem, since 1948."

110 "Resolution Adopted by the National Community Relations Advisory Council," June 21–24, 1956, Atlantic City, New Jersey, Papers of the American Council for Judaism, box 6, folder 7, American Jewish Archives, Cincinnati, OH.

111 Beth Din of America (American Board of Rabbis) press release, June 10, 1956, American Council for Judaism Records, box 1, folder 1, American Jewish Archives, Cincinnati, OH.

112 Sol Kolack to Robert E. Segal, January 7, 1949, Papers of the Boston Jewish Community Council, box 124, Activities, Israel and the Middle East, Anti-Zionism and Arab Propaganda Organizations, folder 3, New England Historic Genealogical Society, Jewish Heritage Center, Boston, MA (emphasis in original).

113 Jewish Community Council of Greater Boston to Aaron Bronstein, Sidney Cohen, et al., May 11, 1959, Boston Jewish Community Council Activities, box 124,

Activities, Israel and the Middle East, Anti-Zionism and Arab Propaganda Organizations, folder 3, New England Historic Genealogical Society, Jewish Heritage Center, Boston, MA.

114 Dr. Carl Seltzer of the New England Zionist Council to Mr. Robert Segal of the Boston Jewish Community Relations Council, October 21, 1957, Papers of the Boston Jewish Community Relations Council, box 123, Israel and the Middle East, Anti-Zionism and Arab Propaganda, 1946–1961, folder 1, New England Historic Genealogical Society, Jewish Heritage Center, Boston, MA. Seltzer wrote that the materials were "very anti-Israel."

115 "An Interim Recommended Religious School Curriculum," July 1952, American Council for Judaism, Papers of the American Council for Judaism, box 6, folder 2, American Jewish Archives, Cincinnati, OH; Leonard Sussman, *Current Events and Judaism: A Syllabus for the Religious School Curriculum* (New York: American Council for Judaism, n.d. [195?]), Library of Hebrew Union College, Cincinnati, OH.

116 Conference pamphlet, *Lessing Rosenwald Reports On: "What Happened in San Francisco? The President of the American Council for Judaism Tells about the Highlights of the Tenth Anniversary Conference,"* May 7, 8, 9, and 10, 1953, American Council for Judaism, Moses Lasky Papers, box 2, folder 6, American Jewish Archives, Cincinnati, OH.

117 Advisory for parents, June 28, 1962, American Council for Judaism Papers, box 18, folder 3, American Jewish Archives, Cincinnati, OH.

118 "Zionists in Nationwide Campaign to Nationalize All Jewish Camp Children," *Council News*, June 1950, Papers of the American Council for Judaism, box 1, folder 18, Center for Jewish History, New York.

119 Leonard Sussman to Philip Amran, June 25, 1956, Moses Lasky Papers, box 2, folder 5, American Jewish Archives, Cincinnati, OH.

120 Bill Gottlieb, publicity director, American Council for Judaism, memo with "To" line left blank, subject: "Your Zionist Programming without Suitable Balance," n.d. [1961?], Papers of the American Council for Judaism, box 9, folder 4, American Jewish Archives, Cincinnati, OH.

121 Minutes of the National Executive Committee Meeting, June 24, 1960, box 8, folder 7, Papers of the American Council for Judaism, American Jewish Archives, Cincinnati, OH.

122 Leonard Sussman, American Council for Judaism memorandum "not for publication" on "background on the Eichmann trial," December 12, 1960, box 8, folder 8, Papers of the American Council for Judaism, American Jewish Archives, Cincinnati, OH.

123 Elmer Berger published his correspondence from this 1955 trip in *Who Knows Better Must Say So!* (New York: American Council for Judaism, 1955); Geoffrey Levin writes about Berger's trip as well as the 1953 Middle East trip of Rabbi Morris Lazaron in *Our Palestine Question*, chap. 5. Historian Hugh Wilford notes that Berger's 1955 trip marked "the single most imaginative contribution" to the

"comprehensive Anglo-American effort to resolve all the outstanding points of contention between Israel and its Arab neighbors" (184, 176). The CIA, notes Wilford, was "informing Arabs about the existence of non-Zionist American Judaism and the Eisenhower administration's policy of friendly impartiality." Hugh Wilford, *America's Great Game: The CIA's Secret Arabists and the Shaping of the Modern Middle East* (New York: Basic Books, 2013).

124 Rabbi Elmer Berger to Clarence Coleman Jr., April 10, 1959, Papers of the American Council for Judaism, box 1, folder 5, American Jewish Archives, Cincinnati, OH (emphasis in original).

125 A *Time Magazine* column titled "Organizations: What Is a Jew?" spotlighted the World Zionist Organization, the American Jewish Committee, and the American Council for Judaism, May 19, 1961, box 9, folder 3, Papers of the American Council for Judaism, American Jewish Archives, Cincinnati, OH. In a mass mailing, the Council called the article a "major Council Break-Through!"

126 Sussman, *Passion for Freedom*, 60.

127 Council leadership cited "serious differences with respect to Council policy and programmatic emphases extending over a long period of time." Memo from Clarence Coleman Jr., acting president, to members of the American Council for Judaism, March 6, 1969, Papers of the American Council for Judaism, box 22, folder 6, American Jewish Archives, Cincinnati, OH. The four-page letter notes that some members of the Council resigned their membership and followed Rabbi Berger to his new organization.

128 Quoted in "Berger Forms Group after Break with ACJ," *Daily Star*, Beirut, Lebanon, October 1, 1969, Papers of American Jewish Alternatives to Zionism, box 1, folder 2, Center for Jewish History, New York. Membership in AJAZ appears to have been very small.

129 "Berger Forms." Information about the American Jewish Alternatives to Zionism came from Mark Glickman's thesis, "One Voice against Many," esp. 163–64. Glickman relied on Berger's papers as well as interviews and correspondence with Berger in his final years.

130 Levin, *Our Palestine Question*, 180. Berger's repeated trips to the Middle East educated him on the history of the region and pushed him further into activism on behalf of Palestinians and against Zionism. In 1959, for example, he visited Lebanon, Tunisia, Egypt, Syria, and Jordan and spoke with former diplomats and policy experts along with ruling elites. Rabbi Elmer Berger, "1959 Itinerary to Middle East and Europe," 1959, Papers of the American Council for Judaism, box 1, folder 5, American Jewish Archives, Cincinnati, OH.

131 Rabbi Elmer Berger to Mrs. Hayman [founding letter of AJAZ], March 17, 1969, Papers of the American Council for Judaism, box 22, folder 6, American Jewish Archives, Cincinnati, OH.

132 Jonathan Marc Gribetz, "The PLO's Rabbi: Palestinian Nationalism and Reform Judaism," *Jewish Quarterly Review* 107, no. 1 (Winter 2017): 110.

133 Lustig, "Resigning to Change," 133.

134 Sussman, *Passion for Freedom*, 64.

135 Geoffrey Moorhouse, "The Rabbi with More Friends in Islam," *Guardian*, February 16, 1970, Papers of Jewish Alternatives to Zion, Center for Jewish History, New York. Mark Glickman writes that by the mid-1950s, Berger "had become solidly critical of Israel and pro-Arab in his orientation." Glickman, "One Voice against Many," 113.

136 Kolsky, *Jews against Zionism*, 86.

137 Kolsky, 120.

138 Kolsky, 201.

139 Murray Polner, "Israel Haunted," review of *Jews against Zionism: The American Council for Judaism, 1942–1948*, by Thomas Kolsky, *New York Times Book Review*, October 14, 1990, 18.

140 Sussman, quoting Glickman, *Passion for Freedom*, 71.

141 Kyle Stanton, "Hyman Judah Schachtel, Congregation Beth Israel, and the American Council for Judaism," *Southern Jewish History* 22 (2019): 127.

142 Stanton, 140.

143 Berkman, "Antisemitism," 136.

144 "Zionism Blamed for Lack of Insight on Israel Crisis," *Atlanta Daily World*, April 30, 1957, 2.

145 Louis Cassels, "Jewish Debate Waxes Hot: Can't Decide Whether They Are Race, Religion or Nationality," *Chicago Defender*, August 23, 1958, 11.

146 Marjorie Mayer Arsht to Syd Applebaum, March 10, 1961, Papers of the American Council for Judaism, box 1, folder 6, American Jewish Archives, Cincinnati, OH.

147 Arsht to Applebaum.

148 Allan Brownfield wrote a brief biography of Marjorie Arsht on the Council website. See Allan C. Brownfeld, "One Woman's Unique Journey and Life of Service," American Council for Judaism, Spring 2006, www.acjna.org. Arsht wrote an autobiography, *All the Way from Yoakum: The Personal Journey of a Political Insider* (College Station, TX: Texas A&M University Press, 2005); George H. Walker Bush, a close friend of the author, provided a blurb for the book's cover.

2. THE JEWS IN REVOLT

1 Tony Michels writes that "Jewish radicals challenged established customs, ways of thinking, and dominant institutions within the Jewish community and American society broadly." Tony Michels, ed., *Jewish Radicals: A Documentary Reader* (New York: New York University Press, 2012), 2. My understanding of the history of territorialists and diaspora nationalists has been aided by Ri Turner, my Yiddish translator, as well as the work of historian Joshua Shanes, "Yiddish and Jewish Diaspora Nationalism," *Monatshefte* 90, no. 2 (Summer 1998): 181; and Madeleine Cohen, "Here and Now: The Modernist Poetics of Do'ikayt" (PhD diss., University of California Berkeley, 2016).

2 Michels, *Jewish Radicals*, 277. Joshua Shanes writes that "Eastern Europe boasted a fair number of non-Zionist forms of Jewish nationalist expression." Indeed, as he

makes clear, some Bund leaders embraced nationalism—only cultural, not political, autonomy—in order to "compete with the Zionists." Shanes, "Yiddish," 181.

3 In the 1940s, natives of Palestine were generally referred to as "Arabs." The term "Palestinian" did not come into wide usage until the founding of the Palestinian Liberation Organization in 1964. See Elon Gilad, "What Israelis Call Palestinians and Why It Matters," *Haaretz*, November 19, 2015. I have tried to use the term "Palestinian" consistently in my own analysis, except when quoting a historical source.

4 Michels, *Jewish Radicals*, 277; Alexander Bittelman, "Israel and the World Struggle for Peace and Democracy," from Bittelman, "The New State of Israel," *Political Affairs* 17, no. 8 (August 1948): 720–30, excerpted in Michels, *Jewish Radicals*, 330. Activist Dorothy M. Zellner explores why American Communist Party Jewish leaders did not work for Palestinian rights after the party accepted partition in 1947 in "What We Did: The American Jewish Communist Left and the Establishment of the State of Israel," Jewish Voice for Peace, 2019, https://jewishvoiceforpeace.org.

5 William Zukerman published his American sources largely, but not exclusively, in English (e.g., his *Jewish Newsletter*). Yiddishists must examine Zukerman's Yiddish-language sources and discern if his messages differed in content from the analysis I provide here.

6 For an analysis of Zionist leaders' "feeling of shame in the Diaspora Jew" and its connection to their war on Yiddish—a war fought with brute force and with laws declaring Yiddish periodicals illegal—see Dovid Katz, *Words on Fire: The Unfinished Story of Yiddish* (New York: Basic Books, 2004), 310. In 1976 in the pages of *Jewish Currents*, Louis Harap noted that "the haughty Zionist rejection of both Jewish history of the past 2,000 years and of Yiddish was hardly an aspect of the Zionist movement likely to attract Jewish—Yiddish-speaking—socialists." Louis Harap, *The Zionist Movement Revisited*, pamphlet reprint of *Jewish Currents* (1976): 20. In her book *Yiddish in Israel: A History*, scholar Rachel Rojanski argues against the standard narrative of Israel's "war" with Yiddish, instead proposing "a complex dialectic between its total rejection and some sense of affinity and even respect" for Yiddish in Israel (Bloomington: Indiana University Press, 2020), 42.

7 William Zukerman used this phrase to describe the state power of Orthodox rabbis in Israel over civic institutions. See, for example, *Jewish Newsletter*, October 15, 1948, 1.

8 Rachel Kranson, *Ambivalent Embrace: Jewish Upward Mobility in Postwar America* (Chapel Hill: University of North Carolina Press, 2017), 95.

9 William Zukerman to David Dubinsky, 1957, William Zukerman Papers, box 1, folder 7, YIVO Archive, Center for Jewish History, New York.

10 Michael Staub's *Torn at the Roots: The Crisis of Jewish Liberalism in Postwar America* (New York: Columbia University Press, 2002) traces these intracommunal Jewish contests over social justice activism's connection to Jewish identity in the 1950s and 1960s, especially those that invoked the Holocaust.

11 William Zukerman to Henry Hurwitz, December 1, 1938, Henry Hurwitz Papers, box 64, folder 10, American Jewish Archives, Cincinnati, OH.

12 George Zukerman, son of William Zukerman, memoir (unpublished), n.d., draft obtained by Dr. Geoffrey Levin and shared with the author. I am grateful to Dr. Levin for sharing this and other materials with me.

13 Zukerman, memoir. Biographical information is also located in Zukerman's online Leksikon entry, Benyomen Elis, "William Tsukerman," Yiddish Leksikon, January 9, 2019, https://yleksikon.blogspot.com.

14 Biographical information was gathered from George Zukerman, unpublished memoir; "William Zuckerman [sic] and His Journalistic Work in the Last 2–3 Years," September 25, 1951, William Zukerman File, Israel State Archives. (No author is listed for this, though it seems certain that Israeli diplomats assembled the information.)

15 In a letter to a friend at this time, William Zukerman announced, "I favour the partition plan. My chief reason is that partition does away with the Balfour Declaration which has been a great misfortune for the Jews, Zionists and non-Zionists alike. I do not believe a Jewish state can be any worse." Zukerman to Henry Hurwitz, August 25, 1937, Henry Hurwitz Papers, box 64, folder 9, American Jewish Archives, Cincinnati, OH. He later wrote that the Balfour Declaration "changed first into a demand for a Jewish Commonwealth and, later, into a Jewish state of the Biltmore Program. The principle of equal partnership with the Arabs was turned into a demand for an outright [Jewish] majority and for dictatorial powers while the Jewish group was still a minority." Of Israel's attempts at peace in this year, 1960, he wrote, "What kind of a peace is it that starts out by sentencing a million civilians who have been made homeless by an act of Israel, and does not permit even the discussion of their chief grievances?" Zukerman, *Jewish Newsletter*, November 28, 1960.

16 William Zukerman, "The Biro-Bidjan Project in Eastern Siberia Stirs Opposition as a Possible Rival of Palestine," *New York Times*, August 26, 1934, 13. In 1932, Zukerman wrote in the pages of the *Morgen Zhurnal* that Birobidzhan would solve the Jewish problem. He noted that it lacked the "grave problems" of the Balfour Declaration. This quote is from Henry Felix Srebrnik, "The Formation of Ambijan," in *Dreams of Nationhood: American Jewish Communists and the Soviet Birobidzhan Project, 1924–1951* (Brighton, MA: Academic Studies Press, 2010), 29–30. Ambijan was the American Jewish organization that raised funds for Birobidzhan.

17 "Soviet Jews Approve Russian Colonization, Says Writer," *American Israelite*, June 30, 1932, 1. Birobidzhan never received adequate resources, and many Jews who arrived there eventually left because of the difficult living conditions and isolation from the main cities. The Great Purge of 1936–39 signaled the end of Soviet support, as many of its leaders were killed and resources ceased to be dedicated to the project. See David Shneer, "Birobidzhan," YIVO Encyclopedia of Jews in Eastern Europe, 2010, https://yivoencyclopedia.org.

18 William Zukerman to Henry Hurwitz, August 1, 1937, Henry Hurwitz Papers, box 64, folder 9, American Jewish Archives, Cincinnati, OH.

19 William Zukerman, *The Jew in Revolt: The Modern Jew in the World Crisis* (London: Martin Secker and Warburg, 1937), 253, 254.

20 Zukerman, 151, 143, 157, 152.

21 Zukerman, 162. Here Zukerman writes that he relies on "the words" of Zhitlowsky, but he does not credit direct quotes. On Zhitlowsky, see Ri Turner, "Confronting the Jewish Rejection of Jewish Particularism: Chaim Zhitlowsky's Anti-assimilationist Intervention in the American Yiddish Press," *Res Rhetorica*, June 2020, 17–32.

22 Zukerman, *Jew in Revolt*, 165.

23 Zukerman, 208.

24 Zukerman, 209.

25 For a discussion on this idea of Jewish exceptionalism, or triumphalism, regarding Israel, see Michael Brenner, "A State like Any Other State or a Light Unto the Nations?," *Israel Studies* 23, no. 3 (Fall 2018): 3–10.

26 Kaplan, *Our American Israel*, 28. Kaplan links this to Zionists who hoped to bring a New Deal to Palestine, the "technocratic fantasy" of white Americans for the Palestinians (43). Like many on the left, Zukerman wrote too with deep affection for the New Deal.

27 Zukerman, *Jew in Revolt*, 195.

28 Zukerman, 207.

29 Benjamin Balthaser, "When Anti-Zionism Was Jewish: Jewish Racial Subjectivity and the Anti-imperialist Literary Left from the Great Depression to the Cold War," *American Quarterly* 72, no. 2 (June 2020): 452, 453.

30 Alain Brossat and Sylvia Klingberg capture this set of contradictions: "The Bundists, for their part, linked the universal definition of their struggle indissolubly to the emancipation of the community from which they came, to the promotion of the positive values and culture of this community, to the promotion and flourishing of the specific identity of this community within the universalism of the 'new world.'" Alain Brossat and Sylvia Klingberg, *Revolutionary Yiddishland: A History of Jewish Radicalism* (1983; repr., Verso: New York, 2017), 18. My thinking here was also deeply influenced by Tony Michels, *A Fire in Their Hearts: Yiddish Socialists in New York* (Cambridge: Harvard University Press, 2005); and Matthew B. Hoffman and Henry F. Srebrnik, eds., *A Vanished Ideology: Essays on the Jewish Communist Movement in the English-Speaking World in the Twentieth Century* (Albany: State University of New York Press, 2016).

31 These are the (clearly self-selected) reviews Zukerman excerpted and sent to friends, colleagues, and potential supporters. "Press Opinions of *The Jew in Revolt*," n.d. [August 1937?], Henry Hurwitz Papers, box 64, folder 9, American Jewish Archives, Cincinnati, OH.

32 William Zukerman to Zalman Reisen, October 17 [1937?], correspondence of Zalman Reisen (Reyzen), 1921–27, box 1, folder 58, Records of the YIVO Institute for

Jewish Research in the Martynas Mažvydas National Library of Lithuania, YIVO Institute for Jewish Research. These letters were translated from Yiddish by Ri J. Turner.

33 William Zukerman, "The Passing of a Generation (in Memory of Peter Wiernik)," *American Hebrew*, January 29, 1937, 835–36, William Zukerman Papers, box 1, folder 7, American Jewish Archives, Cincinnati, OH. The decline of Yiddish schools sped up considerably after World War II with American Jewish social mobility and suburbanization. Rachel Kranson writes that "between 1946 and 1958, for instance, the proportion of American Jewish children studying in secular, leftist Yiddish schools declined by half, leaving those schools to serve less than 2% of the overall population of Jewish schoolchildren." Kranson, *Ambivalent Embrace*, 60.

34 William Zukerman, "In Defense of the Yiddish Press," *Sentinel*, May 27, 1943, 8.

35 Roger Baldwin, Abraham Cronbach, Erich Fromm, J. B. S. Hardman, William Hubben, Morris Lazaron, Dwight Macdonald, et al., preface to *Voice of Dissent: Jewish Problems, 1948–1961*, by William Zukerman (New York: Bookman Associates, 1964), 7. Zukerman's friends and colleagues published this collection of his editorials upon his death.

36 William Zukerman, *Jewish Newsletter*, January 27, 1958.

37 Penslar observes that in 1947 and 1948, American Jewish newspapers were sympathetic to Labor Zionism and largely dismissed the Irgun as "fascist, chauvinistic, and dangerous to the unity of the state." Penslar, "Solidarity as an Emotion," 40.

38 William Zukerman, *Jewish Newsletter*, November 29, 1948.

39 In his biography of David Ben-Gurion, Tom Segev writes, "In his memoirs, Ben-Gurion wrote at great length about the involvement of the village of Deir Yassin in attacks on Jewish neighborhoods, but in general he stayed away from addressing what happened during the capture of the village. After the war, he opposed his justice minister's demand to bring the perpetrators of the deed to trial." Tom Segev, *A State at Any Cost: The Life of David Ben-Gurion*, trans. Haim Watzman (New York: Farrar, Straus and Giroux, 2019), 420n.

40 Albert Einstein et al., letter to the editor, *New York Times*, Internet Archive, December 4, 1948, https://archive.org.

41 Thomas Suárez, *State of Terror: How Terrorism Created Modern Israel* (Northampton, MA: Interlink Press, 2017), 270.

42 William Zukerman, "Begin Farewell N.Y. Talk Is End of a Masquerade," *Jewish Advocate*, December 23, 1948, 1.

43 William Zukerman to Henry Hurwitz, September 23, 1948, Henry Hurwitz Papers, box 64, folder 14, American Jewish Archives, Cincinnati, OH.

44 William Zukerman, "Reply to Rabbi Bick," *Jewish Advocate*, December 7, 1950, 14.

45 See, for example, "Militarization of Antisemitism," *Jewish Frontier*, 9 (March 1942): 10–13. Editors of the magazine later attacked Zukerman. According to Mark Raider, *Jewish Frontier* was "the first Anglo-Jewish journal to publish complete details of the Nazi genocide." Mark A. Raider, *The Emergence of American Zionism* (New York: New York University Press, 1998), 169.

46 "A Call to the Jewish Public, Declaration of the Free Jewish Club," translated from the Yiddish by Ri Turner. This document is on microfilm in the Jewish Labor Committee records at the Tamiment Library, New York University.

47 William Zukerman, *Jewish Newsletter*, November 25, 1949.

48 Adam M. Howard writes that in the early 1920s, even non-Zionist American Jewish labor leaders came to see supporting Histadrut as "aiding a fellow trade union movement and providing a haven for persecuted European Jews." Adam M. Howard, *Sewing the Fabric of Statehood: Garment Unions, American Labor, and the Establishment of the State of Israel* (Urbana: University of Illinois Press, 2017), 110. While Jewish Labor Committee leaders did not publicly support Zionism or Israel until 1947, some leaders, such as David Dubinsky, a supporter of Zukerman's *Newsletter*, advocated for European refugees to be able to enter Palestine (75, 69). On Dubinsky's friendship with Zukerman and support of his *Jewish Newsletter*, see William Zukerman to David Dubinsky, April 20, 1958, William Zukerman Papers, YIVO Archive, New York.

49 William Zukerman, "Have You Heard?," n.d. [July 1949?], Edward S. Goldstein: Jewish Labor Committee Research Files, box 5, folder 93, Zionism and the JLC, Tamiment Library, New York University. Michael Letwin, Suzanne Adely, and Jaime Veve argue that Israeli officials orchestrated support for Israel from US labor leaders. Michael Letwin, Suzanne Adely, and Jaime Veve, "Labor for Palestine: Challenging US Labor Zionism," *American Quarterly* 67, no. 4 (December 2015): 1047–55.

50 William Zukerman, *Jewish Newsletter*, January 11, 1960. In 1961 the Jewish Labor Committee continued to issue statements that disputed the idea that Israel alone was a home for Jews. "We express our conviction that a free, creative, democratic Jewish community in America is also a strong safeguard for Israel." "JLC Replies to Zionist Congress," *Workmen's Circle Call*, March 1961, 6, Clipping in Jewish Labor Committee Research Files, box 5, folder 93, Zionism and the JLC, Tamiment Library, New York University.

51 On the rise of Labor Zionism's influence in the United States, see Raider, *Emergence of American Zionism*.

52 William Zukerman, *Jewish Newsletter*, July 21, 1952. Michael Letwin, Suzanne Adely, and Jaime Veve write that the Jewish Labor Committee joined the "Histadrut's well-orchestrated campaign for a Jewish State in Palestine" and that the Zionism of these labor officials was "closely linked to their support for U.S. imperialism, anticommunism, and racism against workers of color in the United States." Letwin, Adely, and Veve, "Labor for Palestine," 1048. In his history of American Zionism, Mark Raider writes that "American Zionism, by the late 1930s and early 1940s, had incorporated a quasi-Labor Zionist sensibility as its own ethos" (164). This meant that "Arab nationalism . . . attracted the attention of the Labor Zionist intellectual leadership during the interwar period." Raider, *Emergence of American Zionism*, 164.

53 William Zukerman, "The Battle over Yiddish," *Jewish Advocate*, May 18, 1950, 13.

54 William Zukerman, *Jewish Newsletter*, September 30, 1949. One of the very few scholars to study Zukerman, theologian Marc H. Ellis writes of Zukerman's commitment to Palestinian refugees in *Toward a Jewish Theology of Liberation: The Challenge of the Twenty-First Century* (Waco, TX: Baylor University Press, 2004), 76–91.

55 William Zukerman, *Jewish Newsletter*, December 9, 1949.

56 William Zukerman, *Jewish Newsletter*, November 30, 1959.

57 William Zukerman, *Jewish Newsletter*, April 26, 1954.

58 William Zukerman, *Jewish Newsletter*, January 11, 1960.

59 Historian Mark Raider discusses how Mordecai M. Kaplan, the "philosopher of Reconstructionism," worked "to place Zionism at the center of synagogal life." Raider, *Emergence of American Zionism*, 150.

60 "Mr. Zukerman Defends His Newsletter," *Reconstructionist*, March 9, 1951, 32, in William Zukerman File, Israel State Archives. *Reconstructionist*'s managing editor Eugene Kohn wrote to the Israel consulate in New York to ask for "any information you could give in refutation of Mr. Zukerman's conclusion." Eugene Kohn to Abe Harmon, February 9, 1951, William Zukerman File, Israeli State Archives. The United Nations estimates the number of Palestinians displaced in the Nakba at 700,000.

61 William Zukerman, *Jewish Newsletter*, February 19, 1951.

62 William Zukerman, *Jewish Newsletter*, February 3, 1950. Zukerman mailed this article to the leaders of the American Council for Judaism. Papers of the American Council for Judaism, box 1, folder 17, Center for Jewish History.

63 Shira Robinson, *Citizen Strangers: Palestinians and the Birth of Israel's Liberal Settler State* (Stanford: Stanford University Press, 2013). Robinson writes that "translating the name of the 1952 citizenship law as the 'Nationality Law' . . . obscured from international view the government's active effort to separate the Jewish 'nation' from the Israeli state" (108).

64 Robinson writes that in its "explicit privileging of the rights of all Jews in the world at the expense of native non-Jews, the Law of Return became Israel's first legal nail in the coffin against the homecoming of Palestinian refugees, and the cornerstone of racial segregation between Israel citizens" (Robinson, *Citizen Strangers*, 99).

65 The details of the law are complex. For an Arab Palestinian to prove "uninterrupted presence [in Israel] since May 1948" was nearly impossible for many Palestinians because many areas "did not fall under Israeli control" until later and because "proof" was subjected to scrutiny and the pressing of "false claims against people who otherwise had their paperwork in order" was widespread (106–7). Robinson notes that the passage of the law was "riding on the heels of a makeshift and often violent campaign to minimize the number of Arab residents entitled to that status [of Israeli citizenship]." Robinson, *Citizen Strangers*, 111.

66 "Israel Citizenship Will Begin July 14: Nationality Act Gives Resident Jews Automatic Status—Restrictions on Arabs," *New York Times*, April 17, 1952, 8.

67 William Zukerman, *Jewish Newsletter*, September 15, 1952. Shlomo Katz, managing editor of *Jewish Frontier*, the Labor Zionist journal, wrote a furious letter to Thomas about his position on the Israeli citizenship law. Shlomo Katz to Norman Thomas, September 30, 1952, Norman Thomas Papers, New York Public Library.

68 Elmer Berger, William Zukerman, Norman Thomas, and Israel Knox, *Four Articles on the Law of the Return* (American Council for Judaism, 1952), 6, Moses Lasky Papers, box 2, folder 6, American Jewish Archives, Cincinnati, OH.

69 Berger et al., 8.

70 Berger et al., 11.

71 Historian Maddalena Marinari writes of the 1952 Act that "Jewish organizations exhorted Truman to veto 'this Pandora's box of anti-Semitic, anti-Catholic, anti-colonial, anti-European, anti-African, anti-Asiatic, anti-immigrant, and anti-American prejudices.'" The act splintered the coalition supporting liberal immigration reform. Marinari, *Unwanted*, 148.

72 Berger et al., *Four Articles*, 11.

73 Gerald Blank, publicity director for ACJ, to Norman Thomas, May 16, 1952, Norman Thomas Papers, New York Public Library. Blank invited Thomas to contribute to the *Council News* on the topic of the Israeli citizenship law. Berger thanked him for his writing on July 7, 1952. Berger to Norman Thomas, July 7, 1952, Norman Thomas Papers, New York Public Library.

74 Berger et al., *Four Articles*, 12–13.

75 Lessing J. Rosenwald, "Israeli Citizenship Law: Many American Jews Said to Reject Concept of Jewish Nationality," *New York Times*, June 26, 1952, 28.

76 "Israeli Citizen Law Decried," *New York Times*, May 21, 1952, 18.

77 See Katz to Thomas.

78 Shlomo Katz, "For the Record," *Jewish Frontier* 18, no. 2 (February 1951): 28–30.

79 William Zukerman, "Machine Gun Judaism," *Jewish Newsletter*, December 10, 1957.

80 William Zukerman, *Jewish Newsletter*, March 4, 1957.

81 Melissa Faye Greene writes that "ten percent of the bombs from 1954 to 1959 were cast at Jewish targets," as "whites aimed at [B]lacks *through* the Jews." Melissa Faye Greene, *The Temple Bombing* (New York: Addison-Wesley, 1996), 6 (emphasis in original).

82 William Zukerman, *Jewish Newsletter*, January 12, 1959.

83 Zukerman.

84 William Zukerman, *Jewish Newsletter*, June 4, 1956.

85 William Zukerman, *Jewish Newsletter*, January 12, 1959.

86 William Zukerman, *Jewish Newsletter*, November 3, 1958.

87 William Zukerman, *Jewish Newsletter*, March 23, 1959.

88 Zukerman.

89 Paul Hale, "Fight or Run: First of a Series," *New York Amsterdam News*, April 4, 1959, 8.

90 Florence Haynes, "The Jewish Question," *New York Amsterdam News*, May 9, 1959, 8.

91 See Edo Konrad, "The Roots of Anti-Mizrahi Racism in Israel," *972 Magazine*, December 1, 2015, www.972mag.com.

92 William Zukerman, *Jewish Newsletter*, January 11, 1960.

93 William Zukerman, *Jewish Newsletter*, September 7, 1959.

94 William Zukerman, *Jewish Newsletter*, May 16, 1960.

95 Staub, *Torn at the Roots*, 48, 57.

96 Staub, 74.

97 William Zukerman recounts this story in a letter to Henry Hurwitz, April 14, 1954, Henry Hurwitz Papers, box 64, folder 16, American Jewish Archives, Cincinnati, OH.

98 Horace Kallen was himself a Zionist who wrote of Zionism as compatible with liberal US traditions of cultural pluralism.

99 Ira Eisenstein, "Henry Hurwitz: Editor, Gadfly, Dreamer," in *The Other New York Jewish Intellectuals*, ed. Carole S. Kessner (New York: New York University Press, 1994), 191–205. See also Lewis Fried, "The *Menorah Journal*: Yavneh in America, 1945–1950," *American Jewish Archives Journal* 50, nos. 1–2 (1998): 108.

100 Robert Alter, "Epitaph for a Jewish Magazine: Notes on the Menorah Journal," *Commentary*, May 1965, www.commentarymagazine.com.

101 Alter.

102 In writing about Lionel Trilling's career with the *Menorah Journal*, neoconservative and ardent Zionist Norman Podhoretz writes that "by 1944 . . . while retaining the anti-Zionist position espoused by *The Menorah Journal*, he [Trilling] had turned his back on a favorable attitude toward Jewish culture." Podhoretz, *Ex-Friends: Falling Out with Allen Ginsberg, Lionel and Diana Trilling, Lillian Hellman, Hannah Arendt, and Norman Mailer* (New York: Free Press, 1999), 92.

103 William Zukerman to Henry Hurwitz, July 12, 1950, Henry Hurwitz Papers, box 64, folder 17, American Jewish Archives, Cincinnati, OH.

104 Fried, "*Menorah Journal*," 78.

105 Henry Hurwitz to Mr. Max Epstein, February 17, 1944, copy to Rabbi Irving Reichert, Henry Hurwitz Papers, box 45, folder 14, American Jewish Archives, Cincinnati, OH.

106 Henry Hurwitz to William Zukerman, November 11, 1946, box 64, folder 13, Henry Hurwitz Papers, American Jewish Archives, Cincinnati, OH.

107 "American Council Will Be Host to Henry Hurwitz," *American Israelite*, April 7, 1949, 11.

108 Alter, "Epitaph." In her essay "Zionism Reconsidered," Hannah Arendt argued that nationalism and the building up of a sovereign Jewish nation-state would make Jews and the world far less safe. Hannah Arendt, "Zionism Reconsidered," *Menorah Journal* (October 1944): 162–96.

109 Idith Zertal, "A State on Trial: Hannah Arendt vs. the State of Israel," *Social Research* 74, no. 4 (Winter 2007): 1138. Here Zertal connects Arendt's despair over what she saw in Israel during the Eichmann trial to her writings "in the late 1940s," such as "Zionism Reconsidered."

110 Hannah Arendt, "New Leaders Arise in Europe," in *Hannah Arendt: The Jewish Writings*, ed. Jerome Kohn and Ron H. Feldman (New York: Schocken Books, 2007), 256. "New Leaders Arise in Europe" was originally published in *New Currents: A Jewish Monthly* 2, no. 4 (1944).

111 In 1953, William Zukerman quoted from Arendt's 1948 eulogy of Rabbi Judah Magnes: "It has happened that in the last years . . . coincided with a great change in the Jewish national character. A people that for 2,000 years had made justice the cornerstone of its spiritual and communal experience has become emphatically hostile to all arguments of such a nature as though they were necessarily arguments of failure." Zukerman, *Jewish Newsletter*, April 21, 1958. Zukerman wrote to Arendt in the wake of the Kibya massacre in October 1953, asking her to contribute a statement to his *Jewish Newsletter*. She refused, responding only with a brief note in which she said, "The whole business is absolutely nauseating. I decided that I do not want to have anything to do with Jewish politics any longer." Quoted in Elisabeth Young-Bruehl, *Hannah Arendt: For Love of the World* (New Haven, CT: Yale University Press, 2004), 291.

112 William Zukerman, "New York Jews and Country Jews," *Menorah Journal* 33, no. 2 (October–December 1945): 256.

113 Fried, "*Menorah Journal*," 91, 93.

114 Henry Hurwitz to Mr. A. L. Galinsky, January 21, 1954, copy to Elmer Berger, Henry Hurwitz Papers, box 4 folder 6, American Jewish Archives, Cincinnati, OH.

115 Hurwitz, "Israel, What Now?"

116 Hurwitz, 33, 34.

117 Hurwitz, 50–51, 56.

118 Henry Hurwitz to Robert Nyburg, February 7, 1955, box 4, folder 6, Henry Hurwitz Papers, American Jewish Archives, Cincinnati, OH.

119 Henry Hurwitz, "Announcing Menorah White Paper Number One: On the Functions and Procedures of a Jewish Welfare Fund," *Menorah Journal* 43, no. 1 (Spring/Summer 1955): 1–2.

120 Henry Hurwitz, "Three Ways for Israel," *Menorah Journal* 44, nos. 1–2 (Spring/Summer 1956): 1–40.

121 Hurwitz, 14.

122 Henry Hurwitz, "Heritage and Allegiance," *Menorah Journal* 47, nos. 1–2 (Autumn/Winter 1959): 23.

123 Hurwitz, 32.

124 Henry Hurwitz to Henry Moyer (and copy to Rabbi Elmer Berger), November 9, 1954, Henry Hurwitz Papers, box 4, folder 6, American Jewish Archives, Cincinnati, OH.

125 See Levin, *Our Palestine Question*, chap. 4, "Such Distinctions Cannot Be Maintained," which focuses on Dr. Fayez Sayegh.

126 Rabbi Sheldon Singer to Henry Hurwitz, n.d. [May/June 1960?], Harry Hurwitz Papers, box 4, folder 7, American Jewish Archives, Cincinnati, OH.

127 Samuel B. Finkel, "The Need for Dissent," *Jewish Advocate*, May 12, 1960, A2.

128 William Zukerman, *Jewish Newsletter*, November 21, 1955.

129 Zukerman. On the Bund's attempts to merge "a brand of a Jewish secular social-ism with modern Jewish politics and identity," see Gali Drucker Bar-Am, "The Bund in Israel: Searching for Jewish Working Class Secular Brotherhood in Zion," in *Bundist Legacy after the Second World War: "Real" Place versus "Displaced" Time*, ed. Vincenzo Pinto (Leiden: Brill, 2018), 56–69.

130 Katz, "For the Record," 28–30.

131 Eli Kaminsky, "The Editor's Mail: Labor Zionism," *Jewish Advocate*, June 21, 1951, 14.

132 Nathan Ziprin, "The Listening Post: Little Man with a Broom," *Jewish Advocate*, August 4, 1955, 7.

133 Nathan Ziprin, "The Listening Post: Jewish Newsletter's 'Concern' about Israel," *Jewish Advocate*, August 13, 1959, box 125, Zukerman file, Boston Jewish Community Relations Council Papers, Wyner Family Jewish Heritage Center at New England Historic Genealogical Society, Boston, MA.

134 Ziprin.

135 Norman Perlstein to the Joint Committee of Jewish Community Council of Metropolitan Detroit and Zionist Council of Detroit, February 19, 1958, Boston Jewish Community Relations Council, Activities, box 125, William Zukerman File, Wyner Family Jewish Heritage Center at New England Historic Genealogical Society, Boston, MA.

136 William Zukerman to John D. Hertz, Hertz Foundation, June 10, 1957, Zukerman Papers, box 1, folder 1, YIVO Archive, Center for Jewish History, New York; William Zukerman to Aaron Straus, June 10, 1957, Zukerman Papers, box 1, folder 1, YIVO Archive, Center for Jewish History, New York.

137 "Meshugah Is Trump: Willy Rides Again," *B'nai B'rith Messenger*, September 16, 1960, 4.

138 Michael Arnon to A. Harman, October 12, 1951, William Zukerman File, Israel State Archives.

139 Abe Harman to Y. Harry Levin, August 27, 1952, William Zukerman File, Israel State Archives.

140 In 1951, Yehuda Harry Levin, a counselor at the Israeli embassy in Washington, wrote that he was keeping close tabs on Zukerman. Because Levin was "in good with an editor" at one Jewish press, he had convinced the editor to do "rigorous editing" before publishing one of Zukerman's articles. Levin was less confident that he could do the same with other journals. Y. Harry Levin to Abe Harman, December 6, 1951, William Zukerman File, Israel State Archives.

141 Tzvi Zinder to Yerahmiel Yadun, September 8, 1952, William Zukerman File, Israel State Archives. Translated from the Hebrew by Ri Turner.

142 "William Zuckerman [sic]."

143 Y. Harry Levin to Abe Harman, December 8, 1950, William Zukerman File, Israel State Archives.

144 These are the categories listed in a memorandum labeled "Confidential" from September 25, 1951, titled "William Zuckerman [sic]."

145 Y. Harry Levin to Abe Harman, August 27, 1952, William Zukerman File, Israel State Archives.

146 Y. Harry Levin to Abe Harman, April 11, 1951, William Zukerman File, Israel State Archives.

147 J. L. Teller to Y. Harry Levin, August 26, 1952, William Zukerman File, Israel State Archives.

148 See, for example, Eugene Kohn, managing editor of the *Reconstructionist*, to Hon. A. Harmon, February 9, 1951, William Zukerman File, Israel State Archives.

149 Abe Harman to Michael Arnon, Israel Legation, London, October 3, 1951, William Zukerman File, Israel State Archives [in English].

150 Memo authored by or to Louis Lipsky, Jerome Unger, and Rita Grossman, Re: William Zukerman, September 27, 1951, William Zukerman File, Israel State Archives.

151 Geoffrey Levin writes about Zukerman's position on Palestinian refugees and how Israeli diplomats attempted, with some success, to silence his criticisms of Israeli policies with regard to Palestinians. Levin, *Our Palestine Question*, chap. 2, "A Yiddishist's Dissent."

152 Zukerman, *Jewish Newsletter*, December 1, 1958.

153 William Zukerman to Norman Thomas, January 31, 1958, Norman Thomas Papers, New York Public Library. Zukerman found an ally in Norman Thomas, whom he saw as having the "philosophy and approach to social problems . . . of the old Jewish labor movement and particularly of the spirit of humanitarianism and non-conformity which prevailed among Jews of that period." Thomas's biographer notes that beginning in 1948 and continuing through to Thomas's trip to the Middle East in 1957 with Don Peretz, Thomas advocated for Palestinian rights alongside the rights of minority groups in the region. "Thomas was particularly impressed by the great degree of freedom which existed in Israel to discuss controversial issues such as the Arab refugee and minority problems," Fleischman writes. "He found in Israel far more tolerance in discussion of these issues than in the United States, where any public criticism of Israel or Ben Gurion [*sic*] brought scorn." Harry Fleischman, *Norman Thomas, a Biography: 1884–1968*, 2nd ed. (New York: W. W. Norton, 1969), 289.

154 Phineas J. Biron [Joseph Brainin], "Strictly Confidential: On the Grave of a Journalist," *B'nai B'rith Messenger*, October 13, 1961, 20, 22.

155 Rabbi Morris Lazaron, "Words Spoken at the Funeral of My Friend, William Zukerman," October 6, 1961, William Zukerman folio provided by George Zukerman to Dr. Geoffrey Levin and shared with this author.

156 For an excellent review of scholarship on US–Israel early relations, see Geoffrey P. Levin's "State of the Field" essay on H-Diplo, July 19, 2018, H-Net, Humanities and Social Sciences Online, https://networks.h-net.org.

3. "ISRAEL—RIGHT OR WRONG"

1 William Zukerman, *Jewish Newsletter*, June 12, 1961.

2 Pamela Pennock, *The Rise of the Arab American Left: Activists, Allies, and Their Fight against Imperialism and Racism, 1960s–1980* (Chapel Hill: University of

North Carolina Press, 2017), 101; and Salim Yaqub, *Imperfect Strangers: Americans, Arabs, and U.S.-Middle East Relations in the 1970s* (Ithaca: Cornell University Press, 2016), 60.

3 See, among others, Von Eschen, *Race against Empire*; Brenda Plummer, *In Search of Power: African Americans in the Era of Decolonization, 1956–1974* (New York: Cambridge University Press, 2012); and John Munro, *The Anticolonial Front: The African American Freedom Struggle and Global Decolonization, 1945–1960* (Cambridge: Cambridge University Press, 2017). Early Black Power transnationalism was expressed in Lawrence P. Neal, "Black Power in the International Context," in *Black Power Revolt: A Collection of Essays*, ed. Floyd B. Barbour (Boston, MA: Porter Sargent, 1968).

4 See Kaplan, *Our American Israel.*

5 According to historian Eric Goldstein, the "reinvigoration of American Zionism," accompanied by the ethnic revival inspired by Black Power, allowed American Jews to "continue on the path of integration" into white America "with little fear that they were complicit in the misdeeds of an exclusionary society." Goldstein, *Price of Whiteness*, 215. Goldstein writes that "despite their parting of the ways with [B]lack nationalists, Jews retained sufficient ties with some of the less militant elements of the civil rights movement" (215).

6 The Jewish Liberation Project (JLP) sponsored socialist Zionist Simha Flapan, a leading member of the Israeli left party Mapam, on a speaking tour; Flapan spoke about his opposition to "permanent annexation by Israel of the territories it occupies since the Six-Day War." "Mapam Leader Opposes Permanent Annexation of Lands Won in Six-Day War," *Sentinel*, February 5, 1970, 7.

7 Michael Staub writes that the 1967 war "brought the Holocaust (and the concomitant imperatives of Jewish survival) into sharp relief." He also points out, however, that to assert the war as the singular factor in the growth of these imperatives is to ignore "the longstanding conflicts among American Jews over what the Holocaust's lessons for them might be." Staub argues that Holocaust consciousness aligns with the lessons learned from listening to pre-1967 critics of Zionism: "that the Israeli victory over the Arab nations in 1967 tended more to consolidate agendas and arguments whose foundations had already been set before." After 1967, though, the stakes were far higher, and it was "virtually impossible to resist a mood bordering on the apocalyptic" when talking within the Jewish community about "the future prospects for Judaism and Jewish survival." Staub, *Torn at the Roots*, 131–32.

8 Caitlin Carenen, *The Fervent Embrace: Liberal Protestants, Evangelicals, and Israel* (New York: New York University Press, 2012), 117, 125.

9 Carenen, 137.

10 Historian Jason M. Olson writes that after 1967, many mainline Protestants, especially "liberation theologians," became "disgusted with US foreign policy in the East, and Vietnam in particular," and came to see "Western support of Israel as part of this wider problem," viewing both the Vietnamese and the Palestinian

peoples as victims of Western colonialism. Jason M. Olson, *America's Road to Jerusalem: The Impact of the Six-Day War on Protestant Politics* (Lanham, MD: Lexington Books, 2018), 150.

11 Yaqub, *Imperfect Strangers*, 18–19. It is worth noting that many who supported Israel and the US/Israel alliance directed their hostility toward Arab and Palestinian Americans. Yaqub analyzes this moment in his chap. 2, "A Stirring at the Margins: Arab American Political Activism, 1967–1973."

12 Mitelpunkt, *Israel in the American Mind*, 6.

13 Shaul Mitelpunkt writes that "in adoring Israel," Americans "mourned the demise of their own society's once-proud citizen-soldier model." As social movements challenged any fictional American consensus, so too did manipulated images of Israel as a unified society encourage Americans to look to Israel with nostalgia for a time before the US was fractured by liberation and protest movements. Mitelpunkt, 121.

14 Paul Thomas Chamberlain, *The Global Offensive: The United States, the Palestine Liberation Organization, and the Making of the Post-Cold War Order* (New York: Oxford University Press, 2012), 85.

15 See Shaul Magid, *Meir Kahane: The Public Life and Political Thought of an American Jewish Radical* (Princeton, NJ: Princeton University Press, 2021), 82–83, 95. Meir Kahane's "The Jewish Stake in Vietnam," which originally appeared in the *Jewish Press* on June 9, 1967, is reprinted in Michael Staub, ed., *The Jewish 1960s: An American Sourcebook* (Waltham, MA: Brandeis University Press, 2004), 150–52.

16 Magid, *Meir Kahane*, 47.

17 Magid, 37.

18 It's important to note that Black anticolonialist activity began far earlier, perhaps first with the founding of the Council on African Affairs, a "solidarity organization in support of African struggles against colonialism and apartheid." Like other anticolonialist organizations, the COA fell victim to the Red Scare in the early 1950s because its members had ties to the liberal/left. "Council on African Affairs," African Activist Archive, https://africanactivist.msu.edu.

19 Pennock, *Rise of the Arab American Left*, 81.

20 The Suez Canal crisis of 1956 divided Black and Jewish Americans while contributing to solidarity between Black and Arab Americans. Egypt's president Gamal Abdel Nasser nationalized the canal, which had been controlled by France and Britain. He blocked Israel's ships (along with any cargo bound for Israel) from using the Suez Canal and garnered international support for confronting Israel and Western powers—and for his efforts to protect the independence of the Arab world. Black Communist leaders split over supporting Egypt or Israel in the conflict. Conflating Jewish support with support for Israel, Jewish comrades accused Egypt supporters of antisemitism. Paul Buhle and Robin D. G. Kelley, "Allies of a Different Sort: Jews and Blacks in the American Left," in *Struggles in the Promised Land: Toward a History of Black-Jewish Relations in the United States* (New York: Oxford University Press, 1997), 215. While American Jews, including Zionists on the left, supported Israel, President Nasser became a hero of pan-Arab unity

and anticolonialist struggles for liberation across much of the world. Mitelpunkt writes that many (white) Americans saw Israel's role in the Suez crisis as admirable, "cultivating American appreciation of Israel's 'tough little army.'" Mitelpunkt, *Israel in the American Mind*, 33.

21 "Nasser Lauded as Arabs Unite during Summit Meet," *Chicago Daily Defender*, January 30, 1964, 9.

22 K. B. Thakore, quoted in Louis Harap, "The Reality That Faces Israel," *Jewish Life* 11, no. 7 (May 1957): 4.

23 Harap, 5.

24 Hans Kohn, letter to the *New York Times*, November 4, 1956, quoted in Louis Harap, "Suez, Israel, and Peace," *Jewish Life* 11, no. 2 (December 1956): 5.

25 Marjorie N. Feld, *Nations Divided: American Jews and the Struggle over Apartheid* (New York: Palgrave Macmillan, 2014); see also Polakow-Suransky, *Unspoken Alliance*.

26 Marc Dollinger, *Black Power, Jewish Politics: Reinventing the Alliance in the 1960s* (Waltham, MA: Brandeis University Press, 2018), 34–39, 89–103.

27 "Jewish Groups Endorse Anti-Black Power Move," *Jewish Advocate*, October 20, 1966, 1.

28 On the language and literary connections between Black and Arab American communities, see Michelle Hartman, *Breaking Broken English: Black-Arab Literary Solidarities and the Politics of Language* (Syracuse: Syracuse University Press, 2019).

29 "An Appeal by Black Americans for United States Support for Israel," *New York Times*, June 28, 1970, 5.

30 Plummer, *In Search of Power*, 297. Plummer writes that "Israel came to signify for many [B]lacks an egregious example of Western racism and aggression" (297).

31 "Black Civil Rights and Labor Leader, Robert E. Powell, Is Honored by Histadrut, Israel's National Trade Union," Black-Jewish Information Center press releases, Media Project: Black-Jewish Information Center, October 25, 1979, ARC MS 38, Department of Special Collections, UC Santa Barbara Library, University of California, Santa Barbara.

32 See, for instance, William Korey, "Facts Show Israel Trades Far Less with South Africa Than Black Africa, Soviet Bloc, Arab-Oil Producers," Media Project: Black-Jewish Information Center, October 30, 1979, Black-Jewish Information Center press releases, ARC MS 38, Department of Special Collections, UC Santa Barbara Library, University of California, Santa Barbara.

33 Annalisa Jabaily, "1967: How Estrangement and Alliances between Blacks, Jews, and Arabs Shaped a Generation of Civil Rights Family Values," *Law and Inequality: A Journal of Theory and Practice* 23, no. 1 (Winter 2005): 220.

34 Those in attendance included members of the Student Nonviolent Coordinating Committee, the Southern Christian Leadership Conference, the Congress of Racial Equality, the Mississippi Freedom Democratic Party, and the Students for a Democratic Society, along with other antiwar and left political groups. Debates

during the conference—focused on voting power, leadership, strategies, and other issues—were heated, and divisions grew especially between liberal whites and Black militants (76). Simon Hall, "*On the Tail of the Panther*: Black Power and the 1967 Convention of the National Conference of New Politics," *Journal of American Studies* 37, no. 1 (2003): 60.

35 Pennock, *Rise of the Arab American Left*, 89.

36 Martin Peretz, co-author with Michael Walzer of the 1967 *Ramparts* article about Israel and Vietnam, was one of the prominent organizers of the conference who walked out after this resolution. Civil rights leaders Dr. Martin Luther King Jr., Andrew Young, and Julian Bond also walked out. Jabaily, "1967," 222.

37 Ultimately, conference organizers changed the language to a condemnation of the "Israeli government."

38 Robert G. Weisbord and Richard Kazarian Jr., *Israel in the Black American Perspective* (Westport, CT: Greenwood Press, 1985), 48. The delegates divided on what some considered this "anti-Israel" motion.

39 The reference here is to the Bakke case, the *Regents of the University of California v. Bakke*, which upheld the use of affirmative action to accept more minority applicants. The American Jewish Committee, the American Jewish Congress, and the Anti-Defamation League all filed briefs in support of Bakke, arguing that the use of quotas was discriminatory. Thomas A. Johnson, "Black Leaders Air Grievances on Jews," *New York Times*, August 23, 1979, A12. Their stated concerns were that elite institutions would use affirmative quotas to shut Jewish students out of admissions, restoring the Jewish quotas or caps that had been abolished only a few decades before. See also Goldstein, *Price of Whiteness*, 219–20.

40 "Jewish Leader Tells Blacks: No Apologies," *Michigan Chronicle*, November 10, 1979, 1.

41 Adolph Reed, *The Jesse Jackson Phenomenon* (New Haven, CT: Yale University Press, 1986), 102–5.

42 Johnson, "Black Leaders Air Grievances," A12.

43 Israel remained relatively neutral in the conflict, though the United States tried mightily to gain Israeli support through the late 1960s. Israel feared that siding with the US would threaten its image among developing nations in Asia and Africa. Historian Paul Thomas Chamberlain writes that in the late 1960s, "Vietnamese leaders expressed camaraderie with the Palestinian fighters [in the PLO] in their public statements, condemned Israeli attacks as outgrowths of U.S. imperialism, and called for the recognition of Palestinian national rights." Chamberlain, *Global Offensive*, 62. Pam Pennock writes of the Organization of Arab Students (OAS) members who "partnered with campus organizations that represented Third World students and oppositional politics." After the 1967 war, Berkeley's Arab Student Association drew students from "Rhodesia, Cuba, Egypt, and Lebanon"; they "denounced Zionism" and "announced a campaign to raise funds for Palestinian refugees." See Pennock, *Rise of the Arab American Left*, 60.

44 Chomsky, quoted in Chamberlain, *Global Offensive*, 40–41.

45 Israel refused to recognize the PLO in this period. See Chamberlain, chap. 3.

46 Michael Walzer and Martin Peretz, "Israel Is Not Vietnam," *Ramparts*, July 1967, 11, 14.

47 Kaplan, *Our American Israel*, 112.

48 I. F. Stone, "Holy War," *New York Review of Books*, August 3, 1967, reprinted in Karl Weber, ed., *The Best of I. F. Stone* (New York: Public Affairs, 2006), 225–44.

49 Edward W. Said, "Michael Walzer's *Exodus and Revolution*: A Canaanite Reading," in *Blaming the Victims: Spurious Scholarship and the Palestine Question*, ed. Edward W. Said and Christopher Hitchens (New York: Verso, 1988), 172. My thinking here has also been influenced by Michael Staub's introduction to chapter 6, "The Jewish Stake in Vietnam," and the accompanying documents, in Staub, *Jewish 1960s*.

50 Harold Goldberg, "A Lively Debate Is Going on in Jewish Radical Student Press," *Sentinel*, November 20, 1969, 39.

51 McCandlish Phillips, "Jewish Student Press Seeing Swift Growth," *New York Times*, March 13, 1971, www.nytimes.com.

52 Michael Staub, "Selections from the First Jewish Catalog," in Staub, *Jewish 1960s*, 349.

53 Trude Weiss-Rosmarin, "Traditional Attitudes about Israel," in *The Third Jewish Catalog: Creating Community*, ed. Sharon Strassfeld and Michael Strassfeld (Philadelphia: Jewish Publication Society of America, 1980), 318.

54 Strassfeld and Strassfeld, *Third Jewish Catalog*, 327.

55 Weiss-Rosmarin, "Traditional Attitudes," 338.

56 Sharon Strassfeld and Michael Strassfeld, eds., "Political Action for Israel," *Third Jewish Catalog*, 383.

57 The "Radical Zionist Manifesto" is published in Staub, *Jewish 1960s*, 246–47.

58 Laura Krieger, letter to the editor, *Jewish Liberation Journal*, no. 6 (February–March 1970): 2.

59 Arthur Waskow, *The Bush Is Burning! Radical Judaism Faces the Pharaohs of the Modern Superstate* (New York: Macmillan, 1971), 56–57.

60 Waskow, 58.

61 Waskow, 59.

62 Waskow, 60, 65, 66.

63 "Young Radical Jews to Picket ZOA Office against Viet Statement," *Detroit Jewish News*, December 19, 1969, 12.

64 Gershon Freidlin, "JLP Calls Torczyner 'Traitor to Zionism' for Telling US Jews to Support Vietnam War," *Jewish Liberation Journal*, no. 6 (February–March 1970): 1.

65 "Young Radical Jews to Picket," 12.

66 The photo of the students with their signs accompanies Freidlin, "JLP Calls Torczyner 'Traitor.'"

67 "Radical Jewish Students Form Left-Wing, Strongly Pro-Israel Organization," *Sentinel*, December 4, 1969, 3.

68 Freidlin, "JLP Calls Torczyner 'Traitor,'" 4.

69 Moshe Zedek, "Panther Anti-Semitism," *Jewish Liberation Journal*, no. 7 (April–May 1970): 8.

70 David Abraham, "Blind Alley of 'Ein Breira,'" *Jewish Liberation Journal*, no. 9 (February 1971): 2.

71 Jeremy Berson and S. Brent, "Zionism Betrayed," *Jewish Liberation Journal*, no. 11 (Summer/Fall 1972): 1–4.

72 Magid, *Meir Kahane*, 66; Staub writes about the Brooklyn Bridge Collective in *Torn at the Roots*, 236–40.

73 Brooklyn Bridge Collective, "We Are Coming Home," in Staub, *Jewish 1960s*, 263.

74 Interview with Phyllis Bloom, cited in Tamara Ruth Cohen, "An Overlooked Bridge: Secular Women of the Jewish Left and the Rise of Jewish Feminism" (master's thesis, Sarah Lawrence College, 2003), 45.

75 Arlene Cohn [pseud.], "Ten Women Tell . . . the Ways We Are," *Lilith*, January 31, 1977, 4 (emphasis added).

76 Michael Walzer has written that his experiences in 1967—as someone "sharply critical of the [Vietnam] war" and simultaneously "speaking in defence of the Israeli pre-emptive strike against Egypt"—were the "origin of his book" *Just and Unjust Wars*, published in 1977. He notes the impact of Holocaust consciousness on his position, the anxiety and fear, and its impact on "converting" Jewish people on the left and right to Zionism. In this anxiety and fear, he finds the "germ of settler zealotry" that led to further "injustice" in Israel. Michael Walzer, "Remembering the Six-Day War," *Fathom* (Spring 2017), https://fathomjournal.org.

77 Irene Gendzier, foreword to *Peace in the Middle East? Reflections on Justice and Nationhood*, by Noam Chomsky (New York: Random House, 1974), xi.

78 Gendzier, xi.

79 Gendzier, xxi.

80 Chomsky, *Peace in the Middle East?*, 25.

81 Chomsky, 160–61.

82 Chomsky, 162, 188–89.

83 Edward W. Said, "Arab and Jew: 'Each Is the Other,'" *New York Times*, October 14, 1973, 13, https://archive.nytimes.com.

84 Edward W. Said, "Chomsky and the Question of Palestine," *Journal of Palestine Studies* 4, no. 3 (Spring 1975): 95.

85 Said, 94, 97.

86 Michael Walzer, "Noam Chomsky Argues, an Israeli and Arab Talk," *New York Times*, October 6, 1974, 356.

87 Noam Chomsky, "Letters to the Editor: The Middle East" *New York Times*, December 1, 1974, 507.

88 Stuart Svonkin, *Jews against Prejudice: American Jews and the Fight for Civil Liberties* (New York: Columbia University Press, 1999), 134.

89 Emmaia Gelman, "Empire against Race: A Critical History of the Anti-Defamation League" (PhD diss., New York University, 2022).

90 Mel Cooperman to Irwin Suall, Anti-Defamation League, Israel Lobby Archive, May 19, 1975, www.israellobby.org.

91 Papers of the Boston Jewish Community Council, folder 2, 1962–67, Wyner Family Jewish Heritage Center at New England Historic Genealogical Society, Boston, MA.

92 Geoffrey Levin examines what he calls the "Arab-Antisemite nexus," documenting when Arab and Palestinian advocacy did veer into antisemitism. My point here is not to deny these incidents but instead to identify studies that link all non- or anti-Zionism to outside forces, ignoring American Jewish critics of Zionism. See Levin, *Our Palestine Question*, 127–31.

93 Arnold Forster and Benjamin R. Epstein, *The New Anti-Semitism* (New York: McGraw-Hill, 1974), 11.

94 Forster and Epstein, 16.

95 Forster and Epstein, 18.

96 Forster and Epstein, 178.

97 Forster and Epstein, 219.

98 Forster and Epstein, 166.

99 Forster and Epstein, 174.

100 Forster and Epstein, 174.

101 Forster and Epstein, 324.

102 Forster and Epstein, 9.

103 Earl Raab, whose data on antisemitism proved important in the 1970s, reviewed Forster and Epstein's book in *Commentary*. He credited the book with providing evidence of a new antisemitism and also faulted the book's ambiguous categorization of all criticism of Israel as Jew hatred, pointing out that the authors "sometimes even interpret the failure to be pro-Israel as anti-Semitism." Earl Raab, "Is There a New Anti-Semitism?," *Commentary* 52, no. 5 (May 1974): 53. In the 1980s, Raab continued to disentangle antisemitism from anti-Zionism; see Raab, "Attitudes toward Israel and Jews," 288–301.

104 Larry Bush, phone conversation with the author, March 2, 2020.

105 Alan Wald, *Trinity of Passion: The Literary Left and the Antifascist Crusade* (Chapel Hill: University of North Carolina Press, 2007), 207.

106 Morris U. Schappes interview, January 19 and February 2, 1984, American Jewish Committee, Oral History Library, tape 2, 79. The transcript can be found in Morris U. Schappes Papers, Tamiment Archives, box 4, folder 27, New York University, New York.

107 Morris Schappes, "It Happened in Israel," December 1956, American Jewish Historical Society, Morris Schappes Papers, box 17, folder 7, Center for Jewish History, New York.

108 Morris U. Schappes, "Zionism and Anti-Semitism," *Jewish Life* (August 1953): 12, 14.

109 Morris U. Schappes, "Israel and the State of Zionism," *Jewish Currents* 14, no. 9 (October 1960): 35.

110 Morris U. Schappes interview, tape 2, 80.

111 Flyer for "The People's Forum," 30th anniversary season, 1967–68. Schappes's lecture was titled "Israel and the Middle East Today." Isidor Zack's memos indicate surveillance of the organization dated from 1954 through the 1960s. See Isidore

Zack to Robert Segal, March 22, 1966, Papers of the Jewish Community Relations Council, Boston Massachusetts, box 94, folder 17, Jewish Heritage Center at New England Historic Genealogical Society, Boston, MA.

112 See "A Pictorial History of Jews Published," *Jewish Times* 21, no. 35 (April 14, 1966): 15, Wyner Family Jewish Heritage Center, New England Historic Genealogical Society, Boston, MA.

113 Morris U. Schappes interview, tape 2, 84.

114 Melvin Marvin Tumin, *An Inventory and Appraisal of Research on American Anti-Semitism* (New York: Freedom Books, 1961), 153.

115 Wald, *Trinity of Passion*, 208.

116 Douglas Martin, "Morris Schappes Dies at 97; Marxist and Jewish Scholar," *New York Times*, June 9, 2004, C15.

117 Wald, *Trinity of Passion*, 209.

118 The American Jewish Committee, by then staunchly pro-Zionist, "published a series of pamphlets on uniting the Jewish community. Schappes was stunned to learn that he had been invited to a meeting to present his views"; Wald, 209. Abram was president of the AJC from 1963 to 1968, so likely Schappes's meeting with Abram occurred in the late 1960s. Morris U. Schappes interview, tape 2, 85.

119 Morris U. Schappes interview, tape 2, 89.

120 Morris U. Schappes interview, tape 2, 85–86.

121 Morris U. Schappes interview, tape 2, 87–88.

122 Keith Feldman records that Schappes and another of the journal's editors, Louis Harap, engaged in "investigating Zionism's fundamental and enduring contradiction: a socialist-oriented communal structure . . . [which] prohibited incorporation of indigenous Arabs into the structure of its economy." Feldman, *Shadow over Palestine*, 128.

123 Jennifer Young, "Beyond the Color Line: Jews, Blacks, and the American Racial Imagination," *In Geveb*, June 21, 2016, https://ingeveb.org.

124 Jennifer Young, "Unequal Allies: Progressive Jews, the Politics of Race, and the New York Teachers' Strike of 1968," paper prepared for Prof. Hasia Diner, New York University, Post–World War II American Jewry, April 2009, 16. Cited with permission of the author. Young finds that *Jewish Currents* reported on Black-Jewish tensions but "also constantly stressed the theme of Black-Jewish political cooperation and mutual understanding" (15).

125 Feldman, *Shadow over Palestine*, 130.

126 Morris Schappes, "Commentary on Newton's Views," in *The Black Panthers, Jews, and Israel: A Jewish Currents Reprint*, by Rabbi Albert S. Axelrad, Rabbi Robert E. Goldburg, Huey Newton, Morris Schappes, and Dr. George Wald (February 1971), 20.

127 Morris Schappes, "President Johnson, the Jews, and Vietnam," *Canadian Jewish Outlook*, November 1966, 3–4, Schappes Papers, box 18, folder 13, Tamiment Library, New York University. Rabbi Joachim Prinz, long allied with civil rights causes, responded to President Johnson's statement with alarm. He and other

Jewish leaders held a private meeting with Arthur Goldberg, American ambassador to the United Nations, to "clarify the differences arising from the reports." "Jewish Leaders Hold Constructive Talks with Goldberg on Vietnam Issue," *Jewish Telegraphic News Agency Daily News Bulletin*, September 16, 1966, www.jta.org.

128 Morris Schappes, "Six Months after the War," *Jewish Currents*, December 1967, 3–5.

129 Schappes identified "reactionary ideologies" as manifest in the imperialism of Cold War battles for oil as well as the "intransigence" of both Arab and Israeli leaders. He expressed his hope that Arab leaders would move toward "direct negotiations with Israel for a just and lasting peace protecting the basic national interests of Israel, the Arab states and the Palestinian Arabs." He faulted Cold War tensions for the Arab states' threatening posture toward Israel and for emboldening the right wing in Israel, the "annexationist forces" who proposed keeping the occupied territories. Schappes, "Six Months after the War."

130 Amy Weiss, "Billy Graham Receives the Ten Commandments: American Jewish Interfaith Relations in the Age of Evangelicalism," *American Jewish History* 103, no. 1 (January 2019): 16.

131 "JFK Aide Ted Sorenson Decries Nixon Effort to Equate Israel, Vietnam," *Sentinel*, December 4, 1969, 5.

132 Balfour Brickner, "Vietnam and the American Jewish Community," *Christian Century*, April 29, 1970, 531, 532; also quoted in Staub, *Jewish 1960s*, 160.

133 Brickner, "Vietnam," 533.

134 Brickner, 534. That same year, 1970, Rabbi Brickner wrote about the "ordinary American Jew who, at the instruction of most national Jewish agencies over the past couple of years, had often been taught to swallow his anger at the administration." He contrasted this person with someone who, "despite their love of Israel, had long and loudly protested their country's intervention into the Vietnamese Civil War." Brickner, "My Zionist Dilemma: Two Recent Cases," *Sh'ma: A Journal of Jewish Responsibility* 1 (November 9, 1970): 3–5.

135 "West Bank March Condemned," *Jewish Telegraphic News Agency Daily News Bulletin*, April 21, 1976, www.jta.org.

136 Josh Feigelson, "50 Years Ago, Upstart Rabbi Used Jewish Law to Tell Senate to End Vietnam War," *Times of Israel*, May 7, 2020, www.timesofisrael.com.

137 "Religion: Israel: What Is Its Religious Meaning?," *New York Times*, November 1, 1970, 179.

138 Paula E. Hyman, "New Debate on the Holocaust: Has the Popularization of This Tragedy Diluted Its Meaning and Diminished Other Aspects of Judaism?," *New York Times*, September 14, 1980, 67.

139 Deborah Hart, "Holocaust Commission Director Lays Silence to Dual Loyalty Slur," *New York Jewish Week*, December 3, 1978, 43; "Rabbi Irving Greenberg: Test for Jews Is Emerging from Status of Powerlessness," *New York Jewish Week*, October 1, 1982, 4.

140 Professor Marty Blatt traveled with his mother back to Heidelberg when the city invited "former Jewish citizens" for a visit to the city with one guest. Blatt wrote

eloquently of the first visit, which occurred on September 11, 2001, in "Holocaust Remembrance and Heidelberg," *Public Historian* 24, no. 4 (Fall 2002): 81–96. In 2011 he made the trip with his daughter, Rosa, and wrote about it for the presidential address to the National Council on Public History in 2012 and then as "Holocaust Memory and Germany," *Public Historian* 34, no. 4 (November 2012): 53–66.

141 Martin Blatt, work history, January 1985, in Blatt's possession.

142 Uri Davis received his PhD in anthropology in 1975 from the New School of Social Research.

143 Merryl Gibbs, "Black Rejects Grad Student, Overrules Sociology Department," *Justice*, May 18, 1971, 1, 8.

144 "To Be Free," *Justice*, June 8, 1971.

145 Prof. Richard Sennett, "The Matter of Uriel Davis," *Justice*, June 8, 1971, 2, 6. With Jonathan Cobb, Sennett authored *The Hidden Injuries of Class*, an important left critique of capitalism, which was published the following year, 1972.

146 Martin Blatt, interview with the author, January 24, 2020.

147 Martin Blatt, Uri Davis, and Paul Kleinbaum, eds., *Dissent and Ideology in Israel: Resistance to the Draft, 1948–1973* (London: Ithaca, 1975). Quotes and information about the book project and other activist work originated with Martin Blatt and Paul Kleinbaum, "Final Summary Statement" for Cambridge-Goddard School, n.d. [1973?], in Blatt's possession.

148 Phyllis Pomerantz, letter to the editor, *Boston Phoenix*, May 29, 1973, 2; and Phyllis Pomerantz, letter to the editor, *Jewish Advocate*, August 23, 1973, 14.

149 Quotes and information about the book project and other activist work originated with Blatt and Kleinbaum, "Final Summary Statement." The Hillel chapter leadership expelled two members of the Non-Zionist Caucus, Phyllis Pomerantz and Paul Kleinbaum, claiming that they "hurt Hillel financially and socially" by using the Hillel name. Pomerantz and Kleinbaum defended themselves by saying they "do not accept what Hillel defines as Jewish values." Tufts ordered Hillel to reinstate their membership. Ira Tabas, "No Sanction for Disrupter," *Tufts Observer* 7, no. 11 (April 13, 1973): 1, 7.

150 Book titles were listed on the Tufts University store form for "Faculty Listing of Required and Recommended Books and Supplies," in possession of Martin Blatt, dated December 15, 1972.

151 Martin Blatt, "Zionist Reconsidered Exp. 66S, Booklist," in possession of Martin Blatt.

152 The course's enrollment was higher than many others in the Experimental College with sixteen (plus several who were auditing the class). Blatt's sense was that many in the class were Zionists and were at first skeptical of his approach and the course content. Quotes are from "Notes from Second Class," in possession of Martin Blatt.

153 Martin Blatt, interview with the author.

154 Blatt, "Notes from Second Class."

155 Martin Blatt to Board of Experimental College, February 28, 1973. Letter in possession of Martin Blatt.

156 Pomerantz, letter to the editor, *Boston Phoenix*, 2.

157 "Counter Celebration of Israel's Anniversary," *Militant*, May 18, 1973, 2.

158 Seth Kupferberg, "Golda Comes to Brandeis," *Harvard Crimson*, March 10, 1973. The "May 15th Coalition" is cited in the ADL's *The New Anti-Semitism*, alongside the Tufts Hillel Non-Zionist Caucus, as examples of antisemitism in the "radical Left." Foster and Epstein, *New Anti-Semitism*, 136–37.

159 Letters to the editor, *Justice*, March 13, 1973, 2.

160 Frances Hagopian, "A Non-sectarian Jewish Question," *Justice*, March 13, 1973, 3.

161 Greg Perkins, letter to the editor, *Justice*, March 7, 1973, 2, 6.

162 Indeed, it was in the Anti-Defamation League files that I first found reference to Professor Blatt's Zionism Reconsidered class.

163 "Tufts U Reschedules Anti-Zionist Course despite Jewish Protests," *Jewish Telegraphic News Agency Daily News Bulletin*, September 3, 1973, www.jta.org.

164 "Instructor Agrees Class Anti-Zionist," *Jewish Post and Opinion*, October 5, 1973, 10; "Boston Jewish Community Hits Tufts U. Anti-Zionism Course," *Detroit Jewish News*, August 31, 1973, 3.

165 Sid Blumenthal, "Tufts Zionism Course Attacked," *Boston Phoenix*, May 1, 1973, 3, 24, 25.

166 Minutes, Jewish Community Council of Metropolitan Boston, October 4, 1973, Jewish Community Relations Council of Greater Boston Records, I-123, box 7, folder 2, Wyner Family Jewish Heritage Center at New England Historic Genealogical Society, Boston, MA.

167 Herman Brown to Rabbi Richard Israel, November 27, 1973, Jewish Community Council of Metropolitan Boston, I-123, box 12, folder 1, Wyner Family Jewish Heritage Center at New England Historic Genealogical Society, Boston, MA.

168 Minutes, Jewish Community Council of Metropolitan Boston.

169 Gerald W. Wohlberg, "Tufts Anti-Zionist Course Seen as Abuse of Academic Freedom," *Jewish Advocate*, August 9, 1973, 3.

170 Sid Blumenthal, letter to the editor, *Jewish Advocate*, August 23, 1973, 2.

171 Pomerantz, letter to the editor, *Jewish Advocate*, 14.

172 Pomerantz, 14.

173 Dr. Keith Linden to President Hallowell, November 27, 1973, Office of the President Records, 1824–2014, Ex-College, "Zionism Reconsidered, 1973–1974," Tufts University Digital Collections and Archives, Medford, MA.

174 Rabbi Thomas P. Liebschutz to Dr. Burton Hallowell, November 27, 1973, Office of the President Records, 1824–2014, Ex-College, "Zionism Reconsidered, 1973–1974," Tufts University Digital Collections and Archives, Medford, MA.

175 Dr. Harold C. Richman to Mr. Hallowell, May 24, 1973, Office of the President Records, 1824–2014, Ex-College, "Zionism Reconsidered, 1973–1974," Tufts University Digital Collections and Archives, Medford, MA.

176 Martin Blatt, interview with the author.

177 "Scandal at Tufts," *Herut News* 1, nos. 2–3, New England Region, UZRA-Herut USA, Brighton, MA, Office of the President Records, 1824–2014, Ex-College, "Zionism Reconsidered, 1973–1974," Tufts University Digital Collections and Archives, Medford, MA.

178 Mrs. Brenda R. Tanger to President Hallowell, April 2, 1973, Office of the President Records, 1824–2014, Ex-College, "Zionism Reconsidered, 1973–1974," Tufts University Digital Collections and Archives, Medford, MA. In 1994, psychologist Richard Herrnstein co-authored, with Charles Murray, the controversial book *The Bell Curve: Intelligence and Class Structure in American Life* (New York: Free Press, 1994), which argued for connections between race and intelligence.

179 J. Leon King to Mr. Hallwell [*sic*], August 17, 1973, Office of the President Records, 1824–2014, Ex-College, "Zionism Reconsidered, 1973–1974," Tufts University Digital Collections and Archives, Medford, MA.

180 Josef Teplo to Mr. Walter Sobol, associate director, Tufts University Annual Fund, Office of the President Records, 1824–2014, Ex-College, "Zionism Reconsidered, 1973–1974," Tufts University Digital Collections and Archives, Medford, MA.

181 Dr. Burton Hallowell to Dr. Harold Richman, June 22, 1973, Office of the President Records, 1824–2014, Ex-College, "Zionism Reconsidered, 1973–1974," Tufts University Digital Collections and Archives, Medford, MA.

182 Dr. Burton Hallowell to Dr. Harold Richman, June 22, 1973, Office of the President Records, 1824–2014, Ex-College, "Zionism Reconsidered, 1973–1974," Tufts University Digital Collections and Archives, Medford, MA.

183 President Burton Hallowell to Mr. Barnard Florence, April 30, 1973, Office of the President Records, 1824–2014, Ex-College, "Zionism Reconsidered, 1973–1974," Tufts University Digital Collections and Archives, Medford, MA.

184 "Administration Affirms Support for Ex-Coll Class," *Tufts Observer* 7, no. 11 (April 13, 1973): 7.

185 Blatt, Davis, and Kleinbaum, "Editors' Introduction," in *Dissent and Ideology in Israel*, 9, 12.

186 Blatt, Davis, and Kleinbaum, 9.

187 Blatt, Davis, and Kleinbaum, 9.

188 Blatt, Davis, and Kleinbaum, 10.

189 Blatt, Davis, and Kleinbaum, 10.

190 "Tufts Experimental College History Timeline," Tufts University, Experimental College, https://excollege.tufts.edu.

191 In 2020, Tufts University Office of Campus Life presented Students for Justice in Palestine with its 2020 Collaboration Award for bringing twenty diverse student groups together "as part of its '#EndTheDeadlyExchange' campaign, which seeks to end military training trips for the Tufts University Police Department and all other police militarization on campus." These police exchange trips are between the US and Israel. Tufts administrators threatened to revoke the award from SJP. Tufts president Anthony Monaco issued a statement: "We as senior leaders take responsibility for this outcome, which should not have happened, and recognize

that the award has caused a great deal of pain and concern for Jewish members
of our community and others who share concerns about SJP's policy positions,
particularly in light of rising anti-Semitism in the U.S. and around the world."
"Statement on Student Organization Award," Tufts University, Office of the
President, April 24, 2020, https://president.tufts.edu. Jonathan Greenblatt, CEO
of the Anti-Defamation League, praised Monaco's statement and accused SJP of
"regularly fostering antisemitism." Nora Barrows-Friedman, "Boston Students
Vilified for Tackling How Israel Trains Cops," *Electronic Intifada*, May 1, 2020,
https://electronicintifada.net.

192 In his article "Breaking the Taboo: Critics of Israel and the American Jewish
Establishment," historian Jack Wertheimer writes, "Since the founding of Breira
in 1973 and continuing with the establishment of such groups as the New Jew-
ish Agenda and the New Israel Fund, as well as Americans for Peace Now, the
American Jewish community has been challenged to define the limits of diversity
and pluralism, by groups that have publicly dissented from the official policy of
the State of Israel and the consensus of American Jewry's established leadership."
In Jerold S. Auerbach, Ilan Troen, and Walter Ackerman, eds., *Envisioning Israel:
The Changing Ideals and Images of North American Jews* (Detroit: Wayne State
University Press, 1996), 397. In the introduction to the 2nd edition of his *American
Judaism*, Jonathan Sarna writes that "glimmers of dissent" from the idea of Israel
as "the great unifier among America's variegated Jews" appeared with Breira "as
early as 1973." Sarna, *American Judaism*, 377–78.

193 *Proceedings of Breira's First Annual Membership Conference* (New York: Breira,
February 20–22, 1977), 4–5.

194 Malka Rabinowitz, "Breira: Friend or Foe?," *Jerusalem Post*, February 18, 1977, 5,
Breira Papers, box 5, folder 16, Center for Jewish History, New York.

195 *Proceedings of Breira's*, 3.

196 Ezra Berkley Nepon shares this information in their history of New Jewish
Agenda, an organization studied in chap. 4. Nepon, "'Agendas within Agenda':
The Challenge of Mobilizing Diverse Jewish Communities," New Jewish Agenda,
www.newjewishagenda.net.

197 "Breira and the Limits of Dissent" is the title of Michael Staub's final chapter in
Torn at the Roots, 280–308.

198 See Levin, *Our Palestine Question*. Levin notes that Breira connected to the follow-
ing members of the Israeli left, among others: retired Israel Defense Forces (IDF)
General Mattitiyahu Peled; Knesset members Aryeh Lova Eliav, Shulamit Aloni,
Uri Avnery, and Marcia Freedman; and former IDF colonel Meir Pa'il (188).

199 "An Open Letter to Israel's Leaders from Breira," April 7, 1976, Breira Records,
1972–79, box 4, folder 2, "Press Releases, Statements, Open Letters, 1976," Center
for Jewish History, New York.

200 Breira, "Only Those Who Fear Peace," public statement, November 11, 1975, Breira
Records, 1972–79, box 4, folder 1, "Press Releases, Statements, Open Letters, 1975,
2 of 2," Center for Jewish History, New York.

201 "Resolution of Commission 1: Diaspora Jewish Life," Breira Records, 1972–79, box 6, folder 6, "Records of First National Membership Conference," Center for Jewish History, New York.

202 "Resolution of Commission 1."

203 Robert A. Cohn, "Brouhaha over Breira: Serious Schism or Tempest in Teapot?," *St. Louis Jewish Light*, March 16, 1977, 7, Breira Papers, box 5, folder 15, Center for Jewish History, New York.

204 "JDL Exposes Treachery: Hillel-PLO Connection," *Jewish Defender* 1, no. 1 (February 1976), Breira Papers, box 9, folder 2, Center for Jewish History, New York.

205 Alexander Cockburn and James Ridgeway, "Doves, the Diaspora, and the Future of Israel: The Angry Debate among American Jews," *Village Voice*, March 17, 1977, Breira Papers, box 5, folder 15, Center for Jewish History, New York.

206 "ADL for B'nai B'rith Breira Probe, Special Panel to Study Problem," *Jewish Week*, February 1977, Breira Papers, box 8, folder 8, Center for Jewish History, New York.

207 Rabbi Isidor Hoffman to Mr. David Blumberg, February 25, 1977, and Rabbi Isidor Hoffman to Mr. Dore Schary, February 25, 1977, Breira Papers, box 8, folder 8, Center for Jewish History, New York. Schary, a screenwriter and producer, was honorary national chairman of the Anti-Defamation League at that time.

208 David M. Blumberg, "The President's Column," *National Jewish Monthly*, April 1977, Breira Papers, box 8, folder 8, Center for Jewish History, New York. Blumberg noted that these same debates go on in Israel and also asserted that he believed "public criticism of Israel by the Diaspora" should be "behind closed doors."

209 "ADL Stand Harmful," *Jewish Post*, February 18, 1977, Breira Papers, box 8, folder 8, Center for Jewish History, New York.

210 "Bloomberg Rebuffs ADL, Knows of No Violations" and "5 Invade Office of Hillel Rabbi," *Jewish Post*, February 25, 1977, Breira Papers, box 8, folder 8, Center for Jewish History, New York.

211 Joseph Shattan, "In the Community: Why Breira?," *Commentary* 63, no. 4 (April 1977): 60.

212 Robert Loeb, executive director of Breira, responded to Shattan's article with a letter to the editor. Robert Loeb, letter to the editor, *Commentary* 63, no. 6 (June 1, 1977): 4.

213 David Holzel, "Max Ticktin's Second Act," *Washington Jewish Week*, October 7, 2015, www.washingtonjewishweek.com.

214 Letter to "Breira member" from Arnold Jacob Wolf, January 1978, box 3, folder 7, "Letters and Notices to Membership, 1974–1979," Breira Papers, Center for Jewish History, New York. Some of the members of Breira went on to found the New Jewish Agenda, a progressive Jewish organization discussed in the following chapter.

215 "Factual and Other Errors in 'Why Breira' by Joseph Shattan," April 1977, Breira Records, 1972–79, box 4, folder 3, Center for Jewish History, New York.

216 See, for example, "Breira's Pride in Being Used Was Offensive," *Jewish Week*, February 20–26, 1977, Breira Papers, box 5, folder 15, Center for Jewish History, New York.

217 Rael Jean Isaac, *Breira: Counsel for Judaism* (New York: Americans for a Safe Israel, 1977), 28.

218 Scholar Judith Butler, in her critical review of journalist Bari Weiss's *How to Fight Anti-Semitism*, charts this silencing of dissent in the post-1967 era. "Bari Weiss's Unasked Questions," *Jewish Currents*, September 23, 2019, https://jewishcurrents .org.

219 On the silencing of dissent from within the Jewish community using the label "antisemitism," see also Allan Brownfeld, "Anti-Semitism: Its Changing Meaning," *Journal of Palestine Studies* 16, no. 3 (Spring 1987): 53–67.

220 The sum total of these developments meant a "crisis" for Jews and human rights. In his book *Rooted Cosmopolitans*, historian James Loeffler writes of Amnesty International's connections with Jewish leaders and with Israel: "Some [Jews] held fast to their Amnesty activism, often while adopting an explicitly anti-Zionist ideology." Loeffler, *Rooted Cosmopolitans*, 275, 288. "After 1967," however, Loeffler writes, "Jewish human rights activists could no longer avoid being ensnared in the political web of claims and counterclaims about Israel and human rights. Whether they wished to fight for the rights of Jews, Palestinians, or others, they were forced to answer for Israel's sins, again real or imagined" (294).

4. THE THRESHOLD OF DISSENT IN THE 1980S

1 Mitelpunkt, *Israel in the American Mind*, 277.

2 Magid, *Meir Kahane*, 74.

3 The Shalom Network, composed of twenty-five to thirty groups, brought speakers from Israel's peace movement to the US and lobbied Jewish groups to consider the goal of Palestinian self-determination. Their archival website notes, "Their goals were to strengthen two-state activism, promote honest and meaningful dialogue with Palestinians, and express solidarity with Peace Now in Israel." Once the New Jewish Agenda was founded, this network merged with its Middle East Task Force. Aliza Becker, "Peace Movement History, Section 8: The Shalom Network," Brit Tzedek v'Shalom / Jewish Alliance for Justice and Peace, http://btvshalom.org. See also "'Peace Now' Growing in Israel; 37 American Jews Offer Support," *American Israelite*, May 11, 1978, 12.

4 Shaul Mitelpunkt notes that the election of Menachem Begin as Israel's prime minister in 1977 "brought many American observers to believe Israel was becoming nationalistic and messianic, rather than sober and rational." Mitelpunkt, *Israel in the American Mind*, 23.

5 "Mann Joins in Criticism of Nablus Settlement, Upholds General Policy," *New York Jewish Week*, June 24, 1979, 1. The use of the place names "Samaria and Judea," terms used in the Bible, is meant to justify the occupation of the Palestinian land of the West Bank.

6 Jack Wertheimer, "Jewish Organization Life in the United States since 1945," *American Jewish Yearbook 1995*, (Philadelphia: American Jewish Committee, 1995), 72, accessed through https://ajcarchives.org.

7 Marvin Pave, "Boston Jews among 37 Who Signed Peace Message," *Boston Globe*, April 22, 1978, 22.

8 "Mann Joins in Criticism," *New York Jewish Week*, June 24, 1979, 1.

9 Abraham S. Karff, "Answer to Rabbi Gittelsohn," *Jewish Advocate*, August 21, 1980, 13.

10 Rabbi E. C. Armond, "Who Speaks for American Jewry: To the Editor of the Jerusalem Post," *Jerusalem Post*, September 2, 1980, 10.

11 "Begin Rejects U.S. Jews' Advice on Israel Security," *Los Angeles Times*, July 25, 1980, 1.

12 Leonard Fein, "Criticism Is Not Fatal," *New York Times*, July 19, 1980, 17.

13 Meir Merhav, "Begin v. Fein," *Jerusalem Post*, August 1, 1980, 6.

14 Others who criticized Foreign Minister Moshe Dayan's comments included army secretary Clifford Alexander and American Jewish Committee president Maynard I. Wishner. See "Denounce Racial Slur of Black Soldiers by Israel's Moshe Dayan," *Jet Magazine* 59, no. 17 (January 8, 1981): 5.

15 "SCLC, PLO Embrace in Beirut: Israel Snubs Black Group," *Afro-American*, September 29, 1979, 1.

16 Carenen, *Fervent Embrace*, 189.

17 As Carenen notes, in 1991 the National Council of Churches voted to support the United Nations resolution calling for Israel to withdraw from the Palestinian territories. Carenen, 195.

18 Weiss, "Billy Graham Receives."

19 Some scholars link American Jewish opposition to affirmative action to Jews' experiences with quotas in colleges and universities before World War II.

20 David L. Chappell, *Waking from the Dream: The Struggle for Civil Rights in the Shadow of Martin Luther King, Jr.* (New York: Random House, 2014).

21 Murray Friedman, "Intergroup Relations," *American Jewish Yearbook 1982*, vol. 82 (Philadelphia: American Jewish Committee and Jewish Publication Society of America, 1981), 110, accessed through https://ajcarchives.org.

22 "Blacks Blast Carter," *New Pittsburgh Courier*, August 6, 1977, 8.

23 "Polls Show Blacks Favor Jews, Split on Carter, Deplore Job Bias," *Atlanta Daily World*, January 24, 1980, 5.

24 In 1987, the Orthodox rabbi representative of the Jewish Welfare Board Commission on Jewish Chaplaincy announced his movement would withdraw from the organization in protest over the decision of the Reform movement's representative to ordain a woman rabbi. The ensuing soul-searching led to a new assessment titled "American-Jewish Disunity: An Overview," authored by sociologist Samuel Heilman for the American Jewish Congress. Quoted in Lawrence Grossman, "Jewish Communal Affairs," *American Jewish Yearbook 1988*, vol. 88 (Philadelphia: American Jewish Committee and Jewish Publication Society of America, 1988), 191, accessed through https://ajcarchives.org.

25 Stephen Martin Cohen, "The 1981–1982 National Survey of American Jews," *American Jewish Yearbook 1983*, vol. 83 (Philadelphia: American Jewish

Committee and Jewish Publication Society of America, 1982), 95, accessed through https://ajcarchives.org.

26 Cohen, "1981–1982 National Survey," 95. The survey also measured demographic information among American Jews (age, marital status) as well as levels of "Jewish identification" and "ritual practice."

27 Cohen, "1981–1982 National Survey," 109.

28 The position of Professor Stephen Cohen, specifically, is complicated by his long pattern of sexual harassment of colleagues, linked closely to his pathologizing Jewish women—especially those who were not parents and those who are lesbian, gay, bisexual, transgender, or queer. Kate Rosenblatt, Lila Corwin Berman, and Ronit Shahl, "How Jewish Academia Created a #MeToo Disaster," *Forward*, July 19, 2018, https://forward.com.

29 "Reform Rabbi Says Israeli Leaders Must Pay Attention to Changing Mood in U.S. Jewish Community," *Jewish Telegraphic News Agency Daily News Bulletin*, January 11, 1982, www.jta.org.

30 "Reform Rabbi."

31 Grossman, "Jewish Communal Affairs," 196.

32 Edwin Black, "The Cutting Edge," *Jewish Press*, March 28, 1986, 5.

33 Nathan Glazer, "New Perspectives in American Jewish Sociology," *American Jewish Yearbook 1987* (Philadelphia: American Jewish Committee and Jewish Publication Society of America, 1987), 5, accessed through https://ajcarchives.org.

34 "AJCommittee Debate Examines How Far Jews Should Defend Narrow Interests," *Jewish Telegraphic News Agency Daily News Bulletin*, May 16, 1988, www.jta.org.

35 "New Jewish Agenda National Platform," adopted November 28, 1982, copy obtained from Harvard University Library, Judaica Division.

36 Interview conducted by Ezra Berkeley Nepon with Reena Bernards and Rabbi Gerald Serotta, New Jewish Agenda, July 2004, https://newjewishagenda.net.

37 "New Jewish Agenda National Platform."

38 "New Jewish Agenda National Platform."

39 Ezra Berkley Nepon, "New Jewish Agenda: Middle East Task Force," New Jewish Agenda, https://newjewishagenda.net.

40 Becker, "Peace Movement History."

41 "Progressive Movement Uses Breira List, Has No Room for Reporter," *New York Jewish Week*, January 4, 1981, 2.

42 "Jesse Jackson, Advocating Talks with P.L.O., Meets Critics in Israel," *New York Times*, September 25, 1979, A2.

43 Ari Goldman, "Head of Jewish Group Says Jackson Is an Anti-Semite," *New York Times*, June 1, 1984, B6. In addition to noting the activities of the Jewish Defense League, Goldman reported that Nathan Perlmutter, national director of the Anti-Defamation League, wrote in his annual report that Jackson was an antisemite and that if the Democratic Party did not repudiate Jackson's statements on Jews, "the party could forfeit its historic Jewish support in November's Presidential election."

44 "Jesse Jackson Unfairly Labeled," *Michigan Chronicle*, April 7, 1984, 6.

45 Reed notes that this is why "Jackson's incidental remarks provoked a shrillness strikingly absent from reaction to the more programmatic and ideological anti-Semitism emanating from such quarters as the Moral Majority." Reed, *Jesse Jackson Phenomenon*, 94.

46 "Jewish Group to Inquire about Rights in Nicaragua," *Atlanta Daily World*, August 21, 1984, 3.

47 Marjorie Hyer, "Jewish Group Finds No Anti-Semitism by Sandinista Regime," *Washington Post*, August 25, 1984, www.washingtonpost.com. About fifty Jewish Nicaraguans did indeed flee the country after the Sandinistas took power, partly because of business connections that would have left them vulnerable to new confiscatory policies and partly because of the Sandinistas' anti-Zionist rhetoric, which sometimes veered into antisemitism. See Lawrence Bush, "July 19: The Sandinistas, the Contras, and the ADL," *Jewish Currents*, July 18, 2015, https://jewishcurrents.org.

48 Indeed, scholars of "the growth of Jewish feminism" often elide criticisms of Israel with antisemitism; sociologist Sylvia Barack Fishman wrote that Jewish feminism's growth "was helped, ironically, by the presence of anti-Semitism within the ranks of the general feminist movement," including "a tidal wave of anti-Israel criticism" at the UN international women's conferences. Sylvia Barack Fishman, "The Impact of Feminism on American Jewish Life," *American Jewish Yearbook 1989* (Philadelphia: American Jewish Committee and Jewish Publication Society of America, 1982), 12, accessed through https://ajcarchives.org. Referring to American Jewish Zionist women at the UN Women's conferences, historian Joyce Antler writes that "for women's liberationists who had resisted or ignored their identity as Jewish women, the contentious Zionism question became a pathway to claim their Jewishness." American Jewish anti-Zionists, she writes, believed their anti-Zionism "was not a contradiction to their Jewishness but a component of an anticolonialist worldview." Echoing the findings of this study, she continues, "Criticizing American Jewish feminists' 'identity work,' these and other anti-Zionist women declared that failure to denounce the Israeli state rendered anticolonial alliances impossible." Antler notes that "the problem of confronting anti-Semitism and distinguishing it from anti-Zionism remained in the new [twenty-first] century." Joyce Antler, *Jewish Radical Feminism: Voices from the Women's Liberation Movement* (New York: New York University Press, 2018), 316, 318, 347.

49 Quoted in "Nairobi Conference Brought Jewish, Arab Women Together," *Philadelphia Tribune*, August 6, 1985, 6.

50 L. E. Scott, "Reflecting on Nairobi," *Jewish Exponent*, August 9, 1985, 4.

51 Hayyim Feldman, "Reports of Our Demise Are Greatly Exaggerated," *Jewish Advocate*, September 24, 1992, 9.

52 Quoted in "Nairobi Conference."

53 "Brooklyn Feminist Dialogue," *New York Amsterdam News*, October 5, 1985, 40.

54 Hayyim Feldman, "Reports of Our Demise," 9.

55 Feld, *Nations Divided*, 87–106.

56 David Friedman, "Klutznick: Israel Harmed by U.S. Jewish Leaders Who Appear to Act as 'Rubber Stamps' for Israel Policies," *JTA News Bulletin*, April 20, 1982, 4. Steven T. Rosenthal writes that Klutznick and Nahum Goldman joined "former French premier Pierre Mendez-France in calling on Israel to lift its siege of Beirut and to negotiate with the PLO on the basis of mutual recognition." Steven T. Rosenthal, *Irreconcilable Differences? The Waning of the American Jewish Love Affair with Israel* (Waltham, MA: Brandeis University Press, 2001), 67.

57 Fay S. Joyce, "McGovern Stands Apart, Criticizing Israeli Policy," *New York Times*, February 4, 1984, 8; Wolf Blitzer, "Advocate of Dissent," *Jerusalem Post*, February 3, 1983, 5.

58 "Progressive Movement," 2.

59 In June 1987, the New Jewish Agenda "Unsung Hero" Award went to Schappes, and the award program called him "one of the genuine giants of progressive Jewish culture." "A Song for the Unsung," New Jewish Agenda National Convention, July 1987, Schappes Papers, box 4, folder 3, Tamiment Library, New York University.

60 Irving Greenberg, "The Untold Story: American Jewish Reaction to Lebanon," *Jewish Press*, July 30, 1982, 4.

61 Mitelpunkt, *Israel in the American Mind*, 299.

62 Colin A. Moore, "Lebanon, a New Vietnam?," *New York Amsterdam News*, October 29, 1983, 15; Mitelpunkt writes about Israeli protests over the war in Lebanon and their impact on American audiences; see Mitelpunkt, *Israel in the American Mind*, 299–305.

63 George E. Gruen, director of Middle East Affairs for the American Jewish Committee, writes, "From this perspective, the war in Lebanon—including Israel's decisive blow against Kremlin-backed terrorism, the IDF's destruction of Syria's Soviet-supplied SAM-missile sites and large quantities of Syrian aircraft and tanks, the apparent superiority of American over Soviet weapon systems this revealed, and the impotence displayed by the Kremlin in the final months of the Brezhnev era by its failure to save the PLO or its Syrian ally from humiliating defeat—served to enhance America's prestige in the power struggle with Russia." See George E. Gruen, "The United States and Israel: Impact of the Lebanon War," *American Jewish Yearbook 1984* (Philadelphia: American Jewish Committee and Jewish Publication Society of America, 1982), 73, accessed through https://ajcarchives.org; Mitelpunkt, *Israel in the American Mind*, 13.

64 "No matter how many Lebanese are killed by Israeli bombs and rockets, until the Palestinians get justice, Israel will be insecure," Rowan writes. "And there will always be a PLO, saying that the only thing that prevents an Arab wipeout of Israel is the massive supply of modern weapons that Israel gets from the United States." Carol Rowan, "Onrushing Tragedy in the Middle East," *New York Amsterdam News*, August 1, 1981, 17.

65 "This Is Not the Way!," New Jewish Agenda (National), advertisement, *New York Times*, June 30, 1982, B4.

66 Mitelpunkt writes that the "Israeli invasion of Lebanon troubled many elite observers who had previously expressed unreserved sympathy for Israel." Mitelpunkt, *Israel in the American Mind*, 24.

67 Quoted in Arthur J. Magida, "Radical Gadflies: Always on the Outside, the New Jewish Agenda Wants to Heal the Rift between Jews and Progressive Politics," *Baltimore Jewish Times*, August 3, 1984, 55.

68 "Excommunicated," an interview with Betsy Cohen (Batya Kallus), Reena Bernards, and Clare Kinberg, American Jewish Peace Archive, n.d. [2017?], https://myemail.constantcontact.com. See also "'Excommunication' of Jews Challenged by Rabbis' Group," *New York Times*, November 26, 1982, A21; Joanne Omang, "Three Rabbis Excommunicate Hundreds," *Washington Post*, November 25, 1982, www.washingtonpost.com.

69 "American Friends of 'Peace Now': A Call to Peace," *New York Times*, July 4, 1982, E7; quoted in Paul L. Montgomery, "Discord among U.S. Jews over Israel Seems to Grow," *New York Times*, July 15, 1982, www.nytimes.com.

70 Greenberg, "Untold Story," 4.

71 American Israel Public Affairs Committee, action memorandum from Thomas Dine, executive director, August 6, 1982, Boston Jewish Community Relations Council Records, I-123, box 249, folder 8, Wyner Family Jewish Heritage Center at New England Historic Genealogical Society, Boston, MA.

72 Embassy of Israel, Washington, DC, June 22, 1982, "The Truth about Civilian Casualties and Refugees in Southern Lebanon," Boston Jewish Community Relations Council Records, I-123, box 249, folder 8, Wyner Family Jewish Heritage Center at New England Historic Genealogical Society, Boston, MA.

73 Theodore R. Mann, Conference of Presidents of Major Jewish Organizations, Middle East memo: "'Morality' and the War in Lebanon," August 18, 1982, Boston Jewish Community Relations Council Records, I-123, box 249, folder 8, Wyner Family Jewish Heritage Center at New England Historic Genealogical Society, Boston, MA.

74 "Update: National Zionist Affairs Department of Hadassah, July 19, 1982," from Mrs. Henry Goldman, chairman, National Zionist Affairs Department, and Marc Brandriss, director, Zionist Affairs Department, to presidents, education vice presidents, and Zionist affairs chairmen, Boston Jewish Community Relations Council Records, I-123, box 249, folder 8, Wyner Family Jewish Heritage Center at New England Historic Genealogical Society, Boston, MA.

75 Tony Schwartz, "ADL Criticizes TV over Coverage of Lebanon," *New York Times*, October 21, 1982, C30.

76 Mitelpunkt, *Israel in the American Mind*, 301.

77 Rosenthal writes about the poll in *Irreconcilable Differences?*, 65, 66.

78 Paul L. Montgomery, "Discord."

79 Montgomery. By the early 1980s and especially after Israel's invasion of Lebanon, Podhoretz had become well known—and highly controversial—for accusing journalists and other public figures of antisemitism after they voiced criticism

of Prime Minister Menachem Begin's policies in Israel. Brownfield recounts the intense confrontations between Podhoretz and various people in "Anti-Semitism," 53–67.

80 Montgomery, "Discord."

81 Montgomery. Decades later, in Brickner's obituary, the *New York Times* observed that friction with the American Jewish community often resulted from his analogies between Israel and Vietnam: "Rabbi Brickner raised hackles among fellow Zionists for his opposition to the Israeli invasion of Lebanon in 1982 and was criticized for calling Lebanon and the occupied Palestinian territories 'Israel's Vietnam.'" Wolfgang Saxon, "Balfour Brickner, Activist Reform Rabbi, Dies at 78," *New York Times*, September 1, 2005, www.nytimes.com.

82 Norman Podhoretz, "J'Accuse," *Commentary* 74, no. 3 (September 1982): 21.

83 "The Media Assault on Israel," *New York Jewish Week*, October 29, 1982, 16.

84 Rosenthal, *Irreconcilable Differences?*, 73.

85 "Americans for Ethical and Just Conduct in the Middle East" to Ambassador Moshe Arens, September 23, 1982, Ronald W. Fox Papers, box 1, folder 35, Wyner Family Jewish Heritage Center at New England Historic Genealogical Society, Boston, MA.

86 Roger Hurwitz, "The Logic of Invasion," *Jewish Advocate*, June 17, 1982, A3.

87 "Protests, Cables to Begin Urge End to War," *Jerusalem Post*, June 25, 1982, 3.

88 On New Jewish Agenda's protest outside of Sharon's appearance, see Michael D. Schaffler, "Sharon: Troop Plan Endangers Israel," *Philadelphia Inquirer*, May 12, 1983, 16.

89 Quoted in Michael Kramer, "American Jews and Israel: The Schism," *New York Magazine*, October 18, 1982, 28-29.

90 Kramer, 28. Schindler's relationship with the prime minister endured until Begin's death in 1993. Lawrence Joffe of the *Guardian* wrote, "Although the pair later clashed publicly over Israel's conduct in Lebanon, they remained intimate confidants until Begin's death in 1992." Lawrence Joffe, "Alexander Schindler," *Guardian*, November 30, 2000, www.theguardian.com.

91 Kenneth A. Briggs, "Reform Leader Cautions Jews on Israeli Ties," *New York Times*, December 5, 1982, 24.

92 Briggs.

93 Laurie Goodstein, "Feeling Abandoned by Israel, Many American Jews Grow Angry," *New York Times*, November 16, 1997, 8.

94 Rosenthal, *Irreconcilable Differences?*, 75.

95 See, for example, Howla Jackdall Mitchell, letter to the editor, "'Safe' Criticism," *In These Times* 6, no. 40 (October 20, 1982): 15.

96 Manning Marable, "Jobs, Peace, Freedom: A Political Assessment of the August 27 March on Washington," *Black Scholar* 14, no. 6 (November/December 1983): 2.

97 Claude Reed Jr., "A Moment of Pride," *Los Angeles Sentinel*, October 26, 1983, B4.

98 Robert Greene II, "The 1983 March on Washington and the Age of Reagan," *Society for US Intellectual History* (blog), June 29, 2014, https://s-usih.org.

99 Marable, "Jobs, Peace, Freedom," 6.

100 Marable, 9, 15.

101 Walter Lewis, "Jewish Groups Facing Dilemma on D.C. March," *New York Jewish Week*, July 1, 1983, 4.

102 Donald Feldstein, "Why AJCommittee Won't 'March on Washington,'" *New York Jewish Week*, July 29, 1983, 4.

103 "Israel Wins Support from Caucus Members," *Atlanta Daily World*, August 26, 1975, 3.

104 Milton Coleman and Thomas Morgan, "Jewish Leaders Denounce Fauntroy Mideast Effort," *Washington Post*, September 25, 1979, www.washingtonpost.com.

105 Lewis, "Jewish Groups Facing Dilemma." Lawyer and former congresswoman Bella Abzug, a prominent feminist, antiwar activist, and Zionist well known in the Jewish community, offered one of the final speeches on the program. She was not connected to any formal Jewish organization and used her fiery speech to attack President Reagan for moving the economy "to the rich, and out of our hands." Through the 1970s and especially when she was running for political office, Abzug was assailed for not being sufficiently "pro-Israel" and faced protests by the Jewish Defense League. C-SPAN has a recording of the speeches of the march. "Twentieth Anniversary of the March on Washington," C-SPAN, August 27, 1983, www.c-span.org. On Abzug and the Jewish Defense League, see Grace Lichtenstein, "The Abzug Farber Contest: Plenty of Color," *New York Times*, October 30, 1970, 48.

106 Helen Silver, "Special Services Held on the Eve of the March on Washington," *Jewish Telegraphic News Agency Daily News Bulletin*, August 29, 1983, www.jta.org.

107 Albert Vorspan, "UAHC Defends Decision to Join Controversial March," *New York Jewish Week*, July 15, 1983, 4.

108 Vorspan, 4.

109 George Collins, "Then and Now," *Afro-American*, August 27, 1983, A2.

110 Ken Smikle, "The Woman Who Organized the March on Washington," *Michigan Chronicle*, October 29, 1983, D22.

111 Walter K. Lewis, "Controversial Protest in Washington: New Jewish Agenda Leaders Still Seek Widespread Communal Support," *New York Jewish Week*, July 29, 1983, 4.

112 Karlyn Barker and Eric Pianin, "Attempt to Soothe Jewish Groups," *Washington Post*, August 11, 1983, www.washingtonpost.com.

113 "UAHC Is Assailed on Joining March," *New York Jewish Week*, August 12, 1983, 5. Bernice S. Tannenbaum later worked to have President Reagan repudiate the UN "Zionism Is Racism" resolution and remove any mention of it in the condemnation of Zionism or Israel in the conference declaration for the UN Conference for Women in 1985 in Nairobi, Kenya. This story is told in Marlin Levin, *It Takes a Dream: The Story of Hadassah* (Jerusalem: Gefen, 1997), 343–44.

114 Karlyn Barker, "Marchers: Let's Move Forward: Marchers Put Aside Their Differences," *Washington Post*, August 14, 1983, B1.

115 Schindler, quoted in Mark Joffe, "After 20 Years, They March Again for Social Change," *Jewish Exponent*, September 2, 1983, 5.

116 Silver, "Special Services," 3.

117 Patrick Owens, "Sabbath Fire Kindles Unity on Eve of Civil Rights March," *Newsday*, August 27, 1983, 4. One Jewish newspaper noted that King "made no formal public mention of the Jews who had decided not to participate in this year's march or the Jewish organizations that had refused to endorse it." They quoted him as saying he "felt no bitterness toward them." M.J., "Heschel-King: A New Generation," *Jewish Exponent*, September 2, 1983, 5.

118 Scott Simon, "Hundreds of Thousands March on Washington for Jobs, Peace, Freedom," National Public Radio, August 27, 1983, www.npr.org.

119 Rael J. Isaac, "The Messenger Is the Message," *Jerusalem Post*, July 29, 1990, 4. In this work, Isaac likens AJCongress's decision to participate in the march to the anti-Zionism of the American Council for Judaism, the non-Zionism of the early American Jewish Committee, and the critical stand of the New Jewish Agenda.

120 Emanuel Rackman, "Better Live Jews Than Empty-Gestured Martyrs," *New York Jewish Week*, November 4, 1983, 27.

121 Lewis, "Jewish Groups Facing Dilemma."

122 Anti-Defamation League of B'nai Brith, Memorandum to the National Executive Committee from Nathan Perlmutter, September 30, 1983, Jewish Community Relations Council of Greater Boston Records, I-123 and I-123A, box 259, folder 2, Wyner Family Jewish Heritage Center at NEHGS, Boston, MA.

123 Anti-Defamation League.

124 Vorspan, "UAHC Defends."

125 Magida, "Radical Gadflies," 54–56.

126 Magida, 56.

127 Magida notes that the Baltimore chapter, however, strove *not* to join the local federation: "Once you're a part of the establishment," said Mike Tabor, "It's hard to change it." Magida, "Radical Gadflies," 56.

128 Wertheimer, "Jewish Organization Life," 76.

129 Ezra Berkley Nepon, "Author's Conclusion," New Jewish Agenda, https://newjewishagenda.net.

130 Ethan Bloch, "One Voice Less for the Jewish Left: New Jewish Agenda, 1981–1993," New Jewish Agenda, https://newjewishagenda.net.

131 Rael Jean Isaac, "New Jewish Agenda: Outside the Consensus," *Midstream*, December 1990, 14–19.

132 The 1989 New Jewish Agenda report, titled *NJA's Preliminary Response to "New Jewish Agenda: Dissent or Disloyalty,"* can be found here: New Jewish Agenda, https://newjewishagenda.net.

133 "NJA's Preliminary Response."

134 Magida, "Radical Gadflies," 56.

135 Wertheimer, "Jewish Organization Life," 76.

CONCLUSION

1 Zukerman, *Jew in Revolt*, 207.

2 "Listening in on Lessing J. Rosenwald."

3 Lazaron, "Israel and Jewish Nationalism."

4 William Zukerman, *Jewish Newsletter*, November 21, 1955.

5 Hagopian, "Non-sectarian Jewish Question," 3.

6 *Proceedings of Breira's*, 4–5.

7 Rabbi Michael Lerner, quoted in Alice Rothchild, "Wrestling with an Old Demon," *Boston Globe*, October 18, 2003, A15.

8 Journalist Peter Beinart, quoted in Joel Brown, "BU's Rabin Lecture Outlines Split among American Jews," BU Today, April 16, 2019, www.bu.edu.

9 James Baldwin, "On Being 'White' . . . and Other Lies," *Essence*, April 1984, reprinted in David R. Roediger, ed., *Black on White: Black Writers on What It Means to Be White* (New York: Schocken Books, 1998), 178, Bannerker Institute, https://bannekerinstitute.fas.harvard.edu.

10 Goldstein, *Price of Whiteness*, 6.

11 Goldstein, 236, 237.

12 "JVP Response to the Movement for Black Lives Policy Platform" (2016) and "Our Approach to Zionism" (2018), Jewish Voice for Peace, https://jewishvoiceforpeace.org.

13 "Our Approach to Zionism."

14 Founded in 2014, IfNotNow writes in their founding statement that "for decades, politicians have used Jewish safety as justification for sending a blank check to the Israeli government, paying no mind to the oppression of the Palestinian people. . . . And the American Jewish establishment wants us to side against our natural allies, to choose isolation and despair." Further, they write, "Unfortunately, too many self-appointed leaders in our community have been all too willing to play along with this deadly game, all so they can silence criticism of Israel and to advance Israel's expansionist policies. They believe that in America, Jews must fear other marginalized peoples because of their solidarity with Palestinians. . . . The world is on fire and the failed Jewish establishment has chosen the interest of the Israeli government over those of our own community. It is a choice that has led to blacklists of our community's bravest voices, attacks against our strongest allies, and partnerships with global far-right authoritarian leaders." "Who We Are," IfNotNow, www.ifnotnowmovement.org.

15 Mari Cohen, "The Complex Reality of Black-Jewish Coalitions in Georgia," *Jewish Currents*, January 26, 2021, https://jewishcurrents.org.

16 Mari Cohen writes, "The Boston JCRC, a coalition of Boston's Jewish organizations, stated in 2016 that it would reject 'participation in any coalition that seeks to isolate and demonize Israel singularly amongst the nations of the world' and 'dissociate ourselves from the Black Lives Matter platform and those BLM organizations that embrace it.'" In the summer of 2020, however, "JCRC no longer displays the statement on its website." Cohen noted that "JCRC Executive Director Jeremy Burton said in an interview that he now believes the JCRC made a series of mistakes when it attacked the Movement for Black Lives platform in 2016." Mari Cohen, "Jewish Groups Embrace BLM, with Conditions," *Jewish Currents*, June 23, 2020, https://jewishcurrents.org.

17 "Black Lives Matter" advertisement by Jewish organizations and synagogues, *New York Times*, August 28, 2020, A17, www.nytimes.com.

18 "Black Lives Matter" advertisement.

19 "Together for Freedom," promotional video, Jewish Voice for Peace, 2019, https://jewishvoiceforpeace.org.

20 Max Fisher, "As Israel's Dependence on U.S. Shrinks, So Does U.S. Leverage," *New York Times*, May 24, 2021, www.nytimes.com.

CODA

1 Fein, "Criticism Is Not Fatal," 17.

2 Emily Tamkin, "Can American Jewish Support for Israel Survive This New Government?," *New Republic*, March 7, 2023, https://newrepublic.com.

3 "Smotrich Declares There's No Palestinian People, Declares His Family 'Real Palestinians,'" *Times of Israel*, March 20, 2023, www.timesofisrael.com.

4 Tamkin, "Can American Jewish Support?"

5 Published under David Weigel, "The Trailer: Your Hour-by-Hour Guide on What to Watch in Four States Tonight," *Washington Post*, August 9, 2022, www.washingtonpost.com.

6 Ron Kampeas, "AIPAC's PAC Endorses Dozens of Republicans Who Refuse to Certify Joe Biden as President," *Jewish Telegraphic Agency*, March 3, 2022, www.jta.org.

7 See, for example, the ADL report "Hate in the Empire State: Extremism and Antisemitism in New York, 2020–2021," Anti-Defamation League, May 19, 2022, https://adl.org.

8 "Jewish National Fund Whitewashes Theft of Palestinian Land," *Haaretz*, August 4, 2022, www.haaretz.com.

9 "Israel's Apartheid against Palestinians: A Cruel System of Domination and a Crime against Humanity," Amnesty International, February 1, 2022, www.amnesty.org.

10 "American Jews Hold First Protest against Israel's New Apartheid Government," IfNotNow Movement, November 4, 2023, www.ifnotnowmovement.org.

11 Quoted in Ali Harb, "Israel's US Backers Face 'Moment of Reckoning' as Far Right Rises," *Al Jazeera*, November 3, 2022, www.aljazeera.com.

12 Tamkin, "Can American Jewish Support?"

13 "American Jewish Committee Issues Statement on Israeli Election," American Jewish Committee, November 2, 2022, www.ajc.org.

14 "ADL Statement on the Formation of a New Israeli Government," Anti-Defamation League, December 22, 2022, www.adl.org.

15 "Anti-Defamation League Expresses Concern over Likely Inclusion of Extremists in New Israeli Coalition Government," Anti-Defamation League, November 3, 2022, https://adl.org.

16 Paul Berman, Martin Peretz, Michael Walzer, and Leon Wieseltier, "We Are Liberal American Zionists. We Stand with Israel's Protestors," *Washington Post*, February 3, 2023, www.washingtonpost.com.

17 Berman et al.

18 "Statement from American Jewish Leaders: Smotrich Should Not Be Given a Platform in Our Community," Israel Policy Forum, March 3, 2023, https://israelpolicyforum.org.

19 The (undated) letter can be found here: Yonat Shimron, "Hundreds of US Rabbis Protest New Israeli Government in Public Letter," *Washington Post*, December 28, 2022, www.washingtonpost.com.

20 Halie Soifer, "Why Pro-Israel U.S. Jews Like Me Are Protesting the Israeli Government," *Haaretz*, March 13, 2023, www.haaretz.com.

21 Jodi Rudoren, "Why This Zionist Rabbi Has Stopped Saying the Prayer for the State of Israel," *Forward*, January 6, 2023, https://forward.com.

22 Rabbi Jeremy Kalamofsky, "Comments on the Incoming Israeli Government and Our Prayers for the State of Israel," *Ansche Chesed* (blog), December 15, 2022, https://anschechesed.org.

23 Stone, "Jewry in a Blind Alley," 543–44.

24 Hillel Halkin, "On That Distant Day," *Jewish Review of Books*, Winter 2023, https://jewishreviewofbooks.com.

25 Philip Weiss, "Another Prominent Zionist Admits the Project Failed," *Mondoweiss*, January 9, 2023, https://mondoweiss.net.

26 Mari Cohen writes that "a close read shows that, on a few key debates, the Biden administration has incorporated the advice and perspectives of progressive Jewish groups—and rejected the more conservative organizations' agenda." See Mari Cohen, "Thursday Newsletter," *Jewish Currents*, June 1, 2023, https://jewishcurrents.org.

27 Nicholas Fandos and Jonah E. Bromwich, "After Attack on Israel, Politicians Are Asked, 'Which Side Are You On?,'" *New York Times*, October 10, 2023, www.nytimes.com.

28 Jeremy Buron, "Statement Accepting Resignation of Boston Workers Circle as JCRC Boston Member," Jewish Community Relations Council of Greater Boston, October 24, 2023, https://JCRCboston.org.

29 Israel Palestine Committee, "Boston JCRC Moves to Expel Founding Member Boston Workers Circle over Calls for Ceasefire," Boston Workers Circle Center for Jewish Culture and Social Justice, n.d. [October 2023?], https://circleboston.org.

30 Yonat Shimron and Jack Jenkins, "US Jews Fracture over Support for Israeli Retaliation," Religion News Service, October 26, 2023, https://religionnews.com.

31 Goldstein, *Price of Whiteness*, 235. As Eric Alterman writes, "Today . . . young American Jews have been voting with their feet—running, not walking, away from the Israel-and-the-Holocaust-grounded Judaism of their parents and grandparents." Alterman, *We Are Not One*, 409.

32 Arielle Angel, "Shabbat Reading List," *Jewish Currents*, October 27, 2023, https://jewishcurrents.org.

33 Saree Makdisi, "No Human Being Can Exist," *n+1*, October 25, 2023, https://nplusonemag.org.

INDEX

Abourezk, James, 184
Abram, Morris, 123
Abrams, Elliot, 165
Abzug, Bella, 261n105
Adler, Cyrus, 20
Adler, Felix, 17
affirmative action, 156, 183, 243n39, 255n19;
    Black-Jewish conflict over, 104, 155, 156,
    243n39; New Jewish Agenda and, 161
African Americans, 80, 155–56, 178; and an-
    ticolonialism, 54, 97, 101, 119, 164, 178–79,
    194, 241n18; attitudes of, toward Israel, 101,
    102–5, 154, 156, 182, 194; status of, com-
    pared with that of Palestinians, 80, 82. *See
    also* "Black antisemitism"; Black Power;
    Black press; civil rights movement
Agro-Joint project, 25
Ahad Ha'am (Asher Zvi Hirsch Ginsberg),
    10, 88
Algeria, 80, 101, 105, 106
Alter, Robert, 85, 86
Alterman, Eric, 4, 265n31
America First Committee, 29, 221n50
American-Arab Anti-Discrimination Com-
    mittee, 180, 184
American Council for Judaism, 24, 25–33, 37,
    39–41, 47–52; and American Jewish Com-
    mittee, 24, 36–37, 38–39; and Eisenhower
    administration, 41–42, 43–44, 224n92,
    224n99; founding of (1942), 8, 24, 25–26,
    27–28; Henry Hurwitz and, 86, 87–88, 89;
    and Reform Judaism, 8, 23, 24, 26, 29, 31,
    32, 35, 220n43; size of, 49; on US immigra-
    tion laws, 32; vision expressed by, 28–35;
    William Zukerman and, 59, 60, 67, 75,
    76–77, 82, 93, 95, 163–64
—leading figures in: Elmer Berger in, 11,
    26, 36, 43, 44, 48, 49–51, 52, 220n43,

221–22n61; Lessing Rosenwald in, 24,
    28–32, 37; Leonard Sussman in, 43–44,
    49–50, 52, 58
—as prominent critics of Zionism, 8, 11, 24,
    26, 30–35, 45, 47–51, 54–55, 147; attacks
    on, 24, 33, 35–36, 46–47, 68, 74, 75, 82,
    95, 119; concern of, for Palestinians, 28,
    30, 31, 34, 45–46; and historical continu-
    ity of Jewish dissent, 8, 11, 147; on Israeli
    citizenship law, 76–78; on Judaism as
    exclusively a religion, 26, 32, 34
American Friends of the Middle East, 46, 49
American Israel Public Affairs Committee
    (AIPAC), 43, 170, 201–2, 207
American Jewish Alternatives to Zionism
    (AJAZ), 50–51
American Jewish Committee (AJC), 7–8, 25,
    123, 145, 159, 203, 247n118; and American
    Council for Judaism, 24, 36–37, 38–39;
    and American Jewish Congress, 8, 23, 36;
    and Blaustein–Ben-Gurion understand-
    ing, 38, 39; and civil rights issues, 104, 156,
    164, 178, 181, 243n39; founding of (1906),
    7–8, 11, 23–24; and marginalization of
    dissent, 134, 151; and Reform Judaism,
    7, 20, 53; social base of, 7–8, 20, 219n24;
    surveys by, 157, 172, 187–88, 189
—and non-Zionism, 8, 20–22, 23, 87,
    217n23, 220n44; shift away from, 8,
    36–39, 53, 87, 217n23, 247n118
American Jewish Conference (1943), 60,
    220n44, 221n54
American Jewish Congress (AJCongress),
    22, 23, 36, 123; and American Jewish
    Committee, 23, 36; and civil rights is-
    sues, 79, 104, 156, 164, 181, 182, 243n39;
    founding of, 22, 219n28; social base of,
    22. *See also* Siegman, Henry

ABOUT THE AUTHOR

Marjorie N. Feld is professor of history at Babson College, where she teaches courses on US labor and gender history and food justice and sustainability. Her first book, *Lillian Wald: A Biography*, won the 2008 Saul Viener Book Prize of the American Jewish Historical Society. Her second book, *Nations Divided: American Jews and the Struggle over Apartheid*, was published in 2014.